LEGACIES OF LIBERATION

Legacies of Liberation

The Progressive Catholic Church in Brazil at the Start of a New Millennium

JOHN BURDICK
The Maxwell School, Syracuse University, USA

LONDON AND NEW YORK

First published 2004 by Ashgate Publishing

Reissued 2019 by Routledge
2 Park Square, Milton Park, Abingdon, Oxon, OX14 4RN
52 Vanderbilt Avenue, New York, NY 10017

Routledge is an imprint of the Taylor & Francis Group, an informa business

Copyright © 2004, John Burdick

The author has asserted his moral right under the Copyright, Designs and Patents Act, 1988, to be identified as the author of this work.

All rights reserved. No part of this book may be reprinted or reproduced or utilised in any form or by any electronic, mechanical, or other means, now known or hereafter invented, including photocopying and recording, or in any information storage or retrieval system, without permission in writing from the publishers.

Notice:
Product or corporate names may be trademarks or registered trademarks, and are used only for identification and explanation without intent to infringe.

Publisher's Note
The publisher has gone to great lengths to ensure the quality of this reprint but points out that some imperfections in the original copies may be apparent.

Disclaimer
The publisher has made every effort to trace copyright holders and welcomes correspondence from those they have been unable to contact.

A Library of Congress record exists under LC control number:

Typeset in England by Author and Publisher Services, 11 North End, Calne, Wiltshire

ISBN 13: 978-0-8153-9020-6 (hbk)
ISBN 13: 978-1-138-35637-5 (pbk)
ISBN 13: 978-0-429-24325-7 (ebk)

Contents

List of Abbreviations   vii
Preface   ix

Introduction: Looking for Legacies   1

1   Pastoral Negro: Progressive Catholicism and the Anti-racist Struggle   17

2   The Black Pastoral in the Secular World   37

3   Redefining Mary: Women's Changing Roles at Home and in the Church   57

4   The Progressive Church, Domestic Violence and Abortion   79

5   Searching for the Promised Land: Progressive Catholicism and the Shaping of MST Leadership   99

6   Finding the Promised Land: Liberationism and MST Rank and File   119

Conclusion   139

Select Bibliography   145

Index   157

List of Abbreviations

AMZOL	Associação de Mulheres da Zona Este
APN	*agente de pastoral negro* (Black Pastoral agent)
CDD	Católicas pelo Direito de Decidir
CEB	*comunidade eclesial de base*
CFC	Catholics for a Free Choice
CFEMEA	Centro Feminista de Estudos e Assessoria
CIMI	Conselho Indigenista Misionária (Missionary Council for Indigenous Affairs)
CPT	Comissão Pastoral da Terra (Pastoral Land Commission)
CNBB	Conferência Nacional do Bispos do Brasil (National Brazilian Bishops' Conference)
INCRA	Instituto Nacional de Colonização e Reforma Agrária (National Institute of Colonization and Agrarian Reform)
MEB	Movimento de Educação de Base
MMTR	Movimento de Mulheres Trabalhadoras Rurais (Women Rural Workers' Movement)
MNU	Movimento Negro Unificado
MST	Movimento dos Trabalhadores Sem Terra (Landless Workers' Movement)
PMM	Pastoral de Mulheres Marginalizades (Pastoral of Marginalized Women)
PT	Partido dos Trabalhadores (Workers' Party)
PVN	*pré-vestibular para negros* (forerunner of the PVNC)
PVNC	*pré-vestibular para negros e carentes* (college examination preparation course for blacks and the poor)

Preface

The past 20 years have been hard on progressive Catholics in Latin America. Since the early 1980s, progressive clergy, pastoral activists and liberation theologians across the continent have found it necessary to shift from talking about the growing influence, if not immanent triumph, of the progressive Catholic 'model', and towards public acknowledgement that the model is in crisis. I, for one, could read no writing on the wall in 1983, when Pope John Paul II visited Nicaragua. I can vividly recall watching on television as the pontiff moved along the reception line of Sandinista leaders, greeting each one, until he reached Ernesto Cardenal, the ordained priest who served in the government as minister of culture. Cardenal knelt, but there was no mistaking the pope's reprimanding finger: an ordained priest was not supposed to serve as a minister of state. I watched this drama without alarm, confident that Cardenal would remain in his post, inspired by a vision that, I believed, could never be contained by papal authority. Indeed, for me, Cardenal was living proof that reading the Bible as a manifesto for social justice had cracked the shell of the old Church; here was a Church that would no longer take 'no' for an answer, would grow irresistibly larger and stronger, and would continue in its mission to give voice to the numberless masses. When, the following year, the pope called the Brazilian liberation theologian Leonardo Boff to Rome to silence him, my impression became even more solid that the institutional Church was feeling threatened to its very core. The Church, I was sure, could never silence all the voices for change. In my view – which, it turns out, was also the view of many progressive Catholics at the time – the effort to stifle Boff was the last gasp of a decaying ecclesiastical model that would soon be overrun by a million voices clamouring for a church of small, self-sufficient, politically conscious Christian communities.

As it turned out, the attack on Boff, far from being the defensive manoeuvre of a cornered Church, was the Church's first major offensive in a war that would eventually reveal its extraordinary staying power and the liberationists' vulnerability. It was a war that the traditional Church would, in the view of many, dominate and win. At first, many observers were reluctant to recognize this. But as the Vatican alternated between a policy of frontally attacking liberation theology and seeking to coopt it, what eventually came to light was the fragility of the progressive Church's own social base. By the late 1980s utopian hope had turned to resignation, or worse. These feelings were deepened by the crisis of socialism in 1989 and most searingly by the electoral defeat of the Sandinistas in 1990.

Over the course of the following years, an increasing number of progressive commentators admitted that the liberationist Church might not triumph after all. What was happening? Progressive bishops in Brazil and elsewhere in Latin America were rapidly being replaced by conservative ones. Socialist ideals were everywhere on the defensive. And Ernesto Cardenal had been voted out of power. While one should not make the mistake of reducing the political significance of liberation theology to its occupancy of the halls of state, the fact that Cardenal no longer walked those halls became an apt symbol of the passing of an era. Liberation theology, if not yet dead, was mortally wounded. The newspapers and 'talking heads' rubbed salt into the wound. In the early 1990s, as history 'came to an end', it was difficult to escape declarations that liberation theology was but a shard of the great dream of the Left, shattered by the onrushing train of neo-liberal, post-Marxist modernity. By the 1990s most observers were saying that too much rationalism, and too many high-flying expectations, had undone both the theology and its practice, and helped hasten both its decline and the growth of those other less-than-rational movements, Pentecostalism and the Catholic charismatic renewal. Reflecting this overall mood, in 1993 I published *Looking for God in Brazil*, which gave voice to the view that the days of the progressive Catholic project were numbered.

Yet the very year that book was published I was already beginning to sense that despite the People's Church's retreat, the ideas and dreams articulated by liberationists seemed to have spilled over into a variety of powerful social processes that were changing the face of Brazil. Late in 1993 I had a memorable, though brief, conversation with an activist in the MST, the Movimento dos Trabalhadores Sem Terra, the Landless Workers' Movement. I had asked him to tell me what the aims of the movement were. His reply astonished me. 'Our goal is to live on the land the way God wanted us to, it is to return to the land He promised us.' My astonishment came from something almost intangible: a certain lilt of voice, a certain confident, upturned chin as these words were spoken. I had seen and heard that confidence for years in the Christian base communities of the Catholic Church. Then, in 1994, Chiapas exploded. At first, like many others I understood the Zapatistas to be a secular, radical movement. Yet the more I learned, the more the deep influence of liberation theology upon Zapatista leadership and base became apparent. Among the MST and the Zapatistas, perhaps two of the most significant social movements in Latin America in the early 1990s, liberation theology had left an unmistakable imprint. Could it be, I wondered at the end of 1994, that this theology was not, after all, irrelevant to the post-1989 world?

By the mid- to late 1990s, to this question was added my growing awareness that, despite the overall decline in the number of politically active *comunidades eclesials de base* (CEBs),[1] the national meetings of CEBs were remarkably well attended and vibrant. In 1997 I followed with great interest the national meeting of CEBs in São Luiz de Maranhão, where almost 5000 delegates from all around the country sang, danced, and communed joyfully together for over four days, all the while describing their work and dreams as the slow, arduous struggle for the promised land. If the CEBs were dying, somehow the news had not reached these delegates.

By 1998 I had become convinced that the story of the liberationists' survival into the post-1989 world needed to be told. While completing another project, I continued to place items into a 'New Liberationism' file. The file grew thicker as cases accumulated of old liberationist projects that refused to die, of others that experimented with new approaches, and of others that were regaining ground once lost. From consciousness-raising around Afro-Brazilian rights, to facing the challenges of feminism, to articulating and sustaining a revolutionary reading of Exodus that to this day motivates and inspires landless workers throughout the country, liberationist Catholicism appeared increasingly rich with dynamism and hope for the future. History had not yet quite ended for the liberationist Church.

In writing this book I have accrued many personal debts. I met César Soeiro at the national CEBs' meeting in 2000, and have in subsequent years imposed more than once on his and his family's hospitality, as I have come to know the world of liberationist Catholics in Maranhão. For this I am grateful to both César and his wife Lusinete. Also in Maranhão, I was the beneficiary of the support and insight of Padre Evandro, Padre Waldemar, Padre Flávio, and the team at Comissão Pastoral da Terra (CPT), including Paulo and Idomar. In Pôrto Alegre, Maurilio Galdinho and Charmain Levy were exceptional hosts, helping me to navigate the often turbulent political waters of the place. Also in Pôrto Alegre, I was honoured to receive guidance from Frei Wilson Dallagnol, Frei Orestes, and Zander Navarro. In Rio Grande do Sul, in connection with the MST, I was pleased by the welcome I received from Nina and the CPT team. In Rio de Janeiro, I have, over the years, benefited from the support and hospitality of Frei David Raimundo dos Santos and his team. Also in Rio, over the years of researching this book I have continued to benefit from the friendship (and not infrequent criticism) of colleagues including Peter Fry, Yvonne Maggie, Márcia Contins, Olivia da Cunha, Regina Novaes, Livio Sansone and Cecilia Mariz. Andréa Damaeceno was especially helpful to me in talking through a variety of issues pertaining to this book's central themes. In the United States, my thinking about the Church and social movements has continued to be sharpened by conversations with Randy Stoecker, Kenneth Serbin, Marc Edelman, Margaret Crahan, Carol Ann Drogus, Dave Dixon, and Heidi Swarts. My mother, Dolores Burdick, showed once again that she is the world's best editor, and my father, Harvey Burdick, showed once again that he is the world's best curmudgeon. Whatever there is of value in this book derives much of its merit from my association with these people. The guilt for all that is blameworthy in it is mine alone.

A special expression of thanks goes to my wife, Judy, who has been far more patient with me than the academic life deserves. My two children, Benjamin and Molly, are, in the most important sense, the reason I write at all. To them and to their mother I owe everything.

Note

1   The *comunidades eclesiais de base* (CEBs) are Catholic congegations in which a progressive reading of the Bible is actively pursued and implemented.

Introduction

Looking for Legacies

The Emergence of a Liberationist Catholicism

If, in the early years of the twentieth century, an incautious soothsayer had hazarded the prediction that Brazil's Catholic Church, for more than four centuries a bastion of authoritarianism, would soon become one of the hemisphere's most vigorous defenders of progressive ideals, he would no doubt have been dismissed as a lunatic.[1] As late as the 1940s, bishops and clergy in Brazil's rural areas remained staunch allies of large landholders; in the cities they took the side of order against the rabble; and everywhere they stood arm-in-arm with state power. Perhaps no moment better epitomizes the Brazilian Church before mid-century than the day in 1931 when Rio de Janeiro's Cardinal Leme looked down upon the *cidade maravilhosa* from the towering peak of Corcovado, as he and the recently instated dictator Getúlio Vargas together inaugurated the stupendously large statue of Christ the Redeemer that, to this day, stands guard, arms outstretched, over a glistening white and brown sea of skyscrapers and shanty towns.[2]

And yet the soothsayer would have been right. Within a generation the arch-conservatism typified by Leme's visit to Corcovado would be challenged to its very roots, from within the Church itself. Beginning in the late 1940s, a variety of powerful forces would beget a movement of young, idealistic clergy and laity committed to a politically progressive vision of the Gospel.[3]

After the Second World War Brazil underwent rapid urbanization, as the rulers of state strove to develop heavy industry in urban areas and mechanize production in rural ones.[4] At the same time, new post-war ideals of justice, liberty and basic rights for all were flowing into Brazil's courts, press and political meeting halls. A charismatic president, Juscelino Kubitchek, raised Brazilians' hopes that their needs would soon be met through rapid economic development.[5] By the end of the 1950s, when Kubitchek promised '50 years of progress in 5', a youthful generation of Brazilians were ready to believe him.[6]

Yet just as they were being spoken, such promises were already beginning to sound hollow to the millions pushed off their land and towards overcrowded cities where jobs were scarce and the infrastructure non-existent.[7] High hopes stimulated by populist politicians gave way to widespread frustration as the dream of progress foundered on the hard reality of landlessness, unemployment and urban squalor. New ideologies tapped into growing resentment and longing. Rural workers in the north-east rallied to the call of the Peasant Leagues; parties of the Left found a growing number of adherents; and evangelical Christianity swept through urban shanties and rural hamlets.[8] The Catholic Church responded to these pressures in a number of ways, the most pertinent to our interest being to create a more active clerical presence among the poor.[9] In the north-east, the bishops initiated literacy campaigns and rural Catholic unions; elsewhere they created Catholic Action groups; everywhere they strove to reach out to poor, unattended Catholics.[10] For rounds of duty among the poor the Church found recruits among the growing number of regular priests arriving from Europe, armed with the 'see–judge–act' method of Joseph Cardijn, in which Christians combined engagement in the world with judgement illuminated by the Christian ideal of justice.[11] The Church also found recruits among young Brazilians inspired by Catholic social doctrine.[12] While many bishops endorsed the doctrine as a way of drawing the poor away from the temptations of socialism,[13] in the eyes of young pastoral agents the important thing was that their Church was finally taking to heart the lives of the downtrodden.

By the early 1960s a growing number of regular clergy, pastoral agents and clergy-in-training were working in Brazil's poor neighbourhoods and rural areas, where they could bring the Word to what they saw as the wretched of the earth. Perhaps not surprisingly, living closely with the poor and witnessing their daily humiliations had a radicalizing effect on this generation of religious. In the late 1990s a Franciscan monk who had worked in the north-east recounted the following memory to me:

> I was there in the community, and the place was really miserable. There was no clean running water, and no sewage, just the stuff running open in the street. And in a situation like that, what difference does charity make? You can give some clean water to a family, but so what? There was only one way to deal with that – to put pressure on the authorities to do what they were supposed to do. So seeing this really impressed on me the need for action together, not just individual charity.

By the time of this memory, the Church had begun to experiment with another solution to the lack of an institutional Catholic presence: to train laypeople to perform sacraments, lead Bible readings and administer the day-to-day details of the Church. The early efforts took root in Rio de Janeiro during the late 1950s and in Natal at the start of the 1960s.[14] Within a few years, laypeople across the country had been formed into community-level councils to manage the affairs of their local churches. These were Latin America's first *comunidades eclesiais de base* or Christian base communities.[15] In addition, in the north-east, the energetic bishop, Dom Helder Camara, helped conceptualize the Movimento de Educação de Base (MEB), a programme of radio literacy campaigns that sought to strengthen progressive consciousness among the rural poor. The MEB eventually in the early 1960s had at its head an educator named Paulo Freire, who used a method rooted in confidence that the poor could be moved from a fatalist to a radical–agentive consciousness. Central to the method was 'reflecting on everyday life' through guided discussion of key words,[16] a method soon transferred to base communities.[17] All these activities received a major boost from the council of bishops assembled in Rome from 1962 to 1965. In *Gaudium et spes*, the Council's final document, the pope urged his Church to move 'forward together with humanity and experience the same earthly lot which the world does'.[18] Clergy busy at the grassroots took these words as a vindication of their work.

Despite the Brazilian military regime's efforts after 1964 to reduce progressive influence within the Church,[19] by the end of the decade liberationist Catholicism was thriving. Catholic progressives had received a shot of legitimacy from the Latin American bishops' conference in 1968, in Medellín, Colombia.[20] In a final document that was to prove among the most progressive ever produced by an official Catholic body, the bishops of Latin America apologized for centuries of complicity with the ruling class[21] and called on Catholics to confront the poverty and 'institutionalized violence' of the continent by 'creat[ing] and develop[ing] their own grassroots organizations for the redress and consolidation of their rights and the search for true justice'.[22] In 1969 a series of military assassinations of clergy provoked moderate and conservative bishops to join in a unified front with their progressive colleagues.[23] By 1970 Brazil's national bishops' conference was making public statements against state repression; by 1973 it was engaged in a national campaign for human rights; and by 1975, after the murder of journalist Vladimir Herzog, the bishops rallied to the cause of return to civilian rule.[24]

The decade from the early 1970s to the early 1980s would, in retrospect, come to be regarded as a Golden Age of the liberationist Church.[25] It was during this decade that progressive Catholics threw themselves into mobilizing base communities for social and political activism, catalysing thousands of grassroots social movement groups,[26] creating national institutions, seating their leaders in publishing houses and seminaries, and training a generation in the 'see–judge–act' method.[27] Never before nor since have progressive Catholics in Brazil exercised so much tangible, and visible, institutional influence.[28]

It was also a period that saw the efflorescence of original and eloquent progressive theological writing.[29] Catholic liberationists insisted that reflection upon God must begin with the question: how does God wish humanity to act in relation to misery and oppression?[30] Their answer: God expects His children to join forces, oppose social evil, and bring about a world of social equality and justice. 'To work for a just world', wrote Peruvian theologian Gustavo Gutierrez, 'where there is no servitude, oppression, and alienation is to work for the advent of the Messiah.'[31]

According to the new theology, misery and injustice were the consequences of human greed. Some liberationists believed that the elimination of greed could come only through the elimination of capitalism and the triumph of socialism; others accepted that a well-regulated capitalism could approximate the justice they longed for.[32] Either way, the poor should be the primary beneficiaries, the group for which Christians had a 'preferential option'. In the liberationist view, the poor were not just passive recipients of the Church's charity; they were agents of their own liberation, endowed with a wisdom that could break through layers of oppressive socialization. With the guidance of pastoral agents, the poor could discover in the Bible the causes of oppression, God's love of social justice and the need for human collective action.[33] In the liberationist view, Christian base communities were those congregations where Christians could activate their commitment to making the world a juster place. 'Christian life in the base communities', Boff wrote in the late 1970s, 'is characterized by the absence of alienating structures, by direct relationships, by reciprocity, by a deep communion, by mutual assistance, by communality of gospel ideas, by equality among members.'[34] These were no mere worldly relations; these were a harbinger and a sign of the coming Kingdom of God on earth.

As stimulating as this theology was, the greatest excitement of the period lay in the base communities' involvements in social movements. The years 1977–82 were a whirlwind of base-community activity to bring about improvement to urban areas in the areas of transportation, health, education, sanitation, and water. Adopting clearly progressive rhetoric, the National Brazilian Bishops' Conference (CNBB)[35] in 1977 endorsed all such organizing initiatives, insisting that 'people and social groups have duties to society, such as the duty to participate in politics … . Society, which is full of injustice, needs to be totally transformed … . The role of all Christians is to participate in building this new society.'[36]

In the context of the military regime's policy after 1977 to refrain from intervening in Church-based grassroots initiatives, thousands of base communities across the nation were soon calling meetings, leading marches, and collecting petitions.[37] By the start of the 1980s researchers were awash in evidence that Brazil's neighbourhood movements were led, above all, by people from the CEBs.[38]

During this period Church activists played a key role in many other social struggles. In organizing labour, CEBs were essential in the formation of the first independent construction workers' unions.[39] Church-based activists took a leading role in the São Paulo metalworkers' strikes in 1978–80 and were closely involved in the formation of the Workers' Party in 1980.[40] In rural areas, in 1972 Catholics created the Conselho Indigenista Misionário (CIMI), the Missionary Council for Indigenous Affairs, dedicated to defending the rights of native peoples.[41] In 1975 they founded the Comissão Pastoral da Terra (CPT), the Pastoral Land Commission, to defend the rights of Brazil's rural labourers and smallholders. The work of these commissions and groups was dangerous. Church-based activists risked and lost their lives throughout the country every year during this period.[42]

Also during this period the Church remained steadfastly committed to the fight against human-rights abuses, as well as for Brazil's return to electoral democracy. In São Paulo, Dom Evaristo Arns gathered evidence to expose torture under the military[43] and, in so doing, created the national Peace and Justice Commission. The Church publicly denounced censorship and called for amnesty for political prisoners.[44] And when the military regime issued a decree in 1979 guaranteeing a return of elections, pastoral agents and clergy dedicated themselves to educating and getting out the vote.

By the early 1980s progressive Catholicism was clearly a major force in Brazilian society. This influence fostered a robust optimism among Church activists about the future of the Church in a democratic Brazil. By the late 1970s Leonardo Boff became convinced that the key to genuine democracy in Brazil lay in the Church. In 1977 he published the first Portuguese-language edition of *Ecclesiogenesis: The Church that is Born from the Poor*, which argued that bishops and priests should eventually relinquish their authority in favour of a loose network of base communities. By the start of the 1980s most progressive Catholics agreed optimistically, if only in principle, to this model, so it was not surprising that the rubric chosen in 1981 for the national interecclesial CEB meeting was 'seed of a new society'.[45] A priest interviewed years later spoke of this optimism:

> It seemed like there was a new model of church really being born. We were developing a lot of lay leadership and a lot of deep formation. Political courses and those kinds of things were flourishing ... . It seemed that this was the way: a way of transforming church and – indirectly – society. There was a lot of hope.[46]

It was a hope, however, that was soon to fade. If the heyday of the politically radical Church in Brazil was between 1968 and 1985, after that the country witnessed a return – with a vengeance – of a Church that placed more value on prayer and devotion than on mobilizing people for social and political action.[47]

The Crisis of the Progressive Catholic Church

A variety of social and political forces converged in the 1980s to slow down and reverse the progressive trend. First, the 1980s saw an aggressive policy on the part of the Vatican to marginalize the liberationist Church, wherever it lived and breathed. The pope saw liberationism as a potentially dangerous ideology and sought to eliminate it through selective excision and appropriation. In 1984 he summoned Leonardo Boff to Rome and ordered him to cease writing for a year, and he issued documents that denounced liberation theology's 'materialism' and anti-authoritarianism.[48] For the rest of the decade, John Paul II replaced progressive bishops, divided their dioceses, fired liberationist professors, and gutted the institutional power of the progressive Church.[49] Further, the Vatican 'warned progressive bishops, intervened in religious orders, censored publications' and 'curtailed the power of the [National Brazilian] Bishops' conference'.[50]

At the same time the Vatican was undermining the progressives, it threw its weight behind conservative Catholicism.[51] Throughout the 1980s and 1990s the Church sought to renew its mission to save souls through inner conviction, devotion and individual spirituality.[52] In this, wrote Daudelin and Hewitt in the early 1990s:

> the bishops seem to be backtracking from social activism. These bishops now adopt a much lower profile in the discussion of social and political issues, and show openness and at times sympathy toward movements, like the Charismatic Renewal, which give little if any attention to these issues.[53]

In dioceses with conservative bishops, priests were told to desist from all radical activities, such as direct organization and support for unions, leftist political parties and protest movements, or face suspension. Funds for such activities were cut everywhere.

The other face of John Paul's hostility to liberation theology was his call for a 'new evangelization'. In 1992 he announced, on the occasion of the Quincentennial, that the Church was embarking on a great mission of just such a 'new evangelization' to strengthen the authority of the Church and to evangelize the world, not to bring about a world of justice and equality. As Libânio writes, the new project 'shows itself to be intransigently against any Marxist element that infiltrates Church or theology. Thus its cases against theologians of liberation and the official pronouncements against the theology of liberation.'[54] Within the ocean of New Evangelization, the islands of liberationism 'suffer pressure and restriction by the dominant model of evangelization'.[55] 'The churches, theologies and catechisms positioned by the model of an evangelization based in the spiritual power of the poor', writes Libanio, 'suffers reprisals on the part of the larger and hegemonic New Evangelization project.'[56] In particular, so thorough was the 'New Evangelization's' assault that, by 1996, the pope could pronounce the 'end' of liberation theology.[57]

The number of Catholics making an active link between faith and the struggle for social justice began to decline. Christian base communities, long regarded by academics, journalists and theologians as hotbeds of Christian radicalism, began turning to 'traditional pursuits'.[58] Laypeople in the CEBs began to devote more time to the sacraments, Bible study, devotions and catechesis, and less to organizing petition drives and delegations to local politicians. By the early 1990s large numbers of the original CEB activists had left the Church, leaving a space overtaken by traditionalists who prioritized devotions and *promessas* to the saints. A priest in São Paulo told a US researcher in the early 1990s that:

> In my novitiate class, all of them are from lower-class backgrounds but they are far more pious and far less political than before 1985. Out of fifteen, only two have any interest at all in learning about politics, much less doing anything about it. Five come from the Opus Dei, and seven are charismatics ... Overall, the religious type [of CEB] has grown, while the political has subsided ... .[59]

By the start of the 1990s, laypeople still committed to an explicitly liberationist agenda found they had few ecclesiastical resources left to conduct political struggle. Ana Dias, a lay activist in São Paulo, said in 1993 that, since her region had been assigned to a conservative bishop, she had seen friends and colleagues in the Church abandon political struggle. 'People have sacrificed so much,' she said. 'It's easier to give up. If you look back over twenty years, you can see that the results have been meager in relation to the hardship you've endured.'[60] The turn to a heavier emphasis on the spiritual at the expense of the political has been cause for consternation on the part of inveterate liberationists. They have sadly registered the trend that the CEBs are 'not growing, that work at the base level has stagnated ... '.[61] A pastoral agent lamented that 'I feel that the community stopped growing four, five years ago ... we see that the community has stagnated; it stopped.'[62] By the mid-1990s, two long-standing observers of the Church could write that: '[t]he size, the effective mobilization capacity and the influence of the "popular" Church appear not only to have been almost universally exaggerated but also to be everywhere declining'.[63] As the 1990s began, accounts of the progressive Church were pervaded by weariness. 'I belong to the generation that went through the whole process of the late 1970s and early 1980s,' Father Luiz Carlos Marques said to Berryman. 'We were carrying around lots of truths from grand systems ... . We thought things were going to change quickly. Today we're left with a lot of questions.'[64]

While the pope's hostility was key to wearing down the liberationist Church, other forces were important as well. Brazil's return to electoral democracy in the 1980s drew many of its best leaders from the progressive Church, and bequeathed to those who remained uncertainty about their political role.[65] The arrival of normal politics seemed to diminish the need for a 'voice of the voiceless', since presumably now the 'voiceless' would find their voice in public politics. After the installation of civilian rule in 1985 the Church was no longer involved in a titanic struggle for democracy over dictatorship: '[s]uddenly gone', as Daudelin and Hewitt observe, 'were most of the questions to which a simple, yes or no, moral answer could be given'.[66] Many argued that new political questions were better addressed by secular political parties, unions and movements rather than by the CEBs.[67] 'With the shift to civilian government,' a priest in São Paulo told Berryman, 'the church returned to its "specific function".'[68] Unsurprisingly, the 1980s witnessed an exodus of leaders from the CEBs. 'When the unions became stronger and louder,' the priest told Berryman, 'and especially when the Workers Party emerged, a lot of the leadership from the community of the *pastoral operária* [the Workers' Pastoral] went into that, and this created a vacuum of leadership in the communities.'[69]

But this exodus was not just a migration into the arms of political movements. After 1990 a growing number of progressive Catholics seemed to give up on politics altogether. For many, the collapse of socialism in 1989–91 felt like a violent body blow,[70] and although liberationist theologians insisted that their vision was wedded not to Marx but to the poor, not to any single model of socialism but to the Kingdom of God, still the 'triumph of capitalism' in the autumn of 1989 and the defeat of the Sandinistas in February of 1990 left many liberationists reeling. Leonardo Boff himself wrote of 'the general crisis of left-wing thought' brought on by the collapse of socialism; the liberationist theologian Jon Sobrino wrote of 'the closing of a period'.[71]

Many progressive Catholics are convinced that their loss of adherents was also due in no small part to the growth of evangelical Protestants, especially Pentecostals. As long as these churches expanded, Catholics believed, the pool of recruits to their vision of Christianity would shrink.[72] As the evangelicals' low valuation of human agency and collective action spread, liberationists felt, it crowded out the idea of human agency and collective action as central to God's plan.[73] Whilst there is some evidence that the expansion of the evangelicals has been at the expense of the progressive Catholics,[74] it is nevertheless likely that had the progressives offered a message that resonated better with its targeted base, evangelical competition would not have mattered much. In the early 1990s, researchers argued that the *igreja popular*'s base was never as deep or broad as the theology had led many to believe, but was, rather, always limited to a relatively small working-class elite.[75] In addition, there had always been a certain 'disconnect' between the rationalistic and abstract ideas of liberationism and the longing of its targeted constituency for concrete, emotional, immediate support. Father Gonzaga in São Paulo, for instance, preached socialism and liberation, but later regretted having kept his sermons so limited, because 'people are thirsty for spirituality. They are so thirsty for God that we often don't know how to read it.' He was convinced that 'God is much greater than our own ideas and schemes'.[76] Padre Tição, also of São Paulo, admitted that '[o]ur discourse was that of liberation theology and we imagined – I imagined – that the people were understanding our discourse, and that even the poor were understanding. But they didn't accept it.'[77] What the poor wanted, these pastoral agents realized, was not so much talk about 'more struggle', but rather something to satisfy deep spiritual needs and longings.[78]

The evolution of theological content after the mid-1980s may be understood in part as the clergy's struggle to adjust to this newly recognized reality. Those religious who earlier saw activities such as saint worship, blessing with holy water and repetitive prayers to be distractions from political struggle, sought increasingly in the 1990s to embrace these things.[79] Others began to focus more on individual family and health issues, without always immediately emphasizing the need for better social services and resources.[80] In the *Santas Missões Populares*, conceived as a new activity for CEBs in 1990, congregants learned to visit their neighbours door-to-door, to be ready to talk not just about the need for new health clinics, but also about headaches and domestic difficulties.[81]

Critiquing the Current Conventional Wisdom

In the early 1990s, while many observers lamented the passing of the liberationist Church, others began to find such laments overwrought. According to these writers, there were two main problems with such jeremiads: their representation of social influence was too narrow; and they underestimated the continued presence and in some cases gentle growth of progressive Catholic institutions.

With regard to the first point, it may be conceded that if the influence of liberationist-inspired ideas and values be measured solely in terms of the number of clergy and laity embracing a coherent liberationist vision, or in terms of the number of base communities involved in launching struggles for social justice, then, indeed, one should feel disappointed by the Church's post-1985 trajectory. But this is not our only choice. The influence wielded by the liberationists since the late 1980s may be defined and evaluated differently, and more broadly. Specifically, one may witness social influence, for example, in the persons of leaders who carried what they learned from the liberationist Church into their non-Church-based activism;[82] one may see it in the inclusion into legitimate discourse of issues that Church progressives introduced into the political arena long ago;[83] one may detect it in the shift to the left of the ideological centre of the Brazilian episcopacy, such that it now includes basic social reformism;[84] and more besides. Focus on such spheres of influence clearly complicates the notion that the progressive Church is no longer a force to be reckoned with on the Brazilian political scene.

With regard to the second point, the notion that the progressive Catholics themselves are now 'nowhere to be seen' could not be further from the truth. Catholic progressives remain vigorous institution-builders in Brazilian social life, although the institutions they build look and sound rather different than they did in the 1970s and 1980s. One cannot grasp the full complexity of political life in Brazil if we ignore institutions such as the national Encontro das CEBs, the Black Pastoral, the National Conference on Indigenous and Black Theology, the pre-vestibular courses, Educafro, the Land Pastoral Commission, the Centre of Indigenous Missions, Catholics for a Free Choice, the Pastoral of Marginalized Women, and many others. All these institutions continue to be shaped profoundly by liberationist ideas and views.

In this book I try to return the study of present-day liberationist Catholicism to its proper place, as central to our understanding of Brazilian society.[85] In order to do this I have sought to identify and investigate the political agendas and struggles through which Catholic liberationist ideas and values continue to make themselves felt in that society.

In order to appreciate this influence, it is important to set aside the expectation that it would usually take the visible form of mass mobilization or dramatic social change. In doing so, I join current scholarship on social movement outcomes. Some of this analysis has focused on what Jennifer Earl calls 'extramovement outcomes' – that is, on the policies and legislation of the state, and on the cultural values of the society in which the movement 'moves'.[86] In the case of the liberationist Church, however, our efforts will bear greater fruit if we also attend to 'intra-movement' outcomes – that is, to how the liberationist Church has affected the thinking and action of people who have been directly involved in it. We can then begin to see how individuals exposed to liberationist ideals and values have made these their own, have sometimes reshaped them, and have applied them in a variety of ways within different fields of social action. As Meyer and Whittier argue, 'one movement can influence subsequent movements both from outside and from within: by altering the political and cultural conditions it confronts in the external environment, and by changing the individuals, groups, and norms within the movement itself'.[87] When we attend to this sort of effect, we can better appreciate how liberationism continues to exert its influence even when it no longer has large numbers on its side, nor is being applied in direct CEB-led activism.

There are three main sources of data for this book, collected in a variety of contexts over the past decade. First, there are in-depth interviews. On the topic of the Church and women's issues, I conducted 18 interviews with women involved in CEBs, either as leaders or non-leading participants, and with five women who had once been participants but who were no longer. I also interviewed leaders in the Associação de Mulheres da Zona Este (AMZOL), Pastoral de Mulheres Marginalizadas (PMM) and Católicas pelo Direito de Decidir (CDD). These were conducted in São Luis de Maranhão, Rio de Janeiro, São Paulo, and Pôrto Alegre. On the issue of the Church and the landless workers' movement, I interviewed nine pastoral agents at the Comissão Pastoral da Terra (CPT), five leaders of the Movimento dos Trabalhadores Sem Terra (MST) and eight rank-and-file participants in an MST settlement. The interviews were conducted in the region of Pôrto Alegre and in São Luis de Maranhão. On the theme of the Church and anti-racist struggle I interviewed 15 clergy and pastoral agents, 20 rank-and-file

Introduction: Looking for Legacies

participants in the afro liturgy and pre-vestibular courses, and five people who regarded themselves as peripheral to the Black Pastoral but who have strong anti-racist commitments. I also interviewed six leaders in the black consciousness movement, in both Rio de Janeiro and São Luis de Maranhão.

In addition to interviews, I participated in, or witnessed directly, most of the activities and groups described in this book. During the past decade, I have gathered participant observation material from the afro liturgy and its preparation seminars, the pre-vestibular courses, and race-consciousness-raising workshops. I have participated in meetings of CEBs in both Rio de Janeiro and São Luis de Maranhão, and have extensively observed the interactions between people in these places. I also participated intensively in the week-long 'Popular Missions' in 2001, during which CEBs in the north of the country worked to evangelize their neighbourhoods with their message of liberation and spirituality, and I also took part in several local-level and national meetings of *cebistas*, most notably the July 2000 national interecclesial meeting. I visited several MST settlements, observing meetings and group interactions, and have witnessed diverse meetings organized by the CPT, both at their offices, and in the countryside, in both São Luiz and Pôrto Alegre.

The third main source of data is the large number of primary documents that I have gathered, over the past decade, from the aforementioned groups and organizations, including pamphlets, circulars, newsletters, bulletins, announcements and, increasingly, website material. Finally, I have relied extensively on the published analyses of other scholars. I have endeavoured to bring together the most up-to-date research on the topics I treat, produced by observers with on-the-ground experience.

The argument of the book is that the liberationist stance continues to exert significant, if not always obvious, influence over routines and ideas in three main arenas of social and political struggle. In Chapters 1 and 2 I show how progressive Catholic ideas and practices have contributed to the formation of the movement within the Church to struggle against anti-black racism, with repercussions both within the Church, and beyond it. I turn, in the following two chapters, to the impact of progressive Catholicism on women's struggles. There I argue that, despite sidestepping many issues of concern to women, progressive Catholicism in Brazil has, for the past 20 years, unleashed – not always deliberately – a range of subtle pro-woman energies. In Chapters 5 and 6 I focus on the role of the progressive Church in the landless workers' movement. While much has been written about the Church's role in the early years of the MST, there has been little analysis of the effects of progressive Catholicism on the movement today. I argue in these chapters that Catholic liberationist ideas, perspectives, and practices continue to exert a strong influence on the minds and motivations of both the MST's leaders and its rank and file. I conclude the book by calling for an expansion of the categories used by observers to apply to social movement outcomes, as well as by asking for a greater sensitivity among researchers to the unanticipated and unintended dimensions of social movement legacies.

Notes

1. Pedro Ribeiro de Oliveira, *Religião e Dominação* (Petrópolis: Vozes, 1985), *passim*.
2. Scott Mainwaring, *The Catholic Church and Politics in Brazil, 1916–1985* (Stanford: Stanford University Press, 1986); João Batista Libânio, *Cenários da igreja* (São Paulo: Loyola, 2000).
3. Christian Smith, *The Emergence of Liberation Theology: Radical Religion and Social Movement Theory* (Chicago: University of Chicago Press, 1991); Thomas Bruneau, *The Political Transformation of the Brazilian Catholic Church* (Cambridge: Cambridge University Press, 1974).
4. Thomas E. Skidmore, *Politics in Brazil, 1930–1964* (New York: Oxford University Press, 1967); Robert Levine, *The History of Brazil* (Westport: Greenwood, 1999).
5. Robert Alexander, *Juscelino Kubitschek and the Development of Brazil* (Athens: Ohio University Center for International Studies, 1991).
6. Ronald Schneider, *Brazil: Culture and Politics in a New Industrial Powerhouse* (Boulder: Westview, 1996); Peter Flynn, *Brazil: A Political Analysis* (Boulder: Westview, 1978).
7. Thomas Skidmore, *Brazil: Five Centuries of Change* (New York: Oxford, 1999); Robert Gay, *Popular Organization and Democracy in Rio de Janeiro* (Philadelphia: Temple, 1994).
8. Francisco Cartaxo Rolim, *Pentecostalismo no Brasil* (Petrópolis: Vozes, 1985).
9. Mainwaring, *The Catholic Church*.
10. Vanilda Paiva, 'A Igreja Moderna no Brasil', in V. Paiva (ed.), *Igreja e Questão Agraria* (São Paulo: Edições Loyola, 1985), 52–67; Ralph Della Cava, 'The "People's Church," the Vatican, and *Abertura*' in Alfred Stepan (ed.), *Democratizing Brazil: Problems of Transition and Consolidation* (New York: Oxford University Press, 1989), 146.
11. Daniel Bell, *Liberation Theology After the End of History* (New York: Routledge, 2001); G. Poggi, *Catholic Action in Italy* (Stanford: Stanford University Press, 1967); also see Smith, *The Emergence of Liberation Theology*.
12. Since the encyclicals *Rerum Novarum* (1891) and *Quadragesimo Anno* (1931), which endorsed the right of workers and peasants to organize under the auspices of Catholic unions, the Church has regarded as one of its missions the safeguarding of the welfare of nation's poor. See D. J. O'Brien, 'A Century of Catholic Social Teaching' in J. A. Coleman (ed.), *100 Years of Catholic Social Thought* (Maryknoll: Orbis, 1991).
13. Ibid.
14. Manuel Vasquez, *The Brazilian Popular Church and the Crisis of Modernity* (Cambridge: Cambridge University Press, 1998), 29. On early pastoral experiments that laid the groundwork for the CEBs, see also Mainwaring, *The Catholic Church*.
15. Scott Mainwaring, 'Grass-roots Catholic Groups and Politics in Brazil,' in Scott Mainwaring and Alexander Wilde (eds.), *The Progressive Catholic Church in Latin America* (Notre Dame: University of Notre Dame Press, 1989), 158–159.
16. D. Collins, *Paulo Freire: His Life, Work, and Thought* (New York: Paulist Press, 1978).
17. A key contributor to this early formulation of the Bible circle as ideal consciousness-raiser was Carlos Mesters. See Carlos Mesters, *A Bíblia Como Memória dos Pobres* (Petrópolis: Vozes, 1983).
18. Quoted in Vasquez, *The Brazilian Popular Church*, 21.

19　Kenneth Serbin, 'The Catholic Church, Religious Pluralism, and Democracy in Brazil', in Peter Kingstone and Timothy Power (eds.), *Democratic Brazil* (Pittsburgh: University of Pittsburgh Press, 2000), 48–56; Ralph Della Cava, 'The People's Church', 144.
20　Edward Cleary's analysis of the Medellín conference is still the most profound. See Edward Cleary, *Crisis and Change: The Church in Latin America Today* (Maryknoll: Orbis, 1985).
21　Della Cava, 'The People's Church', 146.
22　CELAM, *Medellin Conclusions* (Washington: National Conference of Catholic Bishops, Secretariat for Latin America, 1979), 56.
23　Della Cava, 'The People's Church', 146; Mainwaring, 'Grassroots Catholic Groups', 161.
24　Central to this process was the São Paulo archbishop's decision to support the secret collection of information about human rights abuses, which, when published in 1985 as *Brasil, Nunca Mais*, led to the creation of diocesan chapters of the Peace and Justice Commission.
25　Iain Maclean, *Opting for Democracy: Liberation Theology and the Struggle for Democracy in Brazil* (New York: Peter Lang, 1999).
26　Contributing to this as a possibility was the fact that after 1974, the military regime finally began to scale back some of the worst of its repressive apparatus.
27　Mainwaring, 'Grassroots Catholic Groups', 151–192.
28　Maclean, *Opting for Democracy*.
29　The year 1971 saw the publication not only of Peruvian Gustavo Gutierrez's seminal *A Theology of Liberation*, but also of Leonardo Boff's *Jesus Christ, Liberator*.
30　Gustavo Gutierrez, *Theology of Liberation* (Maryknoll: Orbis, 1973).
31　Gustavo Gutierrez, *The Power of the Poor in History* (Maryknoll: Orbis, 1983), 32.
32　Paul Sigmund, *Liberation Theology at the Crossroads* (New York: Oxford University Press, 1990); David Lehmann, *Struggle for the Spirit* (London: Polity, 1996).
33　Paulo Freire, *The Pedagogy of the Oppressed*, trans. Myra Ramos (New York: Herder and Herder, 1970). The idea of '*basismo*' is treated by David Lehmann in *The Struggle for the Spirit*.
34　Leonardo Boff, *Ecclesiogenesis: The Base Communities Reinvent the Church* (Maryknoll: Orbis, 1986), 4. See also Lehmann, *Struggle for the Spirit*. Other key writers in this period include Carlos Mesters, José Comblin and Hugo Assmann.
35　The Conferência Nacional dos Bispos do Brasil (CNBB) is the official executive and policy-setting body of the Catholic Church in Brazil.
36　The document is published in Luiz Gonzaga de Souza Lima, *Evolução Política dos Católicos e da Igreja no Brasil* (Petrópolis: Vozes, 1979), 255–266.
37　Ana Maria Doimo, 'Social Movements and the Catholic Church in Vitória, Brazil' in Mainwaring and Wilde, *The Progressive Church in Latin America*, 198. Similar cases have been documented by Paulo Krischke and Scott Mainwaring (eds.), *A Igreja nas Bases em Tempo de Transição* (Pôrto Alegre: CEDEC, 1986); even those CEB members who did not lead these movements provided passive support. See Mainwaring, 'Grassroots Groups', 169.
38　Ana Maria Doimo, *A Vez e a Voz do Popular* (Rio de Janeiro: Relume Dumara, 1995).
39　Doimo, 'Social Movements and the Catholic Church', 201.
40　Margaret Keck, *The Workers Party and Democratization in Brazil* (New Haven: Yale University Press, 1992); Della Cava, 'The People's Church', 156.
41　Paulo Seuss, *A Causa Indigena na Caminhada e a Proposta do CIMI: 1972–1989* (Petrópolis: Vozes, 1989).
42　Regina Novaes, *De Corpo e Alma: Catolicismo, Classes Sociais e Conflitos no Campo* (Rio de Janeiro: Graphia, 1997); Secretariado Nacional da CPT, *A Luta pela Terra: A Comissão Pastoral da Terra 20 Anos Depois* (São Paulo: Paulus, 1995). See also Madeleine Adriance, *Promised Land: Base Christian Communities and the Struggle for the Amazon* (Albany: SUNY Press, 1995).

43 Joan Dassin (ed.), *Torture in Brazil: A Report* (New York: Vintage, 1986).
44 Della Cava, 'The People's Church', 149.
45 Faustino Teixeira, *Os Encontros Intereclesiais de CEBs no Brasil* (São Paulo: Paulinas, 1996).
46 Philip Berryman, *Religion in the Magacity* (Maryknoll: Orbis, 1996), 67.
47 W. E. Hewitt, 'From Defenders of the People to Defenders of the Faith: A 1984–1993 Retrospective of CEB Activity in São Paulo', *Latin American Perspectives* 25, 1 (January 1998), 170–191.
48 Harvey Cox, *The Silencing of Leonardo Boff* (Pak Park: Meyer-Stone, 1988).
49 Kenneth Serbin, 'Religious Tolerance, Church–State Relations, and the Challenge of Pluralism' in Paul Sigmund (ed.), *Religious Freedom and Evangelization in Latin America* (Maryknoll: Orbis, 1999).
50 Ibid. Observers often point out that progressive themes have penetrated the rhetoric of moderate bishops, but this rhetoric is not usually backed by active support for base-level initiatives. See for example, Brian H. Smith, *Religious Politics in Latin America: Pentecostal vs. Catholic* (Notre Dame: University of Notre Dame Press, 1998), 52–56; Serbin, 'The Catholic Church, Religious Pluralism, and Democracy' and Edward Cleary, 'The Brazilian Catholic Church and Church–State Relations: Nation-Building', *Journal of Church and State*, 39,1 (Spring 1997), 253–272.
51 Between 1978 and 1990, of 128 new bishops named worldwide by the pope, 97 were known conservatives. See Smith, *Religious Politics*, 12.
52 Serbin, 'The Catholic Church, Religious Pluralism and Democracy'; see also Manuel Vasquez and Anna Petersen, 'The New Evangelization in Latin American Perspective', *Cross Currents* 48 (Fall 1998), pp. 311–329.
53 Jean Daudelin and W. E. Hewitt, 'Latin American Politics: Exit the Roman Catholic Church?' in Sattya Pattnayak (ed.), *Organized Religion in the Political Transformation of Latin America* (New York: University Press of America, 1995), 178.
54 João Batista Libânio, *Igreja Contempôranea: Encontro com a Modernidade* (São Paulo: Edições Loyola, 2000), 179.
55 Ibid.
56 Ibid., 176.
57 Pope John Paul II, quoted in W. E. Hewitt, 'Introduction: The Legacy of the Progressive Church in Latin America' in W. E. Hewitt and John Burdick (eds.), *The Church at the Grassroots in Latin America* (New York: Praeger, 2000), vii. Brazil, of course, was just one society in the pope's continent-wide assault on liberation theology. By the mid-1990s, many Latin American bishops concurred with Nicaraguan Ernesto Cardenal's statement that 'The pope's attacks have greatly weakened Latin America's church of the poor … There's been an enormous decline'. (http://www.owlnet.rice.edu/~poli354/Mexico_pages/990121_Mexico_theology.html).

Conservative clerics who benefited from the decline made little attempt to hide their satisfaction. Mexican archbishop, Javier Lozano, declared that 'it would be the height of foolishness, ignorance or the malice of some religious leaders to continue sustaining Liberation Theology' (Montevideo/RELIGION-LATAM/ [c] 1999, InterPress Third World News Agency (IPS) http://www.hartford-hwp.com/archives/40/096.html) and San Salvador's Archbishop Sáenz Lacalle proclaimed that 'liberation theology no longer has any place' in his country (http://www.thetablet.co.uk/sample02.shtml). Few comments were as disheartening as that of Cardinal Nicolas Lopez Rodriguez, Archbishop of Santo Domingo, who said in 1996 that '[t]here certainly are some people that still believe in it [liberation theology], but they are just a corpse, a dead body' (http://www.cwnews.com/Browse/1996/02/39.htm).
58 W. E. Hewitt, 'Introduction', ix. For a comparative case, see Sarah Brooks, 'Catholic Activism in the 1990s: New Strategies for the Neoliberal Age' in Christian Smith and Joshua Prokopy (eds.), *Latin American Religion in Motion* (New York: Routledge, 1999), 67–90.

59 Nicholas Demerath, *Crossing the Gods* (New Brunswick: Rutgers, 2001), 22.
60 Berryman, *Religion in the Megacity*, 55. Daudelin and Hewitt, 'Latin American Politics', 179; Robin Nagle, '"Pelo Direito de Ser Igreja" The Struggle of the Morro da Conceição', in Hewitt and Burdick (eds.), *The Church at the Grassroots*, 130.
61 Quoted by Vasquez, *The Brazilian Popular Church*, 69.
62 Ibid.
63 Daudelin and Hewitt, 'Latin American Politics', 177.
64 Berryman, *Religion in the Megacity*, 52.
65 Clodovis Boff already was reading the writing on the wall in 1987. See Clodovis Boff, *Cristãos: Como Fazer Politica* (Petrópolis: Vozes, 1987).
66 Daudelin and Hewitt, 'Latin American Politics: Exit the Catholic Church?', 186
67 Berryman, *Religion in the Megacity*, 68; see also Charmain Levy, 'CEBs in Crisis: Leadership Structures in the São Paulo Area' in Hewitt and Burdick (eds.), *The Church at the Grassroots*, 167–182.
68 Berryman, *Religion in the Megacity*, 67.
69 Ibid., 68.
70 Ivo Lesbaupin, Carlos Steil and Clodovis Boff (eds.), *Para Entender a Conjuntura Atual* (Petrópolis: Vozes, 1996).
71 Bell, *Liberation Theology*, 43; see also Leonardo Boff, *Ecology and Liberation: A New Paradigm*, trans. John Cumming (Maryknoll: Orbis, 1995), 93; Leonardo Boff, 'Christian Liberation Toward the 21st century', *LADOC* 25 (March/April 1995), 1, 3; Jon Sobrino, 'Theology from amidst the Victims', in Miroslav Volf *et al.* (eds.), *The Future of Theology*, (Grand Rapids: Eerdmans, 1996), 164.
72 On the spread of pentecostals, see Clara Mafra, *Os Evangélicos* (Rio de Janeiro: Zahar, 2001); Rubem César Fernandes *et al.*, *Novo Nascimento* (Rio de Janeiro, Mauad, 1998).
73 Some progressives even attributed the growth of Pentecostalism to a US plot to draw people away from liberationist Christianity, and keep them locked in an apolitical Christian cage. See Délcio Lima, *Os Demônios Descem do Norte* (Rio de Janeiro: Alves, 1987). Though largely discredited by scholarship, the theory of the CIA–Pentecostal plot is still alive and well in everyday progressive discourse.
74 John Burdick, *Looking for God in Brazil* (Berkeley: University of California Press, 1993).
75 Vasquez, *The Brazilian Popular Church*, 69; Claudio Perani, 'Notas para um pastoral missionária,' Cadernos do CEAS 127 (1990), 74–83; José Comblin, 'Algumas questões a partir da prática das comunidades eclesiais de base no nordeste', *Revista Eclesiástica Brasileira*, 50,198 (1990), 335–381; Clodovis Boff, 'Desafios atuais da pastoral popular', *Tempo e Presença*, 232 (1988), 30–32; Daudelin and Hewitt, 'Latin American Politics', 184. An early sign of this came in 1982, when Church leaders anticipated a huge turnout in the gubernatorial elections of CEB members voting for the newly-founded Workers' Party. It thus came as a shock that the Workers' Party garnered less than one-third of the vote, and that many CEB participants voted for other parties.
76 Berryman, *Religion and the Megacity*, 61.
77 Ibid., 58.
78 W. E. Hewitt, 'From Defenders of the People to Defenders of the Faith: A Retrospective of CEB Activity in São Paulo', *Latin American Perspectives*, 25, 1 (January 1998), 170–191; also Daudelin and Hewitt, 'Latin American Politics', 179. Beyond such spiritual 'disconnects', some scholars have pointed out that the popular Church's call upon the poor to take history into their own hands seemed, by the early 1990s in the face of the overwhelming odds created by globalization, increasingly unrealistic. The Church told the poor that they had power; but their everyday experience told them they did not. See Vasquez, *The Brazilian Popular Church*, 4.
79 Berryman, *Religion in the Megacity*, 59.
80 Vasquez and Peterson, 'The New Evangelization'.
81 Padre Luis Mosconi, *Santas Missões Populares* (São Paulo: Paulinas, 1996), 15–19.

82 Serbin, 'Religious Tolerance', 212; Anna Petersen, Manuel Vasquez and Philip Williams, 'Introduction: Christianity and Social Change in the Shadow of Globalization' in Anna Peterson *et al.* (eds.), *Christianity, Social Change, and Globalization in the Americas* (New Brunswick: Rutgers, 2001), 3.

83 Serbin, 'The Catholic Church'.

84 Fernando Altemeyer Jr., 'A pastoral católica no ano de 1995', *Tempo e Presença*, 285 (January/February 1996), 23–25; Cleary, 'The Brazilian Catholic Church and Church–State Relations, 253–272.

85 Progressive Catholicism is unfortunately no longer the hot topic it once was in the scholarship of Brazil, whose growth industries are now studies of Pentecostalism, charismatic Catholicism, and non-Christian religions. While these other religious phenomena are obviously important, their magnetism has meant a reduction in scholarship that focuses on how progressive Catholicism has become embedded in Brazilian society. *Religious Abstracts* reports that the decade of 1993–2002 experienced a decline in articles on the liberationist Church in Brazil of about 20 per cent from the previous decade, whilst scholarly articles about Pentecostalism in Brazil increased over the same period by 300 per cent. The percentages are similar when other databases are consulted. See ATLA Religion Online; also see, for example, Sociological Abstracts and Social Science Abstracts. One can also see the trend in doctorates at US universities. While doctorates that dealt with liberation theology in Latin America had expanded rapidly by the end of the 1980s, graduate students in the early 1990s were already learning that the Church's glory days were passing, and that it would be more interesting to watch the rise of its main competitor, the Pentecostals. Between 1995 and 1999 the number of doctoral theses at US universities written on the liberationist Church in Latin America fell almost 50 per cent from the previous five years, while theses dealing with Pentecostalism tripled.

86 Jennifer Earl, 'Methods, Movements, and Outcomes' in Patrick Coy (ed.), *Research in Social Movements, Conflicts and Change* (Stanford: JAI Press, 2000), 3–25.

87 David S. Meyer and N. Whittier, 'Social Movement Spillover', *Social Problems*, 41 (1994), 277–298. See also Doug McAdam, 'The Biographical Impact of Activism' in Marco Giugni *et al.* (eds.), *How Social Movements Matter* (Minneapolis: University of Minesota Press, 1999), 119–146.

Chapter 1

Pastoral Negro: Progressive Catholicism and the Anti-racist Struggle

In this chapter and the next I wish to trace two sorts of influence. First, I want to show how progressive Catholic ideas and practices contributed to the formation of the Pastoral Negro, the Church-based movement against anti-black racism. Tracing how the progressive Church gave birth to this movement helps us see how the liberationist Catholic project has moved beyond a class-based agenda and into identity politics. It also shows that one of that project's legacies to the current generation of young Catholic activists is a well-articulated nationwide Catholic programme to transform racial cultural politics. Second, I want to assess the degree to which this cultural–political project is having an effect on the culture of race in Brazil. I will suggest that this effect is tangible, includes both anticipated and unanticipated outcomes, and that it continues to be a significant presence on the scene of anti-racist struggle.

The two chapters unfold as follows. In this chapter, after a review of the injustices Afro-Brazilians suffer on a daily basis, I offer an analytical history of how the liberationist Church generated and solidified the Catholic Black Pastoral. I then focus on what, from the perspective of black activists in the Church, has been one of their most socially consequential initiatives: the effort to create an 'afro liturgy'. In the following chapter I examine two other key projects of the Black Pastoral: the effort to prepare black (and, as we shall see, poor) youths to pass college entrance exams; and the effort to teach Catholics of African ancestry to identify with the term '*negro*'. With regard to each of these projects, I examine the extent to which progressive Catholic ideas and practices have shaped the initiative, and the degree to which the initiative has reshaped consciousness, norms and everyday practice.

What the Anti-racist Struggle is up against in Brazil

Today, over a century after the abolition of slavery in Brazil, Brazilians of visibly African ancestry are still not free. The society in which they live still assigns the right of rule to white people, while ensuring that the more visible one's phenotypic debt to Africa, the tighter one's limbs are lashed to the deeply implanted posts of poverty, low status and illiteracy. Tales of the indignities suffered by Brazilians whose bodies bear the marks of Africanness fill the pages of analytical and literary writing.[1] While such stories are important for communicating the everyday pain of racism, the grim, unadorned numbers of the statistician are essential to give the lie to those who would claim that anecdotes are exceptions to the rule of Brazil's 'racial democracy'.

Over the past 20 years, those numbers have been depressing. Since 1980, during a period when Brazil's national illiteracy rates have dropped, non-whites have remained roughly three times more likely than whites to be illiterate.[2] During the same period, black and brown children have remained twice as likely as white children never to attend school,[3] and about twice as likely to drop out of school before the eighth grade.[4] And while brown students have been three times less likely to finish high school than whites, blacks have been over four times less likely to do so.[5] Other statistics tell an equally discouraging tale. For the better part of the last decade, black men have earned on average 48 per cent less than their white counterparts in the same or comparable jobs.[6] In the late 1990s over 1000 court actions nationwide resulted in not a single conviction on the charge of racism.[7] And non-whites continue to be conspicuously absent from elected posts, especially at the national level: only a dozen Afro-Brazilians currently sit among the over 500 members of Brazil's Chamber of Deputies; and of 81 senators, only two are of African ancestry.[8]

The Emergence of the Catholic Anti-racist Movement

Clearly, these numbers describe a situation ripe for collective grievance and action. Accordingly, groups dedicated to improving the life chances of Afro-Brazilians expanded rapidly after the waning of military rule.[9] During the 1970s and 1980s literally thousands of groups across the country formed around different aspects of Afro-Brazilians' struggles for equality, dignity and self-respect.[10] By the 1990s the largest contingent was made up of grassroots 'cultural' groups that organized local youths around the development of skill and pride in one or more Afro-Brazilian cultural activities, ranging across music, art and dance.[11] Hundreds of other groups combined cultural work with organizing around political issues such as the legal prosecution of racism, representation of blacks in the media, reparations for slavery, land rights for historic runaway slave communities and, more recently, affirmative action.[12] Some organizations combined a race and class analysis, working to forge unity between poor whites and blacks around citizenship, rights of access to university, an increase in the minimum wage, job training or other economic issues.[13] Black women's groups have grown as well, committed to organizing around self-esteem, non-European standards of beauty, consciousness-raising about the body, women's health, discrimination against black women, gender violence, and forced prostitution.[14]

The progressive wing of the Catholic Church has not been absent from this process. Since the late 1970s liberationist Catholicism has stimulated the formation of institutions dedicated to the struggle against racism and for a strong, positive Afro-Brazilian identity.[15] Currently the main black Catholic organizations, apart from the Pastoral Afro-Brasileira of the CNBB, are the Instituto do Negro Padre Batista, the Atabaque Cultura Negra e Teologia, and the Grupo de Reflexao sobre a Religião Negra e Indígena. Participants in these groups regard themselves as expressions, in one way or another, of the Black Pastoral, the general effort of black pastoral agents to raise public consciousness about race and racism in Brazil. All are involved in creating a pro-black, anti-racist Catholic consciousness, via theology, liturgy, pastoral practice, training, workshops and the media. Shortly I will discuss in detail some of these groups' key activities.

Several forces facilitated the emergence within the Church of these groups. The first was demographic: a relatively small change in the racial composition of Brazilian seminaries in the 1970s. To understand this change, we need to recall that in the mid-1970s progressive bishops predominated in the national bishops' conference, and that the seminaries in the south and north-east were under the sway of liberation theology.[16] These seminaries attracted a whole generation of young Brazilians into clerical service. While it is true that most priests in Brazil continued to be immigrants from Europe,[17] the period after Vatican II saw the entrance into the clerical profession of a growing number of idealistic young men from non-elite homes – the sons of small shopkeepers and workers – and from the popular Christian base communities.[18]

While most of these new recruits called themselves *branco* (white), the interviews I conducted suggest that by the mid- to late 1970s the applicant pool included a growing contingent of non-whites. If it is an exaggeration to say that the seminaries had been lily-white before the 1970s, it nevertheless seems that the decade saw a rise in the numbers of non-white students, at least in the south of the country. One of my informants, a theology professor at a southern seminary, remembered the period in this way:

> Before that it had been white, white. But in the 70s, I saw more of these kids from the *comunidades* – not the really poor, mind you. They were from the stable homes, where everyone always had enough to eat. Small business people, sometimes. But the fact is, many of them were not white. *Moreno*, *pardo*, like that.

Such students, it seems, did not yet think of themselves in terms of race: indeed, if anything, entrance into seminary highlighted class, not racial identity. Samuel, a fifty-something priest in metropolitan São Paulo, calls himself *negro*, but this was not always the case. In the early 1970s he refused to assume this identity, and called himself by the euphemistic term *moreno* instead. The aspect of his own identity that mattered to him most upon arriving at seminary in the mid-1970s was not his race or colour, but the fact that he came from a poor community. 'That was all that mattered,' he said, 'that I was a child of the poor, that I was studying there with the kids of rich families ... . I was very proud of that.'

Samuel was not alone. By the mid-1970s the seminaries saw a growth in the numbers of children of the poor and lower-middle class, and among these were a number of non-whites. But, as Samuel's story indicates, these seminarians did not identify themselves as *pretos* or *negros*; their terms of reference were *pardo* and *moreno*. Arturo, in his fifties and now a regular priest, who was in seminary in the 1970s had distinct memories of the era. 'There were definitely more *negros* entering seminary,' he told me, 'but they didn't think of themselves as *negros*! First of all, because we didn't have that consciousness, to use the term ... . But also because it was difficult for a really dark guy to get into seminary. So what was happening was that it was *morenos*, or *pardos*, coming in.'

It is important to underscore that this cohort, rather than think of themselves as sharing a racial identity, considered themselves as members of a new generation of advocates for the poor. As Father Arnoldo, also in his fifties and who would later become involved in the Black Pastoral, recalled, 'I had come out of the *comunidade de base*. That's where I was inspired, that was what set my future goals ... . I knew one thing: I was going to help bring about the Kingdom, here on earth.' Race was the last thing on Arnoldo's mind when he arrived at the seminary. 'In 1976', he remembered, 'I didn't think of myself as *negro*, [or] the mission of the Church as fighting for *negros*.' Father Manuel, a priest who eventually became active in the Black Pastoral, had a similar memory: 'I wasn't thinking in terms of a question of race,' he explained. 'I wanted to help the poor. I wasn't thinking about *negros* ... . I was inspired by Dom Helder Camara, the liberation of the poor. For me, for us, the thing was the People's Church – we were going to fight for the poor.'

While the existence of this cohort of liberation theology-inspired *morenos* was necessary to the eventual social base of the Black Pastoral, it was not sufficient. The transformation of this cohort from a racially inchoate cluster to a self-conscious contingent could not occur until the broader political environment around the issue of race in Brazil had begun to change. The nature and causes for this change, particularly in São Paulo, in the years 1977–78, have been examined in detail elsewhere.[19] Suffice it to say that the political opening afforded by the military, the arrival, and frustration, in the racist job market of a new non-white college-educated cohort, the drama of decolonization in Africa, and the arrival of powerful models of black identity from the United States all combined to create an explosive racial mix in the late 1970s. In 1977 this mix was ignited by the murder of a black taxi driver, leading to large demonstrations in São Paulo and the formation of the Movimento Negro Unificado (MNU), the first national black identity organization since the 1930s. The MNU set about politicizing the issue of race, publicly declared Brazil's claim to be a racial democracy a lie, and spawned an assortment of offshoots. The result was that, by the late 1970s, a new, ardent collective action frame denouncing Brazilian racism was in the air, making it no longer possible to speak in public about colour or race without taking this frame into account.

Moreno students in Catholic seminaries could not remain untouched by the changing political climate. A few began to note that while white seminarians were being urged to enter the secular clergy, they were being advised to enter the regular orders instead. 'I wondered about this,' said Father Ronaldo, now a member of the Franciscan order. 'Why were so few of us encouraged to become parish priests?' Already attuned to injustice frames because of their exposure to liberation theology, it was but a short step for non-white seminarians in São Paulo to begin to interpret their treatment in the Church as racially discriminatory.

'I concluded', said Ronaldo, 'that this was discrimination.'

'How so?'

'Well, as long as you put blacks into the regular orders, they won't compete with whites, will they?'

Ronaldo found himself questioning the scarcity of non-white clergy at higher ranks. 'I began to question', he said, 'why were there so few black bishops. Was it because whites didn't want us competing with them?'

Progressive Catholicism was crucial in shaping this ideological process. Questions and feelings such as those of Ronaldo originated in an experience of discrepancy produced in part by liberationist thought, and they were further sharpened by progressive Catholicism. To begin with, the contradiction between teachers' progressive pretensions and their discriminatory behaviour had a radicalizing effect. 'The Church was teaching us to seek liberation of the poor,' an ex-seminarian recalled, 'but when it came to our own liberation, there was a real problem there.' Another one-time seminarian remembered sensing hypocrisy among his teachers: 'They were preaching about equality and justice, but they definitely were not practising this when it came to *negros*.' Among some seminarians the sight of hypocrisy in the ranks of the liberationists provoked a growing identity as a *negro*. 'I hadn't really thought of myself as *negro* before entering the seminary,' Ronaldo observed, 'but there, I felt treated as a *negro*; because we knew we would never have the same opportunities as our white colleagues.'

These experiences did not last long without a collective expression. A small number of non-white seminarians in São Paulo began meeting in the evenings in 1977. 'Pretty soon,' recalled one of them, 'we had a few black priests, and laypeople, and religious, talking together ... . And we thought:

this church which says that it wants liberation, let it assume this responsibility fully, let there be no hypocrisy.'[20]

Liberationist Catholic thought influenced the content of these meetings. These young seminarians had learned from liberation theology that their mission included becoming involved in popular political movements. In this case, this meant attending meetings of the Movimento Negro Unificado (MNU). 'We met', remembered Ronaldo, 'and we talked about what was happening all around us, by the MNU ... went to meetings there, one night in the group, one night in the MNU.' The result of this outreach was a deepening of the racial critique of the Church. 'Participating in those groups,' remembered Arturo, 'I came to realize that what I was seeing in the Church was a kind of oppression, racism ...'

The liberationist Catholic desire to identify with the oppressed overlapped with the black movement's insistence that all people of African descent 'assume their black identity'. 'We understood that we could no longer say we were "*moreno*",' remembered Ronaldo, 'but that we had to assume our *negritude* .... That was very liberating for me. I began to think like this: we are all fighting against oppression, but the priest is not really poor; he fights alongside the poor, but he is not poor .... But look, I am *negro*, my fight is both for *negros* and for myself too.'

By the summer of 1978 members of the group had become convinced that their energies needed to focus on fighting racism within the Church. Throughout the summer, a dozen men and women met informally to share their experiences of discrimination, discuss the lack of black priests and bishops, and formulate strategies for putting race on to the agenda of the upcoming 1979 Latin American bishops' conference in Puebla, Mexico. They would, they decided, challenge the bishops to include in the Brazilian delegation's platform, the plight of the 'doubly and triply oppressed' – Brazil's blacks. At a meeting with Dom Paulo Evaristo Arns, the progressive bishop of São Paulo, the group was resolute. Recalled an ex-seminarian who took part; 'We said: "Look, you have not had the courage to say openly that the people you are defending have this physical face."' The meeting led to a significant victory. Dom Paulo lobbied his colleagues in the national bishops' conference, and announced within days that the CNBB would append to their platform a document which highlighted the 'ethnic diversity' of the Brazilian people.

The seminarians viewed the very existence of such an appendix a major victory, as it represented the first time that the Church had publicly recognized that racial difference was connected to oppression. 'After that we felt that we could make a difference,' recalled Arturo. 'We felt that it was our responsibility, as black men and women, to pursue a whole new path in the Church. That we should not simply wait for things to happen.' Encouraged by the incorporation of the issue of racism into the final 1979 report from Puebla, the movement among black seminarians gathered momentum. 'Priests in other cities', recalled Samuel, 'knew what was happening with us, we were in touch with lots of people ... these meetings were taking place all over.'

This ferment nurtured the emergence of a progressive black Catholic perspective, one that synthesized aspects of Catholic liberation theology with the concerns about race then being articulated by the larger *movimento negro*. It is important to appreciate that the black seminarians – increasingly joined by ordained clergy after 1980 – saw themselves not as breaking with the People's Church, but as fulfilling its promise. By 1980 a new named identity was emerging among them, that of *agente de pastoral negro* (APN), or 'black pastoral agent'. This phrase had entered the lexicon early in 1978, based on the earlier liberationist term *agente de pastoral* ('pastoral agent'). 'We simply borrowed the phrase, and added "*negro*" to it,' explained Samuel.

> It was not something we thought too much about ... . But we had all been pastoral agents, and we wanted everyone to know that we were not giving up our fight for the Church of the Poor. It's just that we had this issue, this concern about the liberation of blacks – so we felt we had to add that.

Another ex-seminarian went further:

> We were critical of some points of leaders in the *igreja do povo*, when they were slow to recognize the issue of race ... . But we remained committed to the Church ... . So we were not going to leave the church ... . I think that this term, 'APN', expressed that faithfulness.

The Consolidation of the Black Pastoral Agenda

Through the early 1980s, the number of APNs grew, and their goals became better defined. They aspired to help Afro-Brazilian Catholics build a strong, proud identity, to help Catholics of all colours become more aware of the racism at work in society and in their own hearts, to transform the clergy to better represent the racial composition of Brazil, and to make a contribution to the improvement of life for all Afro-Brazilians. They worked on three main fronts. First was the popular education front, on which they organized local-level seminars and workshops on the history of slavery, Afro-Brazilian heroes, African religion and culture, and racism. I recall from my own exposure to these workshops in the 1980s that the preferred form of pedagogy was to present flipcharts covered with statistics about racial discrimination. Remembering this period, an APN told me that 'I had faith that what we needed to do was show people what the media always denied. A true picture of the racist society in which we lived.'

The second major front of the APNs' struggle in the 1980s was to push toward achieving official recognition of the memory of Zumbi, the seventeenth-century slave leader and martyr.[21] If the image of Zumbi could invade national consciousness, the argument went, *negros*' self-esteem would increase and whites would feel more respect for blacks. 'We had to challenge this image of the black as resigned to slavery,' explained an APN. 'Zumbi was the key figure in this struggle.' Throughout this period APNs organized teach-ins about Zumbi, collected petitions to make 20 November (the date of his martyrdom) a national holiday, sought to convince municipal leaders to name streets after him or erect statues in his honour, and worked to get him into the pages of school textbooks.

But the APNs' most ambitious goal of the decade was to prepare for the Brotherhood Campaign, an annual six-week-long national programme organized by the Church to focus attention on a theme of social significance. In 1986 they convinced the CNBB to adopt the issue of race as the theme of the 1988 Campaign, arguing that the Church must not miss the opportunity presented by the centennial year of abolition, when undoubtedly there would be a media blitz on the issue. The Brotherhood Campaign did not, in the end, unfold as the APNs had hoped, leading to frustrations that I will discuss shortly. Along with the limitations of their other strategies, these frustrations led the APNs by the end of the 1980s to produce a variety of new tactics and initiatives that would eventually shape the black Catholic movement for years to come. In the remainder of this chapter and the next I analyse three of these initiatives: the effort to create an 'inculturated' afro liturgy; the effort to prepare black youth to pass college entrance exams; and the effort to get Catholics of African ancestry to call themselves '*negro*'. How did the progressive Catholic project give birth to, and shape, each of these initiatives? How have these initiatives shaped the consciousness, norms, and everyday practices of the Catholics exposed to them?

The Inculturated or 'Afro' Mass

The afro liturgy in Brazil emerged from a dialogue between the black movement and the liberationist Catholic Church. The primary impulse to create an afro mass lay in the frustrating outcome of the 1988 Brotherhood Campaign. APNs invested the Campaign with near-millennial hopes, seeing it as an occasion when all the consciousness-raising resources of the Church would be dedicated to the single issue of race. It was, after all, the first time the *pastoral negro* would have full and simultaneous access to every parish and *comunidade* in the nation. Understandably, some APNs spoke of the upcoming campaign as a major historical watershed. 'We had incredibly high hopes for the Campaign,' one APN recalled. 'We thought that if we could just get the issue out into the open, change would happen.'

It soon became clear, however, that the popular response to the Campaign was limited in its enthusiasm.[22] People in the *comunidades* were less than swept away by, among other things, the Campaign's adversarial tone. 'We came in very heavily,' an APN recalled. 'We were saying to people who had never thought about these things before, that whites had tortured blacks, and that blacks needed to unite, and all of this ... . It was hard for people to digest.' Another problem, according to several informants, was that people were bored by the content. 'It was no fun,' explained a pastoral agent. 'A lot of people were saying there was nothing enjoyable about it, it was all lecture, lecture.'

The years immediately following the Brotherhood Campaign saw a decline in the Catholic black movement. According to Frei David Raimundo Dos Santos, by 1992 there were 70 per cent fewer people involved in the Black Pastoral than on the eve of the Campaign.[23] This decline, and the disappointing response to the Brotherhood Campaign, were a wake-up call for many activists in the Black Pastoral, who began to take a hard look at their heavily cognitive approach to consciousness-raising. We can hear a new tone in a circular written by Frei David in 1991. 'Some people,' he observed, 'think only from the point of view of the minority (3 per cent) already in the process of consciousness-raising, forgetting the great majority of black Catholics (97 per cent) who have not yet been blessed [*agraciada*] with progressive consciousness.'[24]

The gentle irony of the word '*agraciada*' reveals the sea-change that was taking place in the thinking of black Catholic activists who, a few years earlier, had spoken confidently of how simple exposure to the right statistics would result, more or less automatically, in a rise in consciousness of black oppression. In 1988, before the start of the Campaign, I was present at a meeting for lay leaders at which pastoral agents displayed charts of numbers detailing the unequal treatment of blacks. I can clearly recall noticing the eyelids of some of those in attendance fluttering down to a close. Afterwards, I approached an APN and asked why they had spent so much time on statistics. 'Oh, that's obvious,' he said. 'I tell you now, there is no one who – once they have seen these figures – can remain a racist.'

After the Campaign, however, as the numbers of people coming to meetings declined, such confidence became difficult to sustain. APNs agreed they would have to start thinking of new ways to reach the '97 per cent' that remained 'unblessed'. For some leaders, the issue was how to turn from a focus on the *conscious* to one that tapped into the *unconscious* as well. 'We cannot assume any longer', explained Rogério, a black pastoral agent, in 1991, 'that just knowing about racism will make a difference. We need to touch people's feelings more. ...' But could they do this? If simply presenting truths on blackboards was not the best way to reach an audience, what else was there?

This question echoed the larger quandary facing the progressive Catholic Church at the end of the 1980s. Until then, the model that had dominated progressive Catholic work at the grassroots had been highly cognitive, based on the notion that social change occurred through correct understandings of the world.[25] But, as discussed earlier, by the mid-1980s a growing number of pastoral agents felt frustrated by a model that too often resulted in blank stares. In response, they called on the liberationist Church finally to valorize the core of what made Catholicism appealing to the masses: its ritual and liturgy.[26]

In the late 1980s and early 1990s all efforts to reshape the liturgy implied working under the rubric of 'inculturation'. Anxious for the Church to retain influence in a globalizing world where the majority of Catholics were non-European, Pope John Paul II believed it was crucial for the liturgy to express its message though local cultural practices.[27] For much of the 1980s this was not a model that found many advocates among progressive Catholics, who worried that it disguised the agenda of abandoning structural critique and reinforcing conservative values through celebrations of 'traditional culture'.[28] But as progressives felt increasingly frustrated by the limited popular appeal of their own rhetoric, they turned in hope and anticipation to 'culture' as a way of finally connecting with the masses.

Liberation theological discussion of inculturation soon flourished.[29] After 1990 liberation theologians were writing that the denigration of culture was as devastating as any other form of oppression. Colonization by Europeans had meant not only the domination of bodies, but 'the defeat of souls as well, through the non-recognition of the other as other'. The remedy was a recognition of the 'dignity of the culture of that other' by seeing it as a carrier of liberating values of 'solidarity, sharing, fellowship'.[30] Once understood this way, non-European culture could be incorporated into the liturgy.

Black Pastoral agents seized upon inculturation as a solution to their crisis. They rolled up their sleeves and began in earnest to design the 'afro liturgy'.[31] The liturgy was first fully designed in 1989, in a parish on the outskirts of Rio de Janeiro by a team led by the charismatic Frei David, and soon spread throughout the country, to dioceses and parishes with active teams of Black Pastoral agents. By the mid-1990s the liturgy had become the most visible part of the APNs' struggle to leave their mark on Brazilian Catholic culture. From their point of view, they had finally hit upon the ideal instrument of mass cultural politics. What could be better than using the prestige of the liturgy to raise consciousness about Afro-Brazilian culture and history? What better way to bridge the gap between black activists and rank-and-file Catholics than by turning to the rich resonances of ritual?

A full-fledged, three-hour long afro liturgy is usually only performed at the centrally located church in the diocesan seat. These are big events, performed with much fanfare on special occasions, such as at the end of a black history week. The performances are organized by well-trained teams who plan the liturgy in conformity with well-developed standards. These afro masses are the most elaborate, with every moment filled with rhythm, colour, motion and often the expertise of semi-professional dancers and musicians. At the lower, parish and *comunidade* levels, elements of the afro liturgy are performed occasionally, but do not pervade every moment of the ritual. At this level liturgies are prepared by laity drawn from participating communities, assisted by a corps of APNs. Laypeople are trained in the afro liturgy, but there is ample room for them to suggest their own departures. The events tend to have more of an amateur feel to them.

When performed at the diocesan seat, the afro mass is a big, long affair. Throughout the service, the atmosphere is definitely that of a 'show': audience members are encouraged to dance in place, and take photographs and video. Throughout the three-hour event, in front of large crowds, the air pulsates with the beating of palms on cowskins stretched over the mouths of waist-high *atabaques*, the tall, cylindrical drums used in samba, reggae-samba, and *musica bahiana*, and that also serve sometimes as the instruments in the Afro-Brazilian religions of *umbanda* and *candomblé*. Before the arrival at the altar of the presiding priest, a row of drummers, dressed in brilliant green, red and white, hammer at the drums next to the white tableclothed communion table. There appears before them a troupe of young women, decked out in 'afro' garb, moving to the front of the communion table, arms and legs describing sinuous arcs, silver chalice and white tablecloth flashing intermittently in the curved spaces between bodies. Congregants clap and sway, excited whispers rippling through the crowd.

Later, in some liturgies, two young men, barefoot and wearing only the white cotton pants of the martial art *capoeira*, kneel at the altar, and perform a stylized bout, complete with breathtaking acrobatics. Later, the audience is called upon to intone hymns of praise for Zumbi, for other martyrs in the struggle for black liberation, for all the ancestors who died as slaves, for black saints such as Efigênia and Benedito, and for the *orixás* (spirits) of *candomblé* – Ogun, Olorum, Olodumaré and Oxum. During the liturgy of the Word, the priest, clad in a kente cloth stole and a round, flat, multicoloured headdress, reads from Exodus and offers a homily on how the struggle of the Hebrews to toss off the yoke of slavery showed God's love for the oppressed, and showed He was on the side of all those who fought for their freedom.

Then, during the passing of collection baskets, a half-dozen youths, to the rhythms of *atabaques*, carry in, on their heads, wooden bowls filled with coconut candies, manioc bread, sugar cane and bananas – some of which were 'slave' foods, others commonly offered to the *orixás* – and place them at the foot of the altar. Soon thereafter, the priest leads the distribution of communion. After the final blessing, live drumming is replaced with a recorded tape of secular Bahian music, while pastoral agents circulate with bowls of food.

I want now to consider the extent to which the afro liturgy has accomplished its cultural–political goal of altering popular attitudes toward things 'afro'. First, the afro liturgy aims to challenge the culturally dominant perception that afro religion is 'demonic'. As an APN explained:

> The average Brazilian grows up learning to think of *candomblé* as the work of the devil ... . So that is where we have to work, at the cultural level. And there, I can tell you, people believe that it is a work of the devil. So we have to say, 'No, it really isn't that way', that it is really an expression of African culture.

Clearly, for some rank-and-file Catholics, the afro liturgy does help to de-demonize afro religiosity. In a survey of 40 women, nearly half reported that exposure to the afro mass had effected a tangible shift in their sentiments toward afro religiosity, making them more sympathetic toward it, more ready to tolerate and even value it. The importance of this effect cannot be overstated. As Dona Matilde, a middle-aged woman who has served for many years in the traditional Catholic organization, the Apostolate of Prayer, explained; 'I learned here that all this stuff about it being a work of the devil, that is nonsense ... . I think it is important to learn about it. Before I said, "No, that is witchcraft, I will not even listen to that." Now I listen more.'

If such were the only effect of the afro liturgy it would have served its stated purpose. But the story is more complex than this. Some black movement activists and practitioners of afro religion complain that the afro liturgy, while de-demonizing afro religion in the eyes of some, has done so at the cost of reshaping and distorting it to conform to European-based needs and assumptions. Paradoxically, they say, the afro liturgy has adopted a disrespectful attitude towards the very religiosity it claims to respect, by mixing indiscriminately its sacred elements (for example, the drums, the offering of foods, the invocation of *orixás*) with profane elements such as *capoeira* and the memory of Zumbi, and by shoving them all together with elements that have nothing to do with afro culture at all. Who, the practitioners of afro religion want to know, authorized the Church to do this? As one *candomblecista* put it, 'if the Church feels it can mention *orixás* during Mass, what should keep *terreiros* [*candomblé* temples] from distributing holy Communion?' An ex-practitioner of *candomblé*, now an activist in Rio's black movement, disapproved of the 'instrumentalization' of afro religion for what he called 'narrowly Christian ends':

> Look, it's basically a Eurocentric rite, to make the Mass more exciting, exotic, to attract people back to the Church ... . It's really just another kind of exploitation. Because look: would they accept anyone manifesting a spirit there [possession], if an *orixá* descended? No, of course not. That, they do not respect that, for them that is unacceptable! So they pick only the things that fit easily into the Christian rite: the food, the drums. So that's what's going on there.

Some *mães de santo* express even tougher criticism, saying that they resent what they see as the Church's effort to make afro religion more palatable to Christians by squeezing it into Judeo-Christian molds. Catholics were being taught that *orixás* were deceased African kings and warriors, rather than gods; that veneration of the *orixás* was the same thing as remembering the good deeds of Catholic saints; that Oxalá was the Yoruba name for Jesus, and other falsehoods. 'Oxalá is not Jesus,' a *mãe de santo* said. 'And Olorum is not the God of the Bible. I tell you this: Olorum did not give Moses anything! These are totally different ideas, different entities.'

While these criticisms are no doubt valid, it is still important to maintain a more dialectical perspective on the afro liturgy. For at the very moment APNs are squeezing afro religion into European moulds to make it more palatable to their Christian audience, they are also creating – in ways they neither fully anticipate nor grasp – an important opportunity for people at the grassroots who hold non-Eurocentric views of afro religion to express themselves without fear of ostracism.

In order to appreciate this pattern, we must realize that it is inaccurate to regard the Catholic rank and file as homogeneously prejudiced against afro religion. There exists at the local level, a strain of rich, fairly undistorted knowledge about afro religion. It is not unusual to meet people who, because of a successful encounter in a *terreiro* – a problem solved, a sickness cured, a job obtained – have decided to become familiar with the religion, spend time visiting a *terreiro*, ask questions, listen, read what they can, all the while still identifying themselves strongly as Catholic.

Consider Sonia. A practising Catholic in her forties with an eighth-grade education, who lives in a town about two hours south of São Luis (Maranhão), Sonia some years ago found herself at the edge of despair about her two-year old daughter's chronic cough. After the usual round of doctors and prayer services, she took the girl to a *terreiro* connected peripherally to *tambor de Mina*. Soon after, her daughter got better, and Sonia was filled with gratitude. Alhough she never felt moved to become directly involved in the religion, she decided to learn more about the *tambor*. She asked questions, visited different *terreiros*, observed, read and even went through a couple of cleansing rituals. By 2001, when I met her, Sonia's knowledge of the tambor was rather more nuanced than anything an APN could dish out in a seminar.

Now although people like Sonia are probably outnumbered at the local level by people who demonize afro religion, the very existence of people like her creates difficulties for APNs intent on 'Judeo-Christianizing' afro religion. Consider the case of Lucilene. A thoughtful woman in her fifties, Lucilene had participated for much of her life in her Catholic community in Icatu, a small fishing village in Maranhão. Alhough she had no schooling beyond the sixth grade, she was a lay leader, and a member of her community's liturgy team. When the priest announced a series of training sessions to prepare a parishwide afro liturgy, Lucilene was intrigued and decided to participate. The workshop took place on a humid evening in a badly-lit parish annex, with about 20 laypeople from various communities sitting at rickety wood school desks. At the blackboard, chalk in hand, a young APN spoke animatedly. Lucilene listened while the young man expounded on *tambor de mina*:

> OK, you sometimes hear that *tambor* is polytheistic. No! Not true. They believe in God, just as we do. They have a great, single God, Olodumaré, just as we have Jehovah. These others, they are not really Gods. They are like our saints; they were great people while they were alive. And now this is way the African remembers them, venerates their memory.

I was sitting next to Lucilene, who had begun to fidget. When the young man called Yemenjá, the goddess of the salt waters, an 'African queen', Lucilene could contain herself no longer. She raised her hand. She had, she said, been 'visiting these places for some time'. Further, 'I have friends, and neighbours, even one of my godchildren who are involved in this.' So she felt she had some basis for doubting that the people of *tambor de mina* believed that Yemenjá had once been a human queen. 'The way I understand it,' she said, 'Yemenjá is supposed to come out of the salt waters, she created the oceans of the world. I don't think a queen does that.'

The APN backpedalled. 'Of course, Lucilene, absolutely! I'm just talking about her origins in myth.' This did not satisfy her:

> Yes, but we're talking about whether these *orixás* are the same as saints. And what I see is that there is a difference! It isn't the same thing. These *orixás*, they are rivers, and snakes, and things like that. And the others, they don't seem like saints at all. Saints don't come down and enter into people! But those *orixás*, the people think that they get possessed by them.

The pastoral agent looked sheepish. 'Yes, Lucilene, you certainly are right.' The conversation turned to other things, but the exchange haunted the rest of the discussion.

The exchange, it turns out, had an impact on the content of the liturgy that was eventually prepared by the group. In the days following, I heard Lucilene's intervention referred to by others who had been present. As long as the idea that *orixás* were pretty much like saints had not been subjected to scrutiny, it was possible during the mass to refer to them by name. But once their true natures had been articulated publicly – once it had been stated that they were believed to be real gods, and hence in direct contradiction to Christian monotheism – it became difficult to invoke their names during the mass. I learned later that when the time came for those who went through the training to choose songs from the hymnal, they passed over those that invoked the *orixás*. I asked the team member who told me this why they had done so. 'Well,' she said, 'you were there when we had that discussion about the *orixás*. The inculturated mass is to bring African culture into the Church, it isn't for bringing another religion.'

If it is incorrect to assume that the afro liturgy always purveys Europeanized versions of afro religion to the unsuspecting masses, neither should we presume that APNs always try to do so. In another dialectical twist, it appears that by provoking angry reactions from practitioners of afro religion, the afro liturgy has in some cases opened up new channels of communication between these practitioners and APNs, leading in turn in these cases to significant reforms of the liturgy.

Consider a case from Maranhão. In the early 1990s APNs in a diocese outside of São Luiz undertook to create an afro liturgy, but quite characteristically for the time did not seek input from the practitioners of afro religion themselves. An APN explained that 'we just didn't consult with them. We thought we didn't need to. We were sure we knew what "afro" meant, so there was no need.' Then in 1993 something happened. Some APNs were trying to initiate a dialogue with the leaders of a *terreiro*, without success. While they puzzled over the lack of responsiveness, one of the APNs discovered that the leaders of the *tambor* were angry. 'We learned that the *mães* were infuriated with us. They felt we had offended their religion by bringing the *tambor* [sacred drum] into a Catholic Church without their permission, and by playing it alongside an *atabaque* [in this context, a non-sacred drum]. That was the worst!' This challenge prised open a space for APNs to reflect on what had until then been the taken-for-granted right of Judeo-Christians to manipulate afro religion as they saw fit. 'Well, I tell you that day was very important for me,' the APN stated. 'That changed our behaviour a lot.'

The APNs responded to the criticism by instituting a series of liturgical changes. Henceforth no *tambor* would be played in Church without the permission of a local *mãe de santo*. The *tambor* would be removed from the sacred sphere of the Catholic ritual, and reserved for a special presentation after the ritual was over. And no one would play the *tambor* except for ritually qualified members of the *terreiro*. 'We realized', said an APN, 'that only they had the right to play these drums. Only they understood their powers. None of us were prepared for that.'

This was a path-breaking admission on the part of the guardians of Judeo-Christian truth, which opened a new chapter in the local relationship between APNs and the *terreiros* in Maranhão. Local *mães de santo* welcomed visits from the APNs who began to consult them in greater detail about the afro liturgy. The *mães* were delighted to see shows of respect towards their religion from the Church. When, for example, a *mãe de santo* pointed out that the lyrics to a Catholic hymn inappropriately invoked the name of a specific god, the APNs excised the chant. 'We found this very gratifying,' observed a local *mãe de santo*.

Similar processes occurred elsewhere in Brazil in the early and mid-1990s, though not always as smoothly. In Rio de Janeiro, some *terreiros* threatened to bring a lawsuit against the Church for having allowed the presence of shirtless *capoeiristas* alongside the sacred drums of *candomblé*. Although in the end no lawsuit was filed, the event served as a wake-up call to APNs involved in the afro liturgy. 'After that,' one of them recalls, 'I paid more attention to this … . That has created a strong doubt in my mind about our liturgies, and makes me more careful about what we include in them.'

Conclusion

In tracing the influence of liberationist perspectives on the rise and consolidation of the Black Pastoral and assessing the impact of the Pastoral's leading action, the reformulation of the liturgy, it becomes clear that liberationism has been central to the Black Pastoral from its inception. Indeed, without the power of Catholic liberationism it is unclear how the Black Pastoral could have arisen and consolidated institutionally. As for the afro liturgy, it is also clear that its impact on the Catholic public's perceptions of afro religion is dialectical. While the afro liturgy has succeeded in de-demonizing afro religion, it has often done so at the expense of distorting afro religion to fit the comfort zone of Euro-derived Christianity. By creating contexts in which local people with experience of afro religion feel free to talk openly of their experiences and challenge some of the distorted images of that religion, APNs have unwittingly created opportunities for the grassroots emergence of a more culturally respectful, less Euro-centric version of the liturgy. And by encouraging more open communication between APNs and practitioners of afro religion, the latter have sometimes successfully pressed their concerns upon the APNs. In these sometimes indirect and contradictory ways, then, the Catholic black movement is making an important contribution to an increasingly sophisticated respect for, and appreciation of, afro religiosity in Brazil.

My focus in this chapter has been on the APNs' religious, liturgical interventions in the name of black liberation. But obviously, inspired by a theology that calls for action in the secular world, the APNs could not long remain absent from that world. It is therefore to APNs' efforts to intercede in the non-Church world that I now turn.

Notes

1   There have been numerous studies detailing the psychic and social wounds suffered by Afro-Brazilians. These include Yvonne Maggie and Claudia Barcellos Rezende (eds.), *Raca como Retórica: A Construção da Diferença* (Rio de Janeiro: Civilização Brasileira, 2002); Rebecca Lynn Reichmann (ed.), *Race in Contemporary Brazil: from Indifference to Inequality* (University Park, PA.: Pennsylvania State University Press, 1999); Michael Hanchard (ed.), *Racial Politics in Contemporary Brazil* (Durham: Duke University Press, 1999); Robin Sheriff, *Dreaming Equality: Color, Race and Racism in*

Urban Brazil (New Brunswick, NJ.: Rutgers University Press, 2001); Antônio Sérgio Alfredo Guimarães, *Racismo e Anti-Racismo no Brasil* (São Paulo: Editora, 1999); John Burdick, *Blessed Anastacia: Women, Race, and Popular Christianity in Brazil* (New York: Routledge, 1998).

2   In 1980, illiteracy for the 15–64 age range was placed at 14.5 per cent for whites, and 36.5 per cent for *pretos* and *pardos*. See Carlos Hasenbalg and Nelson do Valle Silva, 'Race and Educational Opportunity in Brazil,' in Reichmann, *Race in Contemporary Brazil*, p. 54. In the year 2000, the illiteracy rate among whites was 10.6 per cent while among *negros* and *pardos* it was 28.7 per cent. See the report by Adriana Ferreira, 'Racismo: reunião define posição do Pais na ONU', in *Estado de São Paulo*, at http://www.estado.estadao.com.br/editorias/2001/07/06/ger015.html. Similar figures for 2001 may be found in the report by Peter Muello at http://aad.english.ucsb.edu/docs/muello1.html.

3   The 1980 figures state that 10 per cent of white children never went to school, against 20 per cent of the *pretos* and *pardos*. See Hasenbalg and Valle Silva, 'Race and Educational Opportunity in Brazil', p. 58. While more recent figures have not been analysed, the authors present the 1980 figures as still indicative of current trends.

4   Ibid., p. 55. Figures may be found in Fúlvia Rosemberg, *Literatura infantil e ideologia* (São Paulo: Global, 1985); F. Rosemberg, 'Relações raciais e rendimento escolar', *Cadernos de pesquisa*, 63 (November 1987), 19–23; Vera Moreira Figueira,'O preconceito racial na escola', *Estudos Afro-Asiáticos*, 18 (1990), 63–71; Rosangela Sant'Anna, 'A fileira da catástrofe: o que a cor pode representar no sistema educacional?', Working Paper, Núcleo da Cor, Universidade Federal do Rio de Janeiro, 1996.

5   In a study of adolescents aged between 15 and 19, according to 1982 regional census, 18 per cent of whites had completed 9–11 years of schooling, but only 4.6 per cent of *pretos* had, and only 6.4 per cent of *pardos* had. See Carlos Hasenbalg and Valle Silva, 'Race and Educational Opportunity in Brazil', p. 56.

6   Nadya Araújo Castro and Antônio Sérgio Alfredo Guimarães, 'Racial Inequalities in the Labor Market' in Reichmann, *Race in Contemporary Brazil*; see also the 2000 statistics reported by the São Paulo State Socio-Economic Research Foundation, as cited by Peter Muello at http://aad.english.ucsb.edu/docs/muello1.html.

7   A recent study conducted by Christiano Jorge Santos for the 1995–2000 period, found that of 1,050 occurrences of racism, in 22 states, none resulted in a conviction. See the analysis in the Estado de São Paulo, 3 August 2001 at http://www.estadao.com.br/agestado/noticias/2001/ago/31/176.htm.
On the more general matter of judicial impunity for racism cases, see also Guimarães, *Racismo e Anti-racismo no Brasil*, (São Paulo: Editora, 1999).

8   See Peter Muello's excellent analysis at http://aad.english.ucsb.edu/docs/muello1.html.

9   The black consciousness movements in Brazil have yet to receive the thorough analytical treatment they deserve. For preliminary analyses, see Márcio Goldman, 'Segmentaridades e movimentos negros nas eleiçóes de Ilhéus', *Mana*, 7, 2 (October 2001), 57–93; John Burdick, 'The Lost Constituency of Brazil's Black Consciousness Movements', *Latin American Perspectives*, 98, 25 (January 1998), 136–155; Michael Hanchard, *Orpheus and Power: The Movimento Negro of Rio de Janeiro and São Paulo*, 1945–1988 (Princeton: Princeton University Press, 1994), John Burdick, 'Brazil's Black Consciousness Movement', *NACLA Report on the Americas*, 25, 4 (1992), 23–27.

10 Caetana Damasceno, *et al.*, *Catálogo de entidades de movimento negro o Brasil* (Rio de Janeiro: ISER, 1988); for a specific case that analyses black movement ideology, see Márcio Goldman and David Rogers, 'An Ethnographic Theory of Democracy. Politics from the Viewpoint of Ilhéus's Black Movement (Bahia, Brazil)' *Ethnos*, 66, 2 (2001), 157–180.

11 David Covin, 'Narrative, Free Spaces, and Communities of Memory in the Brazilian Black Consciousness Movement', *The Western Journal of Black Studies*, 21, 4, (Winter 1997), 272–279; Wivian Weller, 'Identity Construction through the Hip-Hop Movement: A Comparative Analysis between Black Rappers in São Paulo and Turkish-German Rappers in Berlin,' *Caderno CRH*, 32 (January/June 2000), 213–232.

12 For examples see David Covin, 'Learning from Brazil's Unified Black Movement: Whither Goeth Black Nationalism?', *National Political Science Review*, 7, (1999), 84–95; and Christopher Guillebeau, 'Affirmative Action in a Global Perspective: The Cases of South Africa and Brazil', *Sociological Spectrum*, 19, 4 (October/December 1999), 443–465.

13 A good example of this kind of organization is the Centro para Articulação de Populações Marginalizadas (CEAP). See their website at http://www.ceap.org.br/. See also the perceptive analyses of the Grupo Cultural Afro-Reggae by Olivia Maria Gomes da Cunha, 'Black Movements and the Politics of Identity in Brazil' in Sonia Alvarez, Evelina Dagnino and Arturo Escobar (eds.), *Cultures of Politics, Politics of Cultures* (Boulder: Westview, 1998), 220–251; and by George Yudice, 'Globalization and Culture in Brazil: the Case of Grupo Cultural Afro-Reggae', unpublished ms. (2002).

14 Alzira Rufino, '"I, Black Woman, Resist!"', *Gender and Development*, 3, 1 (February 1995), 55–58; Matilde Ribeiro, 'Black Brazilian Women: From Bertioga to Beijing', *Estudos Feministas*, 3, 2 (1995), 446–457.

15 John Burdick, 'The Evolution of a Progressive Catholic Project: the Case of the Black Pastoral in Rio de Janeiro, Brazil' in John Burdick and W. E. Hewitt (eds.), *The Church at the Grassroots in Latin America: Perspectives on Thirty Years of Activism* (Westport: Greenwood Press, 2000), 71–84; Caetana Damasceno, 'Cantando para Subir', Master's thesis, Programa de Pos-Graduação de Antropologia Social, Universidade Federal de Rio de Janeiro, 1990; Ana Lúcia Valente, *O negro e a igreja católica: o espaço concedido, um espaço reivindicado* (Campo Grande, MS: CECITEC, 1994).

16 See Christian Smith, *The Emergence of Liberation Theology* (Chicago: Chicago University Press, 1991); Scott Mainwaring, *The Catholic Church and Politics in Brazil, 1916–1985* (Stanford: Stanford University Press, 1986).

17 See for example, Michel Lowy, 'The French Sources of Liberation Christianity in Brazil', *Archives de sciences sociales des religions*, 42, 97 (January/March 1997), 9–32.

18 This interpretation is largely based on my own interviews with priests in São Paulo, Rio, and São Luiz; but also see the analyses by Madeleine Adriance, 'Opting for the Poor: A Social-Historical Analysis of the Changing Brazilian Catholic Church', *Sociological Analysis*, 46, 2 (Summer, 1985), 131–146; Ralph Della Cava, 'Catholicism and Society in Twentieth Century Brazil', *Latin American Research Review*, 11, 2 (1976), 7–50.

19 See the contributions to Pierre-Michel Fontaine (ed.), *Race, Class and Power in Brazil* (Los Angeles: Center for Afro-American Studies, 1985); Hanchard, *Orpheus and Power*; Reid Andrews, *Blacks and Whites in São Paulo, Brazil, 1888–1988* (Madison: University of Wisconsin Press, 1991); Clovis Moura, *Dialética radical do Brasil negro* (São Paulo: Anita, 1994).

20 For an analysis of the importance of 'free spaces', such as small discussion groups, to the emergence and sustenance of collective action, see Francesca Polletta, 'Free Spaces and Collective Action', *Theory and Society*, 28, 1 (February 1999), 1–38.

21 This goal had been on the agenda of the first wave of black organization in the post-abolition era. See Kim Butler, *Freedoms Given, Freedoms Won* (New Brunswick: Rutgers University Press, 1998).

22 John Burdick, *Looking for God in Brazil* (Berkeley: University of California Press, 1993); Burdick, 'The Evolution of a Progressive Catholic Project'.

23 Frei David, personal communication, September 1996.

24 Frei David dos Santos, 'Uma contribuição ao debate em torno do rito católico afro-brasileiro' mimeo (São João de Meriti: Grupo dos Agentes do Pastoral do Negro, 1991).

25 Here the influence of Paulo Freire was clear. See the analysis of the cognitive basis of the liberationist movement in David Lehmann, *Struggle for the Spirit: Religious Transformation and Popular Culture in Brazil* (Cambridge: Polity, 1996); see also Daniel M. Bell, *Liberation Theology After the End of History* (New York: Routledge, 2001).

26 The change can be seen in the changing foci of the national CEB meetings from the 1980s to the 1990s. See the analysis in Faustino Luiz Couto Teixeira, *Os Encontros Intereclesiais de CEBs no Brasil* (São Paulo: Paulinas, 1996); see also the analysis of Clodovis Boff, 'CEBs: A Que Ponto estão e Aonde Vão' in Solange Rodrigues *et al.*, (eds.), *As Comunidades de Base em Questão* (São Paulo: Paulinas, 1997), 251–306.

27 For cases of inculturation elsewhere in the Latin American Catholic world, see Andrew Orta, 'From Theologies of Liberation to Theologies of Inculturation.' in S. R. Pattnayak (ed.) *Organized Religion in the Political Transformation of Latin America* (Lanham, MD: University Press of America, 1995), 97–124; Diego Irarrazavel, *Inculturation: New Dawn of the Church in Latin America* (Maryknoll: Orbis, 2000); Michael Angrosino, 'The Culture Concept and the Mission of the Roman Catholic Church', *American Anthropologist*, 96, 4 (1994), 824–832; Pablo Richard, 'The Evangelization of Cultures' in Guillermo Cook (ed.), *Crosscurrents in Indigenous Spirituality* (Leiden: Brill, 1997), 225–232; Robert Schreiter, *Constructing Local Theologies* (Maryknoll: Orbis, 1985); David Kozak, 'Ecumenical Indianism: The Tekakwitha Movement as a Discursive Field of Faith and Power' in Elizabeth Brusco and Laura Klein (eds.), *The Message in the Missionary: Local Interpretations of Religious Ideology and Missionary Personality* (Williamsburg: Studies in Third World Societies, 1994), 1–114; Barry Lyons, 'Religion, Authority, and Identity: Intergenerational Politics, Ethnic Resurgence, and Respect in Chimborazo, Ecuuador', *Latin American Research Review*, 36, 1 (2001), 7–48.

28 Harvey Cox, 'Catholicity, Inculturation, and Liberation Theology: the case of Leonardo Boff' in *Struggles for Solidarity* (Minneapolis: University of Minnesota Press, 1992), 105–113; Harvey Cox, 'Inculturation Reconsidered: Indigenization as Form of Continuing Oppression', *Christianity and Crisis*, 51 (13 May 1991), 140-142; Teixeira, *Os Encontros*, 113; Manuel Vasquez and Anna Peterson, 'The New Evangelization in Latin American Perspective', *Cross Currents*, 48 (Fall 1998), 311–329 argue that inculturation was partly a cover for the imposed return of spiritual over political matters.

29 Gutíerrez, in the preface to the 1988 edition of his 1971 *Theology of Liberation*, wrote that 'all theology [is a] dialogue with the prevailing culture' and 'Just as Jesus' accent betrayed him (Matt. 26: 73), our theological language is subject to the same rule; it takes its coloring from our peoples, cultures, and racial groupings, and yet we use it in an attempt to proclaim the universality of God's love' (Gustavo Gutíerrez, *Theology of Liberation* (Maryknoll: Orbis, 2nd edn, 1988), xxxv).

30 Leonardo Boff, *The New Evangelization: Good News to the Poor* (Maryknoll: Orbis, 1991), 44.

31 The impending quincentennial celebration in 1992, by politicizing the themes of slavery, colonization, and ethnocide inevitably focused progressive attention on issues of cultural and racial identity. It was no accident that the theme of 'Oppressed Cultures and Evangelization in Latin America' was chosen for both the interecclesial conference of the Brazilian Liberationist Church, and the Latin American Episcopal conference in the Dominican Republic, both in 1992.

Chapter 2

The Black Pastoral in the Secular World

Whilst, as we have seen, the proponents of the Black Pastoral sought to use religious liturgy to reshape the culture of race, they did not restrict themselves to the religious sphere. In this chapter I will focus on two of the Pastoral's secular struggles. First, I will examine the Pastoral's work to increase Afro-Brazilians' access to higher education. In fighting to improve Afro-Brazilians' ability to compete on college entrance examinations the Black Pastoral catalysed, as its leaders hoped it would, a social process that is still bringing about major changes, both in public policy and in everyday social behaviour. The Pastoral's special commitment to the college entrance project is, I will argue, due largely to the influence of liberationist Catholicism. Second, I will consider the Black Pastoral's effort to persuade parishioners of African descent to abandon any term of self-reference other than '*negro*'. This effort has led, to be sure, to the 'conversions to negritude' so prized by the black movement, but it has also resulted, I will argue, in the formation of an identity not anticipated by movement leaders, in which the valorization of African ancestry coexists peacefully with the insistence that one is not '*negro*', but rather 'mixed'. To the extent that this identity is new, the Black Pastoral is helping to alter the landscape of racial classification in Brazil. Thus, both in intended and unintended ways, the work of the Black Pastoral shows that Catholic liberationism is still alive and well – and leaving an imprint on Brazilian culture.

Getting *Negros* into College

From the perspective of numerous leaders of the Black Pastoral in Rio de Janeiro, their single most consequential initiative in the 1990s was their struggle at the strategic point at which young people enter college. By 2001, Rio de Janeiro's *pré-vestibular para negros e carentes* ('college exam preparation course for blacks and the poor', or PVNC) had grown to a network of over 70 groups, able to prepare every year over 3000 high school students to take the annual college entrance examinations.[1] Nationally, nearly 800 such courses accommodate nearly 60 000 students across Brazil, gaining entry to the best universities for hundreds of them.

The Church chose to emphasize this programme for two main reasons: because the inequality around access to higher education is glaring and easily proven; and because a concern about education fits smoothly with the

Church's historic identity and mission. With regard to the former, until recently, although one in seven Brazilian whites were entering college, less than one in 60 *pretos*, and less than one in 35 *pardos* were making it this far.[2] In other words, 'having white skin in Brazil means having 8.5 times more probability of starting college than *pretos* and almost 5 times more than *pardos*'.[3] By the early 1990s, these disparities were becoming widely publicized, in research and in the popular press, and they became increasingly difficult to deny or sweep under the carpet.[4] With regard to the latter, testimony from several pastoral agents involved in the early years of the prevestibular campaign confirm that they conceptualized the issue as naturally falling to the Church, because of its longstanding association with matters pedagogical. 'What other institution could do this?' was the rhetorical question posed by one of my informants. I will return to this point shortly.

Ironically, through much of the 1980s, the *pastoral negro* paid little or no attention to Brazil's higher educational system. Its energies were focused instead on raising consciousness in the CEBs, valorizing Zumbi, and preparing for the 1988 Brotherhood Campaign. After 1988, however, the idea of preparing blacks for college entrance exams found its way quickly on to their agenda.

The growing popularity of the idea among APNs was due in part to their search for a concrete, practical, experience-near way of appealing to a constituency that had been turned off by the abstract, impractical stance of the Campaign. But the immediate stimulus to the idea was mounting frustration among black clergy about the lack of black Church leadership. While the demand for more black clergy had been on the APNs' agenda for the better part of the preceding decade, they had almost nothing to show for it: by the end of the 1980s only four blacks numbered among the nation's 339 bishops, and only about 500 blacks could be counted among 15 000 priests nationwide. By the end of the 1980s black clergy had realized that simply declaring the need to have more black clergy would not magically increase the number of qualified black candidates for priesthoods and bishoprics. As one of the APNs told me, 'We had been struggling for ten years to get the bishops to increase the number of black clergy. We were reaching a dead-end on that.' A visit to Brazil in 1990 by the papal nuncio was no doubt the clincher. When he met with the nuncio, the well-known black Catholic activist Frei David called upon him to nominate more black bishops. The nuncio's reply, as reported to me by Frei David, was: 'Brazil does not have more black bishops, because the bishops do not present us with black candidates.' David recounted this as the moment when he realized that growth in the number of black bishops 'would happen only with the investment in the training and preparation of the *negro* within the Church'.[5]

Once the notion of 'preparing' *negros* for clerical advancement had been broached, it was a short step for APNs to expand their thinking to include the preparation of *negros* for all professions. The ease of this cognitive move revealed a natural affinity between the values of progressive Catholics and those of secular institutions of higher learning. Progressive Catholics have always echoed the mission of the larger Church, in referring to its own high stake in the role of leaders in society. The Catholic Church in all its forms has always been dedicated to investing in the leadership of an intellectual elite. As one APN explained, 'I think there's something natural, or destined, if you wish, about us getting involved in this [higher education]. We are Catholics! [laughter] I mean, look: the Church runs schools and universities and seminaries, and we have a natural interest in how our youth get educated. And how our young people are prepared for tomorrow through universities.'

But, I wondered, wasn't it one thing to form the Church's own institutions of higher learning, another thing completely to try and interfere with how public universities were run? Not at all, I was told: 'We are no different from the larger Church in this. The Church has always worried about what is being taught there, and tries to make itself available .... ' Here, the special mission of liberationist Catholics to try to intervene directly in the world to bring about social justice weighed heavily. Said one APN:

We cannot keep our 'hands off' any institution. For it is through all institutions that the values, those that we fight for as well as those we abhor, get taught. That applies to us, the Church as an institution as well. If we are willing to work with the Church, to try and transform it from within why shouldn't we also be ready to try and transform the university system from within?

Thus in 1990 it was very much in keeping with their historical identity as Catholics, and with their more recent identity as liberationists, for APNs to begin pursuing preparation for college entrance exams as a site of struggle. As one participant in the early discussions recounted, 'It was like a lightbulb going on. As soon as the idea was mentioned, everyone saw it had to be done.' There were some who thought it was elitist, that they would be turning away from the bases. But the consensus soon became that this might be just what was needed to connect with the base, for it was common knowledge that the working poor longed to see their children make it to college. As one APN recalled, 'I thought this was a great idea, and a great way to organize people. Because what family doesn't want one of its own in college? But I never thought this could happen? So I thought, this will be surely a good way to connect with our base.'[6]

These leaders calculated correctly, for a large base began readily to respond to the Church's call to prepare for the college exams. In 1992, the year before the PVNC began in earnest 'one could have counted the number of Afro-Brazilians taking the vestibular exam on one hand's fingers', according to Frei David, and indeed all witnesses to the era agree that the numbers of blacks in college before the early 1990s was miniscule.

The programme's first year, 1992, saw it prepare no fewer than 50 students to take the exam; 18 of these went on to attend university. It was as if a dam had broken. The news of the first students' success spread like wildfire through the Rio area. By the programme's second year, over 700 poor Afro-Brazilian high school seniors queued up, in the hope of securing one of the 150 places the PVNC could accommodate at that time.[7] The die was cast: Rio's PVNC became a beacon for a national movement of grassroots pre-vestibular courses.

The 'Rio model' included several key features: intense dedication on the part of volunteer teachers, a serious approach by students, concern about nurturing students' self-esteem, and the commitment from successful students that they would eventually return to give back to their communities. In the following years, courses imitating the Rio model appeared in half a dozen other states, and organizers from around the country arrived in Rio to learn about it. As mentioned earlier, about 800 similar programmes serve nearly 60 000 students nationally, and hundreds of these continue to the best universities. Most impressively, in 1997, organizers brought the model to Brazil's largest city, São Paulo, where it quickly caught on. By 2001 there were 55 nuclei in São Paulo, deploying 850 teachers to serve some 3300 vestibular hopefuls.[8]

A Visit to a PVNC núcleo

The model and its continuing reflection of liberationist Catholic values is readily grasped by visiting a '*núcleo*'. At seven a.m. on a Saturday morning, I clutched my windcheater closely and watched little willows of breath rise before me as I ascended the steep cobbled avenue of Rocinha, Rio de Janeiro's largest *favela*, in the shadow of three-story white-plastered clay-brick buildings, a street dense with people returning from night shifts or on the way to their day jobs. As I turned into an alley, the broad blue sky became a sliver between dirty white facades. Walking through the din of radios and past kids kicking a soccer ball, I found my way to the annex of the Catholic Church.

When I entered the classroom where the *Núcleo Resistência* was meeting, a young man with a dreadlocked pony tail and wearing a 'Viva Zumbi' t-shirt was standing at the blackboard, scratching out the name of Malthus. On the walls on either side hung political posters: '100 Years of a Lie', 'Work with Dignity!' and 'Zumbi'. Seated at well-worn chair-desks, 13 students were dutifully writing in their notebooks. The students ranged in age from late teens to mid-twenties, and nine of the students were women.[9] I sat down at a desk, but the atmosphere was so studious that my interruption went unnoticed. One student glanced at me, smiled, then returned to his notebook. The teacher, a high-school instructor named Andre, was a graduate student in economics at the Pontifical Universidade Católica. (The programme, administered by APNs, recruits teachers from the public and private school systems who work on a volunteer basis.) Previously told that I would be visiting today, he sent a gentle nod my way, but refrained from introducing me. In other educational environments in Brazil, the visit of a foreigner was usually a good pretext for distraction, but not here: there was too much to do, time was too precious, aims too urgent. In most classrooms I had visited in Brazil, open doors and windows let in ricocheting noise from cars and hallway conversation. But not here. Here the window to the street remained shut and, when noise began to enter the open door, a student marched over and closed it. After the class had been running nearly two hours, a few side conversations began to bubble up, yet even then, a student glared at the speakers until they stopped.

A *núcleo* comes officially into existence when it has recruited a minimum of 20 students and five teachers (a few have grown as large as 60 students and 15 teachers). Each *núcleo* meets weekly for 15 hours: on Saturdays, from 7 a.m. to 9 p.m., with an hour for lunch, or at night five times a week, from 7 to 10 p.m. Approximately two-thirds of contact time are devoted to mathematics, the hard sciences and economics; and about one-third to history, the social sciences, and the humanities. Low fees are essential to the programme, permitting the poor to attend. Instead of paying the high monthly fee typical of private pre-vestibular courses, students in the PVNC pay just one-tenth of a minimum salary (about $15) once into a fund to buy chalk, books, paper, lunch and travel expenses for teachers. The programme can afford the low fees because its teachers donate time, and classes take place in space provided by community institutions. Meals are also kept cheap: the Church or neighbourhood association provides these, or students bring ingredients and prepare food on-site.

While the programme is defined by its mission to prepare students to pass college entrance exams, it is also designed to be an instrument of consciousness-raising. In the context of courses on 'culture and citizenship', the PVNC seeks to stimulate an awareness of citizenship rights, of the causes of inequality, poverty and racism, as well as the desire to act collectively. As one of the project coordinators explained, 'The objective is to get the student to develop a new consciousness about society, so as not to create the mentality of self-centered individualism.' The political stance of the PVNC is visible in most of the courses, but especially in the social sciences.

The political tone was tangible at *Resistência*, as André was lecturing on the principles of economic growth. As he explained population pyramids and levels of consumption, he conveyed an unmistakeable point of view. Speaking of how the theories of Malthus had been abused by rich countries as a way of imposing population controls on the poorer countries of the world, he suddenly assumed the whiney voice of a Northern businessman: 'Hey! Stop producing so many kids!' The class erupted in laughter. Then suddenly serious: 'But who should stop? Who poses the real threat to the earth's resources?'

The reply: 'They do!'

André: 'Yes!. Those people consume one hundred times more than you or I do here in Brazil. You see? Malthus, applied like that, just doesn't take into account the inequality of consumption. It's useless from our point of view. But it's very useful from theirs!'

Catholicism pervades the movement's rhetoric and practice. The monthly bulletin of Educafro, a PVNC offshoot operating in São Paulo, declares that teachers and coordinators are to undertake their work 'illumined by God, with heart and a sense of civic duty' and regularly effuses, in print, phrases such as 'God be praised', and 'may God bless' the student and her success. In reporting on the growing interest in the PVNC, the bulletin 'praises God for the number of locations that are asking for advice about how to open a new *núcleo*'.[10]

Within this broadly Catholic penumbra, the PVNC's specific emphasis is that of socially committed Christianity. Success in the course and at university are 'gifts' from 'God and society' which must be repaid through service to the community. 'The grantee', affirms Educafro's bulletin, 'takes on responsibly all communal tasks, as a sign of gratitude toward God and society for his entrance into the University.'[11] The PVNC further embraces the progressive Catholic notion of *mística*, or spiritual commitment, periodically holding retreats designed to nurture this *mística* among both leaders and participants. Recently, a group of two dozen coordinators, students and ex-students of a PVNC *núcleo* in Minas Gerais held a three-day retreat on '*mística* and social commitment'. The retreat's final report affirmed that '[d]eveloping the spiritual side in a perspective of social commitment is very important'.[12] 'The work we do in the PV is very spiritual,' said one leader. 'At the retreat we discussed how in this work, this struggle, we have made an option, like Jesus did, to be on the side of the impoverished and the oppressed. It is not easy work, but it was not easy what Jesus did either.'

The everyday lexicon of the PVNC is unmistakeably progressive Catholic. The undertaking of increasing the number of black students in college is *profético* (prophetic); studying for exams, getting into college, and staying through to the end are stages of the *caminhada* (path); students are in the *luta* (struggle) or *batalhando* (in the battle) for *libertaçao* (liberation); one's co-students are one's *companheiros* (comrades), praised for their *garra* (courage/guts).[13] 'There is no question', said an ardent leader of the PVNC, 'that we are involved in a long *caminhada*, that calls upon us to keep faith, and to struggle with much courage.' More expansively, a recent article in *Educafro* editorialized:

> Imbued with a force that certainly comes from God, people at the base find the courage to assume the roles of teachers and monitors ... despite all the obstacles, we have hope that this project, in its very simplicity, will bring the prophetic and transformative vigor that will help the poor of Brazil, especially the historically

oppressed, to liberate themselves from the traps set by a violent economy and political system that are selfish and anti-human. Our people must escape from a prolonged Good Friday to find their Sunday of Resurrection![14]

If the language of the PVNC has been moulded by progressive Catholicism, so has its repertoire of collective action. One hallmark of progressive Church action in the 1990s, especially with regard to land issues, is the use of the pilgrimage. It should come as no surprise that in August 2000, PVNC organizers led a *'romaria* [pilgrimage] for the university', in which several dozen students on courses in the Rio area marched to the state assembly building, intoning progressive Catholic hymns and shouting in support of a bill to set aside 50 per cent of university places for students from the public school system. The students entered the assembly and packed the balconies. Later, in December 2001, no fewer than 100 PVNC students packed the assembly again to urge deputies to vote for a law reserving 40 per cent of all state university openings for blacks and *pardos*.[15]

But pilgrimage is far from the only visible Catholic symbolic resource available to the PVNC; it also taps into the emotive power of Jesus' passion. Thus, in July 2001 30 PVNC students gathered in front of the State University of Rio de Janeiro to protest the school's foot-dragging response to the 50 per cent law. Ten of the students chained themselves to the school's front gate, while a young black man stepped onto a box and was lashed to a wooden cross. Passers-by were riveted; so were newspaper and television crews, who flashed the image across the country. The 'black Christ', as he was immediately dubbed by the media, remained on the cross for a long eight hours, embodying in his performance the themes of sacrifice, blackness and the promise of victory. 'As Jesus was oppressed,' said Frei David, 'so too have been the students at public school, because the right to enter university has been denied.'[16]

Further evidence of progressive Catholic influence over the PVNC may be detected in its ever-growing ideological universalism and inclusivity. When it first appeared in the early 1990s, the PVN (at that time, simply the *'pré-vestibular para negros'*) was conceptualized by APNs as helping only *afrodescendentes*. Within the first two years, however, this position shifted, such that by the end of 1994 it no longer served only *afrodescendentes*, but also *carentes*, poor non-blacks.

The shift was partly due to the fact that, in its first years, the prevestibular faced a severe shortage of volunteer teachers who identified themselves as *negros*, forcing Frei David and his colleagues to reach beyond the black community 'to form the first cohort of volunteer teachers'. By the autumn of 1994 many of these teachers were saying that the PVN ought to make it official policy that the courses aim to serve not just *negros*, but poor non-*negros* as well. 'At first,' remembers Frei David, 'we planned only to have a *"pré-vestibular para negros"*.' But, he added, 'the teachers fought this, they wanted the title to be "*negros and carentes*", there was a long debate, and they finally ended up winning!' The PVN officially became the PVNC – the '*pré-vestibular para negros e carentes*' (prevestibular course for blacks and the poor) – in 1995.

Yet if the only force at work here had been the teachers' preferences, it is unlikely that they would have been successful in pressuring the Church to initiate what was in effect a radical transformation in the ethnic scope of the educational project. The teachers' argument prevailed, I suggest, precisely because the PVN's organizers were endowed with a strong progressive Catholic identity. In contrast with, say, the Biko project in Salvador, which as a secular initiative could afford to winnow its applicants according to race,[17] the Rio initiative, with roots and ongoing guidance from the Church, had little ideological stomach for such things. As an APN explained:

> We wanted a course that prioritized negros, but when it came to excluding anyone, I couldn't see that. It just isn't our way ... . Let us say that in the Church we are used to opening our doors to all. So it was easier for us just to agree with the teachers, and make the PVN open, than to fight that.

In effect, the teachers who argued for the inclusion of the poor in the programme's purview were simply mirroring back to APNs their own progressive discourse about the preferential option for the poor. We know this because the teachers scored a major point in their argument when they observed that many of the shantytown dwellers in their classrooms were not black at all, but called themselves *moreno* or *mestiço* or *pardo*.[18] 'Can we say', argued one teacher, 'that the other inhabitants of the *favelas*, those who are poor and marginalized from society – are we to keep this away from them?' The question was hard to avoid, for it resonated with the PVN's organizers' Catholic liberationist commitment to work for the poor and marginalized in general.[19]

To this day, the '*negros e carentes*' identity has prevailed, and has evolved into the movement's dominant identity. By the end of the 1990s the demographic composition of the *núcleos* in Rio reflected this identity. According to a survey administered by Márcia Contins in 1998, 38 per cent of the students enrolled in the courses identified their colour as *parda*, 21 per cent as *preta* and 24 per cent as *branca*, while only about one-fifth identified themselves as *negro*. And although this is 'blacker' than what one would expect from the distribution of these categories nationally, the numbers indicate that the demographic basis of the PVNC is now considerably more diverse than *negros*.[20] Yvonne Maggie is thus undoubtedly correct when she claims that the PVNC attracts 'people with different conceptions of color, ethnic identity, inequality, exclusion, politics, etc'.[21]

Still, the race-first ideology that motivated the founders of the PVN has not disappeared altogether from the programme; rather, it lives on as a submerged tendency. Those who articulate this tendency use the phrase '*negro e carente*', but interpret it as expressing an alliance taken on by blacks with non-blacks, in which the ultimate goal remains the building of *negro* self-esteem and the righting of historic wrongs against *negros*. This, by all evidence, is the view of Frei David himself. Thus, for example, although he supports educational quotas that include non-blacks, what he really wants are quotas for *afro descendentes*. This position of his has been cited in various publications and he is no less forthright in person: 'Look, the ones who have suffered historically have been *afro descendentes*. We are the ones who need to have those injustices corrected.'

Yet Catholic (and progressive Catholic) universalism and inclusivity triumph at the end of the day. While Frei David still believes that blacks have suffered more intensely than other groups, his liberationist vision of a socially just world for all continues to frame his thinking. In the struggle for the Kingdom, he says, the role of *negros* is to serve as example for the struggles of all marginalized peoples:

> The drama of the *negro* in Brazilian society speaks to every single one of us. The other poor who are not *afro descendentes* should learn from the struggle of *negros* that there are many forms of official discrimination, and that the success of the *negros* can strengthen [*potencializar*] the struggles of other marginalized groups.[22]

Or, as a young APN influenced by David put it:

> Without saying it can happen overnight, I think that getting more *negros* into universities does not only benefit *negros*. It benefits society! Because with these kids who have suffered so much and overcome so much, for them to be in the university, shows other oppressed people what is possible. And when that happens, we will all unite, and that will speed up the coming of the Kingdom.

The Impact of the Program

There can be little doubt that this deeply liberationist programme is leaving its imprint on Brazilian society. It appears that the APNs have discovered in the PVNC an initiative that is powerfully magnetic to a large audience. There has been an unmistakeable growth in the presence of *negros* at university in the past decade. While in the 1980s no more than 5 per cent of students at Brazilian universities were Afro-Brazilian, in the year 2000 Afro-Brazilians had grown to about 16 per cent of graduating university students. Brazil's ministry of education reported in 2000 that 13 per cent of students at private universities, and fully one-fifth of students in public universities were of African descent. Although this increase cannot be traced to the PVNC alone, there can be no doubt that the process it catalysed in the early 1990s has now spread rapidly throughout Brazil. Certainly many observers have pointed to the PVNC and its imitators as a key factor in the trend.[23]

It may still be too soon to assess the effects of the trend on the everyday lives of poor Brazilians. Nevertheless, stories of PVNC students bringing back to their communities the skills they have gained at university may be heard in abundance from the leaders of the movement. To take but one example, in the poor periphery of Rio, Iara Sarmento, 41 years old, had finished high school in 1982, but four years ago decided to study professional teaching at university. She took the PVNC and then took the vestibular exam for PUC-Rio. She gained fourth place, and is now about to graduate. Her dream is to open her own school, in the poor neighbourhood where she grew up. She now teaches as a volunteer in the PVNC, so that others may benefit as she did. 'I think it's time', she said, 'to return a little of what the course did for me.'

Whether or not such stories are indications of a growing trend, they have, not surprisingly, brought increased national visibility to the PVNC, spreading the powerful message of the need to democratize the educational system. In 2001 the PVNC received the Betinho award, one of the nation's highest awards for citizenship, and in 2002 Educafro was awarded the Parlamento Latino-Americano Prize. By 2001, Educafro was regularly sending students to the Catholic TV channel, *Rede Vida*, to participate in a weekly programme for youth, and representatives of Educafro appeared regularly in TV debates with administrators from universities as experts on the matter of quotas in universities.

Capitalizing on such recognition, the PVNC has convinced numerous universities to waive registration fees for poor and black test-takers. A major obstacle in the path of poor youth seeking to take the vestibular exam is the registration fee, which ranges from about $10 to $50. Lawyers volunteering to help the PVNC have brought lawsuits to compel universities to drop the fees, saying that they nullify the constitution's guarantee that public education will be *gratis*. These lawsuits have been very successful. Each case sets a precedent which it then becomes hard for the university to ignore. By 2001, in many regions, students who could prove they had taken a 'community prevestibular course' were exempted from paying the registration.

Beyond the thousands of poor youths who have benefited directly from the PVNC courses, and who in turn may be starting to benefit their communities with skills, leadership, income and social honour, the model of the PVNC has transformed public discourse and debate about education in Brazil. It has contributed in tangible ways to policy and legislative debates, at both the state and national levels, regarding set-asides for *afro-descendentes* seeking entry into public universities. At the national level, the example of the PVNC was central, for instance, to the debate between the ministers of education and justice about how best to increase access to university of *'negros e carentes'*. The education minister stated in a published interview that '[a]n initiative that we want to support are the *cursinhos para negros*, to enter the University, so that there can be better training and preparation of poor populations, where there is a greater concentration of *negros* and *pardos*.'[24] Suspicious of quotas, he announced in February 2001 that he was actively negotiating a 10 million dollar grant from the Inter-American Development Bank for the creation of '*cursos pré-vestibulares para negros*', and in September of that year he identified PVNC-like initiatives as essential partners in the battle against racial inequality. 'In the area of education, for example,' he said, 'we have the *pré-vestibular para negros* that we wish to create.'[25] The minister of justice invoked the PVNC even more directly. The government, he said in February 2001, is using the PVNC as its model. 'In Rio', he stated, 'Frei David has already developed a pioneering work with these courses. We must stimulate these projects that take into account the disparity in educational preparation.'[26]

At the state level in Rio de Janeiro, this debate was transformed into public legislation. There, two recently passed laws bear the PVNC's fingerprints. In August 2000 the state assembly passed a law ensuring that 50 per cent of all places in public universities would be reserved for applicants from public schools. In the debate on the floor of the State Legislative Assembly, Arthur Messias, of the Partido dos Trabalhadores (PT), invoked the PVNC's example:

> Sr. Presidente, in connection to the reality of the city of Rio de Janeiro, there exist today more than seventy alternative pre-vestibular courses. This is an initiative that defends and renders possible, for many, access to higher education for needy students. This experience which, in the Baixada Fluminense, is occurring in the municipality of Rio de Janeiro, has struggled, since its birth, for precisely the extension that this project is insuring: for the number of openings in public universities, and also that there be exemption for students from public schools from registration fees for the vestibular exam. The project has made this possible, and so it is good to recall the struggle of so many people connected to the movement of alternative pre-vestibulars, and, in particular, of the '*pré-vestibular para negros e carentes*', which arose in the city of São João de Meriti, under the inspiration of Frei Davi, who has already taken this experience to São Paulo and to many other states of the country. I would like to honour this movement, along with the organization of students, for this victory.[27]

Over the course of 2001 a flood of letters from PVNC students to deputies, and demonstrations in front of the State University, raised pressure for a more radical bill. This process was accelerated in July 2001 when Rio governor Anthony Garotinho announced he would resign the following April to enter the presidential race, a move that made Benedita da Silva, vice governor and famous black politician, governor-elect of the state. Endowed with unprecedented power, Benedita went to Durban, South Africa, accompanied by the federal minister of justice and 152 other

Brazilian delegates, to represent Brazil in the United Nations Third Conference on Racism. Upon her return, Benedita joined the minister of justice in announcing that the federal and state governments would play a new role in supporting affirmative action. Within weeks, the state deputy for the PT, José Amorim, had introduced law no. 2490 into the state assembly, calling for a set-aside of 40 per cent of all places in the public university system for '*negros e pardos*'. In October, the law was passed, ensuring that 40 per cent of all new openings in Rio's public universities would be set aside for '*negros e pardos*'. Although it is still far from clear how these laws will be implemented, there is little doubt about the high profile of the PVNC in getting them passed.[28]

De-stigmatizing African Ancestry

While the PVNC may be regarded as an example of a major success by the APNs in bringing about social and cultural change, the initiative of the Black Pastoral that I wish to examine now has a rather more complicated record. By looking at the Black Pastoral's effort, through consciousness-raising workshops, to convince Afro-Brazilians' to 'assume their negritude', we will come closer to appreciating not only the intended legacies of the liberationist Church for Brazil's racial culture, but also its unintended legacies.

It has by now become conventional wisdom that the ideology of *mestiçagem* in Brazil is rooted in, and perpetuates, the stigmatization of African ancestry. Most scholars and activists have argued that when someone in Brazil uses one of the numerous 'mixed' categories (for example, *pardo, mestico, moreno, mulato*) to self-identify, he or she is seeking to minimize his or her African ancestry, and to construct in its place an identity 'ennobled' by the presence of European blood.[29] It should therefore come as no surprise that the Black Pastoral, in step with the larger black movement, has called for an end to the use of the whole intermediate categorizing gamut – including terms like *pardo, mestiço* and *moreno* – and to replace them with the proud term *negro*.

To achieve this goal, APNs organize seminars, workshops, lectures and other meetings, at the parish and community levels, in which participants are drawn into discussion of institutional, interpersonal and internalized racism. During the 1980s the pedagogy of such meetings was heavily cognitive and thick with presentations about history. Today these elements have not been entirely excluded, but the meetings have become more rooted in a process methodology that calls for dialogue and the sharing of experience. Though less directive than in the 1980s, a key goal of the meetings continues to be persuading Brazilians of African ancestry to stop defining themselves by intermediate colour terms and to start calling themselves '*negro*'. 'Negros in Brazil must learn that they cannot escape their identity, that they must assume their negritude,' commented a young APN. 'All of these other terms are ways of escaping their identity. So we show that by saying we are "*negros*" we assume our race, our blood, what it is that unites us, rather than accept the white man's effort to divide us by colour.'

In a working-class community on the outskirts of Rio de Janeiro, in the summer of 1996, I attended a seminar organized by Black Pastoral agents in collaboration with the youth group of the *comunidade*. In this community, several of the youths had become involved in a local (non-religious) cultural group in which they were learning to value their African heritage more highly, by mastering traditional African drumming. These youths were eager to invite APNs in to stimulate their elders to see the value of the drumming, and to shake off their prejudice against such things. For this to happen, they were sure, their elders would have to 'assume their negritude', and that is where the APNs' experience in running consciousness-raising meetings on the subject was needed.

The meeting I attended was one of a series, held in the annex of the community church on alternating Tuesdays, for two hours in the evening, after dinner. It was clear that the meeting was not well attended – only six of the community's 'adults' were present, along with five members of the youth group. When I asked why there were not more adults in attendance, I was told that 'they don't want to deal with this issue'. Sitting in a circle, those in attendance were led by an APN from the parish seat to talk about the terms they used to describe themselves and others. 'Think about this,' the APN said. 'We have this mania in Brazil of saying that a little girl has "good" or "bad" hair. Who here has heard someone say ...'

He was unable to finish the sentence, because the room immediately filled with laughter, chatter and volunteered stories. 'Yes, *moço*, that is terrible,' said one of the adults. 'That is prejudice, and that shouldn't exist among us, we who are the children of God, we cannot accept this.' Another participant began to recount an episode in which a neighbour had forced her daughter to straighten her hair against her will, to 'better it'. The APN, visibly relaxed, offered a story of his own, and the meeting proceeded in a highly interactive, informal way.

So far, it seemed, so good. The adults had clearly already been influenced by the anti-racist discourse circulating in Brazilian society, especially in progressive circles, in which it had come to be understood that referring to 'bad hair' was politically incorrect. The conversation became less consensual when the APN asked each person in the room to say what colour they were. While a couple of the non-white adults answered '*negro*', one of them laughed and said, 'Well, you know, I am more *marrom bom-bom*'. Everyone laughed. 'Yeah, I have to say I am *moreno*, that is after all what I am, I am a mixture, like most Brazilians.' At this point, the APN became didactic. 'Well, Dona Marluce, that is where we have to think: isn't this term, '*moreno*', just one more way that we are taught to forget our African blood? Because, that you have African blood, that I have the blood, there is no denying. That we can see! But in our society, we are told we must not value this blood, that it is dirty, that it isn't worth anything, and all those other things.'

The sounds of positive recognition rumbled around the room, and Dona Marluce was nodding her head politely. But there were signs that she was not convinced. She crossed her arms, and I could detect a setting of her lower jaw, and a tightening in the muscles of her cheeks. The APN continued: 'Oh, people, we can see from this our problem in Brazil: whites want to keep us divided, they have introduced this third term – *mulato*, or *moreno* or whatever – and with that we *negros* actually come to discriminate against ourselves!' (A ripple of 'yes, that's so'.) 'It's a neat trick,' he said, his voice rising. 'Just think – they do not have to discriminate directly, they just get us to devalue our negritude, and we do the work for them.'

The discussion then turned to numerous other ways in which those present could think about how people of African descent were discriminated against, and the importance of 'assuming one's blackness' as a way of challenging society's devaluation of the identity. Although this meeting did not include any audio-visual aids, in other similar meetings I had observed the use of slides to teach about the history of slavery and about the many episodes of slave resistance and rebellion. Here, when the APN spoke of Zumbi, it was clearly to help instill a sense of pride in belonging to a people that had been able to stand up and fight against the system that oppressed them. 'We are all children of Zumbi,' he said. 'We who have African blood in our veins have the spirit of the warrior, of the fighter! That is something to be proud of, not to try and run away from!'

I was unsure throughout the meeting whether Dona Marluce was accepting any of this. She participated in the discussion, but she carefully refrained from returning to the issue of her own identity. Later, after the meeting was over, I asked her whether she had been satisfied with the APN's argument about why she should identify herself as *negra*. In a graceful effort to defuse what clearly were some growing negative sentiments on her own part, she laughed and said, 'Oh, *moço*, that is all well, maybe that's so. Maybe Carlito is right. But I have doubts, I have doubts! I agree that more of these youths should call themselves what they want! But how can anyone say that I should call myself *negra*? Isn't that discrimination too, against my white ancestors? For I have blood that is not only black!' She laughed again, and changed the subject to other matters.

In 1996 I gathered some evidence that seminars and workshops of this kind do indeed have a contributory effect on how some participants talk about their identities. While it is difficult to distinguish the effect of any single group, institution or social context on racial identity, especially since powerful anti-racist discourses circulate widely in Brazil in a variety of contexts, the evidence nevertheless suggests that workshops such as the one described above have made a difference. In a sample of 30 women of

African descent who had participated in such groups, I found that fully half said explicitly that their exposure to such group work had been important in helping them to move from feeling shame about their African ancestry to embracing a fully *negra* identity. Seven of these women said they had once called themselves *preta* (a term of strong identification with African ancestry, but without the pride), and eight had once called themselves *morena*; all of them now proudly called themselves *negra*. These 15 women told me that exposure to the Black Pastoral's 'talks' had been 'important' in helping them develop pride in their ancestry. 'When I started coming to these meetings', said Rosana, a woman in her thirties, 'I saw a whole different side to these things. I saw that really my colour has value, that I cannot waste my time denying it. I too have value. And now I have so much pride in this, in my *negritude*.' Or consider the longer account of Deolinda, a woman in her twenties, which may usefully stand for the others I heard:

When I was younger, I always said that I was that thing, you know, '*morena*', because I didn't want anything to do with *negros*. I didn't think I wanted to be on the side of *negros*, I was different, I thought. I refused to assume my negritude. And this whole work of the Church helped me to see that, no, these words were used by slave-owners to separate *negros* from each other, to weaken us so that we could all be denied our rights. And I saw that I really am *negra*, that is my race, there is no such thing as the '*morena* race'. So that was very important. I assumed my negritude, and now I am proud to say 'I am *negra*'.

Having said this, the more complicated response to the seminars among people like Dona Marluce, described earlier, must be taken seriously. Her scepticism points to the possibility that there are ideological and psychological processes at work in the workshops other than that of the straight 'assumption of negritude'. Here my suggestion is not only the obvious one – that the message of black pride did not touch all participants equally – more complexly, I want to argue that the message of black pride seems to have generated, among some people who identify with an intermediate colour term, novel identity processes that APNs have not yet fully grasped. I found that workshops that discouraged the use of intermediate colour terms helped create conditions in which those terms' meanings were – for people who identified with intermediate colour terms – transformed.

To show what I mean, I want to focus on the testimony of six women who: (a) participated in meetings such as the one described above; (b) had once called themselves *morenas*; (c) now called themselves *negras*; but who (d) expressed the feeling that the term *negra* did not adequately describe their identities. Two of these women declared that they used the term *negra* mainly out of political solidarity, but that the term did not resonate subjectively. Most telling was the experience of the four other women for whom the term *negra did* resonate – *but only partially*. These were women who had once called themselves *morenas*, but who now, as a mark of their involvement in consciousness-raising seminars and workshops, had come round to realizing that the term to use for themselves was *negra*. *Yet, according to their testimony, they were not satisfied with it.* 'I say "*negra*",' said Sonia, a woman in her late thirties, 'but I do not feel comfortable with it.' In a comment that was reiterated in a variety of ways by the other four informants, Sonia went on, 'I use the term because I know I'm supposed to, that that is what people expect me to say. And I think that's good, I like the term. But I don't really identify with it.'

At first glance one might be tempted to attribute such ambivalence to internalized racism. Yet what is distinctive about this small but, I submit, sociologically significant contingent of people is that they had considerable involvement with the Black Pastoral, and had therefore encountered and grappled head-on with the critique of internalized racism. These four women were, in fact, insistent in claiming that their discomfort with the term *negra* in no way derived from feelings of shame about their African ancestry. 'I have African blood', said Janete, a woman in her forties, 'and I am proud of that. I was once ashamed, but these things of Frei David have shown me that we are all equal and that I must love my African heritage.'

If not from shame, then, where did this discomfort with the identity of *negra* come from? I found that, as with Dona Marluce, it came from the feeling that the term called upon them to set aside a part of their ancestry that part that was not African. Listen again to Sonia:

> In these meetings we have learned that we must validate, we must value our heritage, our race. Well, I value my African race, but I also value my Portuguese race too. That doesn't mean I am denying my *negritude*. In no way! I take pride in my *negritude*. But I am more than *negritude*. I have ancestors who were *negros*. I am proud of that. I have ancestors who were slaves! And I am proud of that. I am prouder now than I ever was before! But my mother is white, my father *negro*. So I feel I have something from both sides. So when I say that I am '*negra*', I do not really feel this. Because I feel like I am forgetting my mother.

Another source of emotional distance from the term, I found, was that it seemed to these women to call for a deliberate obscuring of the differences in experience between them and people with no visible white ancestry. Listen to Camila, a forty-year old woman: 'I can say I am "*negra*", but my life has been very different from the life of a real *negra*, someone who has suffered for that her whole life. I have enjoyed privileges!' Camila said this without pleasure. For her, the term *negra* short-circuited the possibility of a deeper analysis of racism, in which people of visibly mixed ancestry acknowledge their social power and subject it to critique. 'When I say I am "*negra*",' she said, 'I feel like I am avoiding something. Like looking at how much better you are treated in Brazil if you have that little bit of white. To denounce that!'

I noticed something else significant about these informants. While they used the term *negra* in public contexts, in our private conversations they sometimes referred to themselves as *mestiças* (mixed). While this term has been used as one more way to minimize African ancestry, in the mouths of these women the term appeared to have taken on a new set of connotations. I asked them what the term *mestiça* meant to them. 'To me,' said Camila, 'it is the best term to describe who I am. Because I am *mestiça*. I refuse to say "*morena*", because that is a way to say "no" to your African ancestors. But I am saying "yes" to them, and "yes" to my other ancestors too. So for me, I am a *mestiça*.'

The irony is that while the Black Pastoral has drawn these four women into a process of consciousness-raising that has led to the development of what appears to be a new identity, it provides little or no space for the public articulation of that identity. One of these *mestiças* recounted that she had once referred to herself during a meeting as *mestiça* only to be quickly corrected by a pastoral agent. 'He told me that the term was not strong enough, that I must say "*negra*"', she said with a wan smile. And, indeed, when I raised this question directly with several APNs, I was met with responses ranging from bemused scepticism to outright hostility. The most open response was probably that of Geraldo, a young APN:

> Maybe some day it will be possible to have these other terms out there. But it is too soon. Because unfortunately, still, any time you use one of those terms, you are weakening the *negra* identity, you are dividing us, you are keeping people focused on the benefits they can get by separating themselves out from *negros* and getting closer to the whites. So it is just too soon.

This constriction of space has led to a certain psychic duality in these women's lives: between their subjective identity as *mestiças*, and their public identities as *negras*. So far, the Black Pastoral has been unable to help them overcome this duality. While it seems that these women can live quietly with this duality, at least one of them expressed a strong feeling of frustration with it. 'To be honest,' she said, 'I feel like every time I say "*negra*" that I am forgetting who I am.'

Overall, then, the Black Pastoral is creating the cognitive conditions both for the reinforcement of a proud *negro* identity, and for the emergence of what appears to be a genuinely novel, emergent race/colour identity – that of the *mestiço* proud of her African ancestry.[30] In the case of the identity of *mestiço* it is possible that we are witnessing the emergence of an identity that incorporates one of the Black Pastoral's most important lessons, that of the need to remove and denounce the stigma attached to African ancestry; yet it is also an identity which may simultaneously be seeking to transcend ethnic essentialism and value experiential difference. The political question is whether the Black Pastoral, having catalysed a process leading to this new identity, will doom it to a shadowy, submerged existence, depriving it of air and sunlight, or whether it will carve out a public space for the identity, making its ideological contrast with *morenidade* clear, making available to it the resources of collective articulation, legitimation and intellectual energy.

Conclusion

I have in this chapter and the last endeavoured to show some of the ways in which progressive Catholic consciousness has led both to the emergence and complex development of a Catholic-inspired black consciousness movement. I have tried to suggest some of the ways – some small and some surprisingly large – that the movement has in turn left its mark on Brazilian society and culture. Yet I have also insisted that the lines of influence and impact are not always linear; indeed, in some instances, both progressive Catholicism and its Black Pastoral offshoot have brought about cultural and social changes indirectly, even unwittingly. It would, of course, be a mistake to conclude that these influences are for that any less significant, that the changes they effect are any less consequential. If anything, I suggest that we should be all the more intrigued to follow the proverbial ripples in the pond radiating out from the progressive Catholic pebble, as they encounter, cross and create still other ripples.

But even more, the case of the Black Pastoral should encourage us to shift how we think about the outcomes of social movements. We are used to thinking of social movements as artificial tools – as the hoes or spades used to turn over the land, for example. But perhaps an organic metaphor is more appropriate. The social movement might be viewed as a large dendritic plant, with deep, tendril-like roots and shoots. Even when the dramatic flowers are absent, the roots remain, feeding and fertilizing the soil for other plants. And even when, some day, the plant dies, it continues long after to give its nutrients to the land.[31]

There may be one last unintended consequence of the progressive Church's dendritic influence in this story. I recall an evening I spent not long ago in the company of Rogério, a young black man who had made it to university thanks to the preparatory course he had taken through the PVNC. Rogerio is a member of the Assembly of God Church. When I mentioned to him that the PVNC had originated in the Catholic Church, and continued to enjoy many Catholic influences, he sounded surprised. Somehow, all the Catholic influence at the PVNC had slipped past his notice. 'Really?' he asked. 'I didn't know that.' As I described some of the history to him, he seemed pleased. Finally, he broke into a big smile and commented, 'Wow, that's great. I am glad to hear the Catholic Church is concerned with education, and with the problem of negros. I didn't know that ... . You know, in my Church we learn that the Catholic are all wrong about the

Bible, and they worship idols. But if what you say is true, perhaps they aren't as bad as all that.'

Notes

1. Yvonne Maggie, 'Os novos bachareis. A experiência do pre-vestibular para negros e carentes', *Novos Estudos CEBRAP*, 59, (March 2001), 193–202; Márcia Contins, 'Os efeitos do Pré-Vestibular', paper presented at the 1999 AAA meetings in Chicago; also see the main website of *Educafro*, http://intermega.globo.com/educafro/.
2. Carlos Hasenbalg and Nelson de Valle Silva, 'Race and Educational Opportunity in Brazil' in Rebecca Reichmann (ed.), *Race in Contemporary Brazil: From Indifference to Inequality* (University Park, PA: Pennsylvania State University Press, 1999), 55; Idem, 'Raça e oportunidades sociais no Brasil' in Peggy Lovell (org.), *Desigualdade racial no Brasil contemporâneo* (Belo Horizonte, 1991), 245.
3. C. Hasenbalg and Valle Silva, 'Race and Educational Opportunity in Brazil', 57.
4. Antonio Guimarães, *Classes, Raças e Democracia* (São Paulo: Editoria 34, 2002).
5. Mônica Bairros, 'Os APNS e a Luta Contra Racismo na Igreja', unpublished ms., (1997), 18.
6. Abdeljalil Akkari, 'The Construction of Mass Schooling in Brazil: A Two-Tiered Educational System Reference to Role of Education in Determining Class Status in Brazil', *Education and Society*, 17, 1 (June 1999), 37–51.
7. See the various historical retrospectives on Educafro's website, http://intermega.globo. com/educafro/. Educafro now has satellite initiatives around the country. For the one in Espirito Santo, see http://www.litoralsulcapixba.com.br/educafro/.
8. Educafro website, http://intermega.globo.com/educafro/.
9. These numbers are fairly representative: in a survey of 600 participants in he PVNC in Rio, Yvonne Maggie recently found that 76 per cent were women, and almost 90 per cent were in the 17–25 age range. (See Maggie, 'Os novos bachareis', 196.)
10. *Educafro*, November 2001. See website.
11. *Educafro*, December 2001.
12. Educafro Informe, *Educafro*, October 2000.
13. All these terms are constant throughout the newsletters and reports in *Educafro*. See http://intermega.globo.com/educafro/.
14. *Educafro*, September 2001.
15. Ibid., August 2000, December 2001.
16. 'Vestibulando protestam', http://www.uol.com.br/aprendiz/n_noticias/noticias_ educacao/id260701.htm~1.
17. 'Todos os alunos que estudam na instituição passam por um processo de seleção, em que são avaliados alguns pontos considerados pela direção como fundamentais: motivação e disponibilidade para os estudos, espírito cooperativista, condição financeira (priorizam-se os alunos de baixa renda), pontos de vista sobre a situação do negro no país, acesso ao mercado de trabalho etc. Superada esta fase, a direção seleciona os que mais se aproximam, num primeiro momento, dos ideais da instituição, embora reconheça que o ideal seria aproveitar todos e submetê-los ao programa de formação que oferece. Através do programa Cidadania e Consciência Negra (CCN), o Instituto contribui para a conscientização da realidade e potencialidades do afro-descendentes, motivando-os à busca da ascensão social, objetivando um exercício pleno da cidadania e dos direitos humanos. (http://www.stevebiko.org.br/historico.html).
18. Maggie, 'Os novos bachareis', 193–202.
19. These convergences with the organizers' progressive Catholicism was crucial, but perhaps was facilitated by the fact that already on the black movement scene there existed an ideological tendency that sympathized actively with the inclusion of poor

non-blacks under the umbrella of initiatives that sought blacks as their primary targeted constituency. At the start of the 1990s, several organizations in Rio, particularly the Centro de Articulação de Populações Marginalizadas, under the leadership of Ivanir dos Santos, which had started off exclusively as a black-only movement, had expanded its purview to include the poor as well.

20 Marcia Contins, 'Os efeitos do pré-vestibular', unpublished paper (2000).
21 Maggie, 'Os novos bachareis'.
22 http://www.terra.com.br/istoe/1667/educacao/1667_david_o_abolicionista.htm. Of course, progressive Catholics do not have the monopoly on the vision of a socially just world for all. Similar utopias motivate activists in the secular black movement to come to similar conclusions as Frei David. It is just that the Catholic version of social utopia happens to be what is most present in Frei David's mental world.
23 Peter Muello, 'Brazil Grappling with Racism', http://ead.english.ucsb.edu/docs/muello1.html.
24 *Jornal do MEC* (November/December 2001), 9.
25 Ibid.
26 *Globo*, 4 February 2001.
27 Daily transcripts of state assembly debates, State of Rio de Janeiro, available at http://www.governo.rj.gov.br/.
28 For recent developments in the affirmative action debate and its pertinence to Rio, see Jon Jeter, 'Affirmative Action Debate Forces Brazil to Take Look in Mirror', *Washington Post Foreign Service* (16 June 2003), 401.
29 Donna M. Goldstein, *Laughter out of Place: Face, Class, Violence and Sexuality in a Rio Shantytown* (Berkeley: University of California Press, 2003).
30 On the 'emergent' of new ideologies and identities, see Raymond Williams, *Marxism and Literature* (New York: Oxford, 1977).
31 Some readers may detect an echo here of Deleuze and Guattari's concept of the 'rhizome'. The difference between their metaphor and mine is that the rhizome's roots are not very deep or broad, whereas the dendrite's are deep, broad, and can reappear far away from the head of the plant.

Chapter 3

Redefining Mary: Women's Changing Roles at Home and in the Church

It is common among observers of religious politics in Brazil to maintain that the progressive wing of the Catholic Church, its commitment to universal liberation notwithstanding, has failed to break with the mother Church's less than emancipatory stance toward women.[1] They point out that, whilst liberationist Catholics have opened doors to women to become partners of men in the struggle to end the oppression of the poor,[2] and have declared that in that struggle women may be as heroic as men,[3] they continue to sidestep issues specific to women's lives, such as gender inequality in the household and in the church, sexual violence in the home and reproductive rights.[4]

This critique of the liberationist Church is clearly very important, and I will, in fact, shortly discuss the considerable ideological limits of liberationism's stance towards women. Nevertheless, I argue in the next two chapters that an adequate account of the relationship between progressive Catholicism and women's struggles in Brazil must take note of a range of more subtle, less intended, pro-woman energies that the liberationist project has helped to unleash. While Brazil's progressive Church continues to sweep many issues of concern to women under society's carpet, I argue here that over the past 20 years the progressive Church has – not always in a planned, self-conscious way – offered women important new sources of authority, ideas for challenging traditional gender norms and opportunities to act upon these challenges. To this extent, the Church has been an active participant in the larger movement for change in Brazil's gender relations.

By emphasizing the ideological resources made available to women's struggles by the liberationist Church, I seek to counter the assumption that when radical thinking about gender occurs among Catholic women at the grassroots, this has been due mainly to exposure to non-Catholic, urban middle-class feminists.[5] Without denying the influence of secular feminism (which I touch on), it is important to recognize the ways in which liberationist Catholicism has been impelled by its own logic to stimulate and frame Catholic women's outlook on gender issues.

In order to highlight how the Catholic liberationist project has generated and shaped the views and practices of women at the grassroots, in the next two chapters I will focus on four arenas of women's rights. In this chapter I examine the interaction of progressive Catholicism with women's right to equal treatment within the home and to equal status in church. In the next chapter I will focus on the role progressive Catholicism has played in connection to women's right to live free of gender violence and their right to control the size of their families. This list of rights, though obviously not exhaustive, should offer a fair introduction to how progressive Catholicism has acted over the past 20 years to help articulate and address women's issues in Brazilian society.

An important caveat is in order. Although I argue that Catholic liberationism has indeed contributed in important, and at times unexpected, ways to the remedying of gender injustice, I hasten to add that I am not claiming that Catholic liberationism is the only religious tradition in Brazil to do so. An adequate account of the relationship between religious traditions and gender justice in Brazil would need to describe the activities of numerous religious traditions and groups, including a number of evangelical Christian denominations, the charismatic Catholic movement, and the multiple expressions of afro religiosity. It has been argued, for example, that both Pentecostalism and the Catholic charismatic renewal have been effective critics of *machismo*, not only calling upon men to desist from physical abuse and to commit themselves to the welfare of the household, but placing real, active pressures on them to do so.[6] There is evidence as well that these traditions have been supportive of women who wish to control the size of their families,[7] and that women in these traditions are able to develop new, non-domestic arenas of authority and leadership.[8]

This being said, a focus on the progressive Catholic field is crucial to understanding the full range of religious resources available to Brazilian women in their struggle for equality. While not alone as a religious tradition that supports women, there can be no doubt that Catholic liberationism has a wholly distinctive character, emphasizing practical and ideological elements downplayed or absent in other religious traditions. Among these is the fact that only the liberationist tradition emphasizes the socio-structural context of gender violence and abortion, and conceptualizes the emancipation of women as a means toward strengthening the struggle against class oppression in general. Thus, whilst Catholic liberationism is not the only religious tradition that contributes to the empowerment of women in Brazil, its contribution bears the unmistakeable marks of its ideological origin.

Women's Paradoxical Status in Brazil

In order to proceed with this analysis, it is important to grasp some of the basics about women's status in Brazil. There can be no doubt that the scope of women's freedom in Brazil has expanded significantly in the last 20 years. Starting in the 1970s, the feminist movement in Brazil, along with a variety of demographic and social pressures, have brought about major changes in gender status and relations. Whereas in the 1970s men still outnumbered women in the completion of high school, the figures have now been reversed, with women outpacing men in becoming educated, even in the working class. In the 1960s women were still bearing around four children each; by the 1990s, the spread of contraception and the growing belief among women that their lives could include more than motherhood led to one of the most dramatic drops in the reproduction rate in modern times – now, the average Brazilian mother only has about two children. In addition, women's participation in the job market has steadily increased over the last two decades, and women have found their way into a variety of professions that had once been entirely closed to them.

Nevertheless, the struggle for women's rights in Brazil is just beginning. The words of Maria Lucia Rocha-Coutinho, first written in 1994, remain true: 'Most women, and most of society, have not been able to abandon the old model of the woman, responsible for the house and children.'[9] Certainly, the expectation that women will be primary caretakers at home, preparing meals, seeing to children's welfare and keeping house, remain pervasive and dominant.[10] Brazilian textbooks in public schools, images in popular culture and even comic books reinforce these stereotypes, linking men to public life and women to the household.[11] Household labour continues to be assigned to women, and the severe lack of childcare facilities affects working-class women's access to the wage labour market. Brazil's gender wage gap remains one of the widest in Latin America. Better-educated women still receive lower salaries than less-educated men; Brazilian working women still earn only about 60 per cent of the wages of their male counterparts. As for political representation, women continue to be largely absent from the halls of state power. Although women have gained visibility on Brazil's political scene in several high-profile offices (mayors of São Paulo, governorships of Maranhão), it remains true that only 7 per cent of all federal deputies and senators in the legislative branch are women. Clearly, although the road towards greater gender equality has been taken in Brazil, there is still a long way to go.

Given this enduring inequality, it is a matter of some importance to identify the social forces in Brazilian society that are pushing women to demand and expect a more equal division of labour in the household. The Catholic Church, traditional as well as progressive, has long encouraged women to become involved in activities beyond their households, at the local and regional levels. To this extent, the Church has long exercised a kind of paradoxical force in women's lives – on the one hand divinizing their roles as wives and mothers, on the other urging them to taste a realm of action and authority outside the home. Yet this tension was usually, if not always, resolved in favour of traditional domesticity, as Catholic women kept their trans-household labours limited to Church and charity work ideologically subordinated to the family itself.[12] What is new with the progressive Church is that women are being encouraged more than ever before to become involved in the secular world of political struggle. While it has been clearly shown that a principal motivator for women to enter such struggles is precisely the defence of their ability to fulfil their roles as mothers,[13] the world of political struggle is in many ways more intellectually demanding of women than those of purely church and charity work. As I will suggest, fighting for causes calls upon women to learn more, understand more, analyse more, represent others more and argue high-stakes issues more than pure church and charity work ever did. These new experiences have a real effect on women's ability to accept without complaint all aspects of their traditional roles within the household.

What is true for the household, it turns out, is also true for the hierarchy of authority among the laity of the Church. Having been told they must master whole new intellectual and political worlds, it becomes increasingly difficult to accept relegation to second-class citizenship within the Church. This too, we will see, is a legacy of the progressive Church. But first we need to be reminded of just how traditional even progressive Catholicism is.

Liberationist Catholicism's Gender Conservatism

There can be little doubt that the stance of Catholicism towards women is weighed down by conservative imagery and associations. Progressives, no less than traditional Catholics, define women not by the androgynous qualities of courage and fortitude, but by the essential 'feminine' virtues of nurturance, self-sacrifice and asexuality.[14] The ultimate goal of women, in the view of progressive Catholics no less than of traditional ones, is to emulate the Virgin Mary. The well-known liberation theologians Ivone Gebara and Maria Clara Bingemer, in their exceptionally influential book *Mary, Mother of God, Mother of the Poor* (published in Brazil in 1987) argue, it is true, that the mother of Jesus was a great leader in the fight against injustice; yet they find that her virtues as a leader resided precisely in her selflessness, her sexual purity, her motherliness and her desire to protect all forms of life.[15] Similarly, a dominant motif in progressive Catholic thought is that women involved in the struggle for the Kingdom are reliving the maternal sorrow and triumph of Mary. The following declaration can be found in a pamphlet used in progressive Bible reflection circles in Pôrto Alegre in the late 1980s:

> Just like Mary, woman involved in the struggle, servant of God, we want to respond with happiness to the call of Service that God entrusted us with. We want to renew the desire to live and, like Mary, to help in the struggle of the oppressed people. She who saw her son being persecuted, tortured and assassinated by the powerful of that time, assumed the mission of Mother of the Church, living and acting in the first Christian communities.[16]

Furthermore, the image of the virtuous woman as life-giving, nurturing caretaker of those who cannot care for themselves, permeates the progressive Church's effort to inspire women to become politically active. Consider, for example, the CPT's description of women engaged in struggles for the land:

> Women who fight for land for crops and for housing. Women who build community ovens to guarantee bread for the unemployed. Women who build nurseries to confront the problem of abandoned children. Women who organize teams to sew quilts to keep the sick warm. These activities and others are coming from communities and are signs of the reign of God in action.[17]

Dona Giusepa, one of the oldest members of her *comunidade*'s Mothers Club on the outskirts of Pôrto Alegre, summed up the progressive Church's view: 'We poor mothers of Bairro ... are also bearers of life, just like Mary.'[18]

The irony is that, although such images proclaim the value of women's participation in large, society-wide struggles, they reinforce the notion that women's worth ultimately derives from their ability to set aside their own needs in order to satisfy those of others.[19] A woman may say 'no' to her class oppressors, but in the Catholic liberationist literature there is little mention of her saying 'no' to the man who abuses her; she may say 'no' to Pontius Pilate, or to the king, or to the Pharisee, or to the capitalist, or to the dictator, but there is little mention of her saying 'no' to the expectation that she juggle family, work and the struggle for collective justice; she may say 'no' to the rich exploiter, but there is little mention of her saying 'no' to bringing yet another child into the world. Thus, the dominant position of liberation theology, while calling for the empowerment of women, simply sidesteps key issues that bear upon that empowerment: women's subordination in the household, everyday male–female relations, sexual violence, rape and reproductive rights. And it avoids the issue of women's *de facto* exclusion from the higher positions of leadership in the Church.

But do the dominant motifs of liberation theology tell the whole story? In what follows I will suggest that, despite its conservative gender ideology, Catholic liberationism has generated perspectives, experiences and practices that pose powerful challenges to patriarchy, and has facilitated the struggle against gender injustice in Brazil.

Gender Inequality in the Home

While thundering against huge, societywide economic and social injustices, the theologians, priests, pastoral agents and lay leaders of the liberationist Church have had relatively little to say about gender inequality in the home. One is hard-pressed to find discussion of the gendered division of labour in the writings of liberation theologians, even self-styled feminist ones such as Ivone Gebara,[20] and I have heard no report of the topic in sermons of progressive clerics. The everyday practice of grassroots progressive Catholics is similarly unquestioning. I recently witnessed, in a *comunidade de base* in Maranhão, a staged dramatization of the local land struggle, in which the lead player, a man, sat at a table served by his wife, while he denounced the landlord. Quite clearly, the fact that the woman stood serving her husband was wholly unremarkable for the audience. I have also witnessed such taken-for-granted roles within the homes of progressive Church leaders, from Rio to Bahia to Maranhão, in which husbands expect to be served, and their wives – many of them also participants or leaders in the CEB – serve them. In one instance, the wife worked for wages, while the husband was unemployed; she had earned a college degree, while he only had a high school diploma; and she was a leader in the Church. Yet she served him dinner, made sure he got coffee and a snack at night, and would, with no sign of irritation, stop speaking when he interrupted her. The case is by no means atypical. Dona Iraci, whom Drogus characterizes as endowed with radical political consciousness, and who recognized the difficulties that unequal division of labour had created for her involvement in the Church, still felt it was up to her, as a woman, to 'harmonize things at home'. When her husband objected to her enthusiastic participation in Church, she concluded that it was up to her to 'slow down'.[21]

Such dispositions, however, do not tell the whole story. When one listens closely, one discovers that involvement in the *comunidades de base* has emboldened some women to deal with their male partners in incrementally new ways. Although such new gender orientations do not usually announce themselves in open, politicized debate, they are for that no less important. Working as they do in everyday, often subterranean ways, these orientations have begun to bring about important changes in gender relations within the home.

In order to grasp these changes, we need first to appreciate the subtle ways in which CEB participation affects women's sense of themselves. It is important to understand that becoming involved in a CEB means moving into new spheres of social relations. As the CEB draws women into Bible reflection circles and other neighbourhood-level activities, such as the pastorals of baptism, liturgy and catechism, they find themselves called upon to learn more about the Bible and the Church, and to navigate a new, expanded map of relations – of cooperation, decision-making, communication, visiting, hosting and gossip – with men and women to whom they are unrelated and whom they know mainly as co-residents of their neighbourhood or community.[22] It is in fact common for women to report that an initial motive for becoming involved in the *comunidade* is precisely to escape the isolation of the home and to discover a new circle of friends and companions. Often they seek out the CEB because they long 'to fill an emptiness, to be able to get out of the house'.[23] Zelia, a middle-aged woman who lived in a working-class community to the north of Rio, and who was active in her neighbourhood association and CEB, explained to me that when she had first moved to the area, she had no extended family and knew no one. 'I was very depressed,' she said. 'I felt cut off.' Later, she explained that 'That is why I joined the CEB. I was so lonely, I needed to get out of the house, not just stay cramped up inside and do nothing. So the *comunidade* gave me that chance, to really get out, to meet people.'

To a point, of course, such moves out of the house are not very different from the trajectories towards trans-household experiences women have in connection with other churches or temples. (While men in Brazil will often try to stand in the way of their womenfolk attending other kinds of social gatherings without them, they rarely try to prevent women from attending church.) Yet in the CEB the move beyond the household is framed in terms that are quite different from those used by women to describe their moves out of the house and towards traditional Catholic, evangelical or charismatic Catholic groups. In the latter cases, I have never heard a woman explain her initial involvement as due to the simple desire to 'get out of the house' and seek human companionship. Women's accounts of involvement in these other groups tend to focus on the need for support in a crisis, a search for remedy to an illness or the desire to fulfil explicitly spiritual needs.[24] In my dozens of interviews with evangelical women over the years, I never heard a woman explicitly emphasize her longing to escape the isolation of the home. In contrast, the heavily human-oriented language current in the CEB appears to authorize women to articulate church participation as at least partly about being liberated from the confines of the household. The oh-so-human style of this language is apparent in the account of Adailda, a woman in her forties who lived in a working-class district near São Luiz. Adailda told me that 'The *comunidade* is a place to get to know your neighbours. It is the Church, but it is also like a group of women, where we socialize. So that was very important for me at first, when I arrived here, I couldn't stand staying locked up [*trancada*] in the house, and so when a neighbour came by, and said, "let's go to the *comunidade* meeting", I thought, "Yes, that's where I'm going to go."'

Having escaped domestic isolation, women who become involved in leadership roles in the CEB find an arena of exciting possibility for rough-and-tumble equality with men in an extra-domestic domain. The quality of male–female interactions in a CEB directorate is well illustrated by one on the outskirts of São Luis. Here, in July 2001, local women were involved in every decision in the preparation, implementation and evaluation of monthly activities. At an evaluation session, in two hours of boisterous give-and-take about the strengths and weaknesses of the month's activities, the women on the directorate vigorously challenged and contradicted men's points of view, occasionally raised their voices over those of men, and reprimanded men who dared interrupt them. Such modes of interaction are well established in this place, and the women I spoke with are proud of them. Said Alessandra, a forty-year old mother of three and long-time participant in the directorate: 'What you saw here is the way we always operate, because here we all make decisions. There is no "men over women" here.' In another CEB council, in the south of the country, gender interactions were, if anything, even more egalitarian. For example, I recently saw a woman on the council speak at length in contradiction to a man older than her and who enjoyed considerable local prestige. When the man tried to interrupt her, using a body language that declared 'I am an important man', he was roundly silenced by a wave of verbal protests, mainly from the women.

The rough equality of these interactions are a function of three main factors: the general norm that declares that church matters are a special province of female expertise; the specifically liberationist discourse of human equality; and women's numerical domination of CEB directorates. With regard to the first, both men and women assume that women are able to speak with authority about such matters as the best way of organizing charity drives, house-to-house visits, Sunday school, feasts and so on. 'That is what we are good at,' said Rosane, a thirty-something council member in São Luis. 'We have grown up with running a household, so it is easy for us to run a church too!'

With regard to progressive Catholic ideology, what is striking here is that this ideology celebrates, in sermons, pamphlets and catechism, the human skills and talents that everyone brings into the community. The following text, taken from a pamphlet published in the early 1990s as a guide to *comunidades* faced with electing their councils, gives a flavour of this ideology:

> God has endowed all of us with different gifts. For one, this is the gift of speaking in public. For another, it is the gift of cooking delicious food. Yet another knows how to build with great skill, and another is good with figures. Each has something to offer the community. We must valorize all of these skills, each is essential to the success of the *comunidade*![25]

Whilst these discursive resources are important, they would probably have little room to develop were it not for women's numerical preponderance in the councils. In the dozen or so CEB councils I have known over the years, women have almost always outnumbered men by about two to one. Near Rio, the directorate of one CEB I got to know well had ten women and five men; in the suburbs of São Luiz, in one *comunidade*'s directorate there were seven women and three men; and elsewhere I encountered similar ratios. In explaining these ratios, everywhere I heard from women that they had more time to give, they were around the community more, they were more willing to give of themselves, and they were more interested in religious matters. Whatever the reason, the women I spoke with referred to these ratios quite readily in accounting for their experience of gender equality. The women themselves do not doubt that their numbers make them more at ease to speak openly in front of, and equally with, men. As Madelena, a fifty-year old council member in Ilhéus, Bahia, said to me, 'men can't try to dominate there, because there are more women than men!'

For these reasons, women are able to experience in the CEB a context of unusual equality with men. There are, however, key limits to this equality; indeed, it is precisely these limits that, by producing dissonance with the taste of equality present on councils, lead to women's further radicalization. I shall discuss these processes shortly.

Beyond the CEB council and the immediate co-residential community, some women go on to participate in Church-oriented activities at the wider parish and diocesan levels, including liturgy seminars and workshops, youth group meetings, courses in theology and catechism conferences. Attending such meetings, women find themselves in situations outside the authority of their menfolk, and in which they must rely on their own savvy: on long bus-rides, in navigating strange towns, in lodgings far from their homes, in restaurants or public cafeterias and, perhaps most important, in public discussions in which they officially represent their communities to outsiders. Silvia, a woman in her sixties, a long-time participant in a CEB in Rio de Janeiro, told me what such trips meant to her:

> It really changed my view of things. Because there you are, seeing other places, going anywhere you need to ... . Meeting other people. In those meetings, each person would have a turn to talk. And I would speak, and say what was happening in our community. And everyone listened to that!

In a moment I will return to considering the impact of such trans-local experiences on women's self-concepts. For now I wish to underscore that the examples I have been discussing have focused on women's involvement in specifically Church-oriented matters. But recall that what distinguishes the liberationist Church is its call to participants to transfer the lessons they learn within the Church to the making of a better world outside it.[26] Now, women who enter the arena of secular social action, accustomed to household and neighbourhood and Church-related matters, often encounter a kind of culture shock: they find themselves suddenly immersed in a whirlwind of people, ideas and facts quite different from what they have dealt with inside the Church. Sonia, a forty-year old participant in a *comunidade* in Maranhão, told me:

> Before I became involved in the *comunidade*, I didn't know much about these things. I started with the land pastoral ... it was like going to university – I learned so much ... And we were always going here and there, I would go in delegations to the offices of land records, and you know, that is an amazing thing, to be standing there, and talking to the minister of land records, and this is no joke, you have to have all your facts straight.

Given all these possibilities, there should be little doubt that becoming active in the *comunidade* is frequently experienced as 'life gone hectic', as involvement in ever-expanding circuits of activities beyond the home.[27]

The Politics of Female and Male Authority in the Household

What are the consequences of all this intense activity for women's roles? For a start, it has produced standards of female self-definition that are no longer confined to keeping house and raising children. In practice, some of these women find it difficult to reconcile strict adherence to their traditional domestic duties with their new roles as actors in the public domain. Not surprisingly, it is usually only women with older children who choose to move furthest into public circuits.[28] Yet even women with grown children do not always find it easy to juggle domestic and Church obligations. In Maranhão, Katiane, in her early forties, complains about all the work: 'I have my work for the Church, which I will never give up. But does that mean I have any less work to do at home? No! There are days, I swear, when I get very little sleep ... even now, that my kids are grown!'

Sleep-deprived or not, Katiane's insistence that she will 'never give up' her Church-related work is paradigmatic. Women who have experienced leadership roles in the CEB are reluctant to relinquish them and return to simple domesticity. After all, they are proud of their extra-domestic activities, from which, in their view, their families and communities clearly benefit. 'I think', said Suzane, a thirty-year old woman involved in her CEB's health pastoral in São Luis, 'that we need to be very proud of what we do for the pastoral. This is God's work, it is divine work. I could stay at home and do nothing but feed my family. But I have chosen to do more, that is my calling.'

'It is divine work' – pretty heady stuff, this. And let there be no mistake: what many women in the CEB are experiencing is, for the first time, the unambiguous valorization of their minds over their bodies. For women who have been told all their lives that their political opinions are of little importance, the experiences of learning about matters of public concern and of speaking about them in public is nothing less than transformative. As Carolina, a middle-aged woman active in her *comunidade* on the outskirts of Rio, says:

> As a woman, what are we always told? Growing up, this is what I heard: 'men argue, women gossip'. Like what men say is important, but women, we don't know what we are talking about, we just say nonsense! Before the *comunidade*, I thought that way! I thought: 'Me, a woman, I don't have anything important to say.'

Becoming involved in her neighbourhood's *comunidade* changed Carolina's life and outlook:

I started going places with the others, where I would never have done that. And I thought: 'I'm not stupid, I have ideas. I learned many new things – all this discussion, these readings, all of this.'

Dona Helena, now a minister of baptism in a CEB in Rio Grande do Sul, recounted a similar experience:

I used to be an ignorant person. I always kept quiet, I was afraid to speak up. When I saw these women [female CEB leaders] for the first time I was appalled! Them being women and speaking like that, out loud, about what they felt and thought. But little by little I understood that they were good people. They always invited me to their meetings, they invited me to come, to participate, to speak up. Now I'm much like them, they have become my friends.

Dona Helena, like other women with CEB leadership experience, has translated her new-found confidence into speaking out in public for what she believes. 'The people respect me, I go anywhere in the neighbourhood, I go to the centre [of town], I even go to see the mayor if I want to, to tell him about the problems in the *vila*. I'm a different person now than I was then, a better person, no, a better woman.'[29] Or listen to the female CEB participant in São Paulo who declared that:

Even if we haven't had the chance to study, like me, myself, I don't know much. A person without schooling doesn't know much, not even how to get around, eh? And that was a very important thing ... . And look, nowadays we go to every blessed place trying, looking for things.[30]

What happens when this emerging self-respect collides with a possessive, jealous or protective male? It should come as no surprise that some of these women conclude that men who seek to restrict them to circumscribed domestic roles, must be resisted. 'We women are there not only to make coffee,' said a female CEB participant in Rio Grande do Sul, 'to be at the side of our king [husband], but we are here for life! ... We have to salvage the right to be who we are, not through a war, but we don't need to be subordinate any more. We are adult women, we have faith and fibre, we are no longer girls.'[31]

What do such women do to alter the domestic political economy? How do they show their partners that they 'don't need to be subordinate any more'? And to what extent are they succeeding?

It should be noted that some women are able to become active in the CEB precisely because they are already in relatively gender-equal marital relationships. This pattern is illustrated by Paulo, an activist in a CEB in Pernambuco, who has a personality regarded by some as typical of the CEB male: 'a caring person, visiting the sick, talking to them, giving comfort to the needy' – all patterns associated with femininity in Brazilian gender norms.[32] The example of such men encourages women to question whether they must resign themselves to the intemperate behaviour of husbands and other men. 'Marisa', reports De Theije, '… came to realize – through conversation with the priest and the participating men – that not all men are as brutish and violent as her husband.'[33] Some women go so far as to call upon men in the *comunidade* to cultivate their 'feminine' qualities, such as protectiveness and nurturance, 'as desirable assets not only for women, but for all Catholics who want to effectively contribute to the Kingdom of God on earth.'[34]

Naturally, not all male partners are ready to cultivate their 'feminine' side. Unfortunately, cases of jealous husbands forbidding wives from attending CEB meetings are all too common.[35] Zelia, for instance, was able to become a leader of the CEB-led health movement in São Paulo only after she was widowed:

> He did not let me out on my own, only together with him. He was the type of man who believes 'a woman's place is in the home', taking care of the children. Perhaps if he were alive today, now older, he might have changed a little. But at that time he would not have let me take part in the Movement as I do today.

Now Zelia is relieved no longer to have a man stand in her way. Women, in her view, 'must have their rights, to study, to work, in the Church, in politics. Everyone must see that she isn't an object, a toy.'[36]

Yet for every Zelia there is another woman who refuses to be a doormat while her husband is alive. As one of Caldeira's informants in São Paulo remarked:

> You make friends in the local groups and it opens women up, little by little things become clearer; let's see if we can overcome this fear we have of our husbands. It seems to me that men prefer to see women at home washing clothes, cooking, I think that's what it is. If he goes out that's all right but if the woman goes, she'll see what happens. Women must do something they like; I like it so I do it.[37]

'I like it so I do it' – revolutionary words indeed. Consider their implications for Joanina, in Pernambuco, when her husband tried to stop her from participating in the CEB. 'I said, "You cannot forbid me, hinder my going to my church. If I were to go to a dance, a birthday party, or something like that, then okay, but to my church, where I was born and grew up, you cannot take me from there now, so don't try."'[38] Or for Simone of São Paulo, who became an activist through the CEB and who reported that her husband 'resented the loss of a model wife who kept a perfect house when she became active'. But, she says, 'Now I say to him, that's not why I was born. I was born to live, not to live for you.'[39] Or for Joselina, who reflected that:

> There's that idea you must be submissive to the man, that was put in women's heads. But it can't be that way. Because we have to be free too, we have to be

something. Can it be that we think we're lowered, that the man is the head, we're not the head? But then, don't I have a head equal to his?[40]

Now, certainly some women lose such battles, and find themselves forced to limit or abandon their activism. Olivia, for example, a leader of a *comunidade* outside of Recife, found that she could not attend a diocesan assembly because it would have kept her away from home for two consecutive nights, something her husband would not tolerate. She only began to attend trans-local meetings when her husband got a job in São Paulo, taking him away from home for extended periods.[41]

Still – and this is the key point – in the past 20 years, a growing body of evidence suggests that women win these battles just as often as they lose them. In São Paulo, Iraci's husband opposed her overnight trips, but eventually, moved by his wife's arguments, he relented.[42] Near Brasilia, Vanessa initially faced disapproval from her husband about her late-night meetings in church, but she stood her ground. 'Today', she said, 'I come home at one or two or three, and my husband doesn't dare ask where I was. If he did he would get an answer like "none of your business".'[43] When the husband of a CEB participant in São Paulo complained about her 'going out too much', she simply ignored him:

> Even if there's a fuss, I go. I don't know, he seems to think that I go out too much, that I stay out too long ... But I like it, so I put my foot down and go. Sometimes, when I have the chance to go and celebrate the liturgy, when I get back there's a fight. But he's the one who causes it, I don't want to get involved in arguments, and the following day I'll go again. He'd have to tie me up to stop me.[44]

The Politics of Housework

Resistance such as this to male control over women's time and movement leads ineluctably to the politics of housework. To what extent are leading women in CEBs able to push their husbands and families to take up more domestic chores, so as to facilitate their own involvement in Church-related activities? The available evidence suggests that when it comes to housework, the 'revolution' represented by CEB participation encounters a clear limit. Testimony from around Brazil indicates that most women in the *comunidades* continue to assume that housework is primarily their responsibility. Although ready to defy spousal prohibitions against going out, few women are prepared to lay down pots and pans and wait for men to pick them up.[45]

Still, even if there is no revolution, subtle ideological changes about housework may be afoot. CEB women, like most women in Brazil and elsewhere, ask their husbands and sons to pitch in around the house.

Interestingly, some CEB women report thinking of male help at home not in the limited sense of assistance in the running of the household, but rather as allowing them better to pursue their trans-household project of struggling for the Kingdom. Listen to Dona Salete, a catechist and minister of Baptism in Rio Grande do Sul: 'We need the co-operation of our husbands, children and so on, so that we are free to do this work, to get the training we want and need...in a way we ourselves need to be shared.'[46] Similarly, in a CEB on the outskirts of Rio de Janeiro, I knew a female minister of baptism who insisted that her husband take on the task of cooking one or two afternoons a week 'so that I can go to my meetings. He has to help me, I told him, because otherwise I won't be able to keep up my activities in Church.' Or listen to the CEB activist in São Paulo interviewed by Caldeira:

> At home it was like this: when my husband and children had a bath I would get them towels and lay out all their clothes for them to dress. That was my obligation ... . Suddenly I realized that it wasn't just me, everyone had to change ... I had thought that as a woman, a wife, it was my duty to do all these things for my husband. Then one day I saw that it wasn't so.[47]

Progressive Christian ideas have sometimes been brought to bear on this issue. In Bible reflection circles, housework is sometimes placed under scrutiny in connection with a key passage from Luke. In this passage, Jesus visits Mary and her sister Martha and begins to preach. Mary takes a seat in front of him and listens, while Martha busies herself with household duties. When Martha complains that Mary has left her with the housework, Jesus corrects her: 'Martha, Martha, thou art careful and troubled about many things; But one thing is needful; and Mary hath chosen that good part, which shall not be taken away from her' (Luke 10: 40–42). Els Jacobs witnessed a discussion of this verse among female catechists in Pôrto Alegre. 'On the basis of this verse', she writes, 'the women engaged in a discussion on the difficulties of being housewives. They concluded that they should follow Mary's example and tune into God's intentions.'[48] What followed was rather less traditional: 'They also proposed that in order to be able to do so, childcare and household duties should be more equally divided between them and their husbands.'[49] Jacobs does not report whether this idea was pursued in practice, but the astonishing thing is that it was expressed at all, and that it was facilitated by commentary on a biblical passage.[50]

While such views undoubtedly represent new forms of gender consciousness, it would be a mistake to see them as part of an ideological package that questions the validity of marriage, or that regards men as oppressive of women, or that advocates a woman's right to pursue her individual interests at the expense of family. Rather, these women are rejecting the submissive, long-suffering model of motherhood for a more public, active model. According to these women, the values of motherhood and family do not impede their pursuit of freedom, but are integral parts of it. More generally, they view themselves as largely realized through social ties, not through unencumbered self-realization.[51] It is common to hear women who, while thrilled by their new-found independence, explicitly reject the notion of pure individualism, which they associate with abandoning families. Thus, for instance, Vanessa, a CEB activist in Brasilia, felt that 'the tendency of women to emphasize their own independence in individual terms already bordered on egotism that left negative marks on children and families. She [was] especially worried that women are increasingly leaving husbands and children in order to pursue their own lives.'[52]

Given such sentiments, it should not surprise us that activist Catholic women tend to embrace neither pure familialism nor radical individualism: rather, they tend to advocate a 'balance' between their domestic and extra-domestic lives. 'It's a question of compromise,' said Dona Zilda, in a comment I heard echoed in my own interviews with women in CEBs in Rio and Maranhão. 'I find it absurd that people who are militants in movements and political parties should then forget family and children.' She is quick to add that this is 'absurd' *not* because women must stick to traditional gender roles; it is absurd because forgetting family and children make women unhappy. 'I think that's wrong,' she said, 'it involves too much frustration. The ideal is to have a balanced life. The man needs the woman, and vice versa. If we achieve a balance at home, we do the same outside.'[53]

From this perspective, leading CEB women feel that men may in fact play a constructive role in their lives when they ask them to avoid going overboard in their extra-domestic activities. 'I tell him,' Zelia said, 'I think it's good that he sometimes tries to hold me back – in the heat of the moment you can get overwhelmed and throw yourself into the work, forgetting everything else. That's when he holds me back.'[54]

Although falling short of a feminist utopian dream, such a compromise does represent a cultural shift away from the model of Marian suffering and submission. Participation in the CEB and the broader arenas of action encouraged for women by the liberationist Church may thus be subtly reconfiguring what poor Brazilian women expect from the men of their households.

Equal Treatment within the Church

A common criticism of the People's Church is that, despite its egalitarian rhetoric and despite the fact that over two-thirds of its members are female, women continue to be passed over in favour of men for the *igreja popular*'s highest-status roles. We have already noted women's active presence as leaders and decision-makers in CEB councils. However, when we focus our attention on the specific roles within both the council and the religious ministries, it becomes possible to see tangible gender inequality. Men tend to occupy the highest-profile, highest-status roles, such as ministers of the Word and of the Eucharist, while women tend to be concentrated in the lower-profile, lower-status ministries of baptism, marriage, liturgy, and catechism.[55] In addition, despite the fact that a growing number of women are travelling outside the community, it is still the case that such travel is easier for men who consequently build up the networks necessary for leadership at the diocesan level more rapidly than do women.[56] Consequently, because men are selected as advisers and confidantes to the diocesan clergy more often than are women, the sexism inherent in the priesthood is reinforced.[57]

Earlier I suggested that, at the community and parish levels, women have tasted a kind of rough equality with men. Indeed, this is true – the equality is in fact only 'rough'. On closer inspection, at the community level the division of labour among council members and ministers remains tainted by traditional sex roles. In a CEB in Maranhão, for instance, the men ran the prestigious activities of the church radio station, treasury and construction projects, while the women were expected to ensure that food and drink were provided for church functions and dishes cleared away afterwards. Likewise, in other CEBs, male leaders were expected to manage the church's structural integrity, while women were expected to sweep, cook and clean.[58]

The question, is of course, whether the women resent any of this, and so it is important to note that, for the past 20 years, there has been a growing demand from women in the CEBs that these patterns change. As early as the late 1970s some laywomen were already calling for more equal representation in the higher rungs of leadership. While this demand was no doubt partly attributable to the growing presence in the media (and, occasionally, on the ground) of middle-class, urban-based feminists,[59] a simple exposure to feminism cannot explain why certain feminist ideals – those calling for greater equality of treatment within the Church – would find such a receptive audience among CEB women. It was, in the end, their own everyday experience of contradiction that rendered some outsiders' calls for greater gender equality sensible and appealing. Simply put, as leading women saw themselves, through the 1970s and 1980s, accumulating mastery of every other task in the Church, many of them began to experience their exclusion from the Church's most prestigious roles as a burning insult. Luana, a fifty-something CEB participant in Rio, recalled that in the 1970s and 1980s she had been angry about the unwillingness of the priest to appoint her as minister of the Eucharist. 'He never explained it,' she told me. 'He never said it was because I was a woman, but I knew it. We all understood why Reginaldo was minister and I wasn't.'

Supported and reinforced in their own agenda by the feminism brought to working-class neighbourhoods by urban middle-class activists,[60] in the early 1980s women in CEBs began to demand that the issue of female leadership be articulated at the national inter-ecclesial meetings of the progressive Church, and finally succeeded in getting it on the national agenda in 1986.[61] At that meeting, the women's delegation publicly criticized 'the insufficient or non-existent representation of women in the exercise of the most important ministries in the *comunidades*'.[62] Similar concerns and calls for the election and appointment of women to these ministries, were issued at national CEB meetings in 1989 and 1992.[63]

The combination of pressure from women at the grassroots, as well as the national articulation of the issue, succeeded in bringing about change. Most strikingly, in CEBs across the country, the period of 1989–93 saw women finally getting elected to the much-coveted position of minister of the Word. In Pôrto Alegre, ahead of the rest of the country, a cohort of women became ministers of the Word at the insistence of the priest, who supported them because they 'had so much experience in the community'.[64] In Coroado, a town outside of São Luis, where only men had been ministers of the Word and of the Eucharist until the late 1980s, the early 1990s saw male leaders finally concede that 'women should be full partners in the church', as one of them put it; after that, women in Coroado finally found themselves expounding the Word in front of the congregation. Similarly-timed changes occurred in CEBs on the outskirts of Rio de Janeiro. The testimony of a minister of the Word may represent those of many others. 'When I was young', she said, 'and participated in the Youth Group, I wasn't even allowed to do a reading in church, much less the Bible. Today, I proclaim the Gospel!'[65]

By the end of the 1990s the issue of gender inequality had become less visible at national inter-ecclesial meetings, and this may be taken as a measure of the success of women in CEBs gaining greater representation at higher posts. And yet the issue of gender inequality in leadership had not really disappeared; it had only entered a new phase. For although CEBs grew more gender-equal in the 1990s with respect to formal positions of leadership, in practice the women serving in these positions have not always received the respect they deserve. 'The people have difficulties in accepting a female minister of the Word,' said Dona Zenaide of Pôrto Alegre, in 1994. 'They don't pay attention, perhaps they think it's all nonsense that leaves my mouth.'[66] Parishioners are notorious for preferring male over female ministers of the Eucharist. 'When I distribute the host,' said Dona Clarete, also in Pôrto Alegre, 'together with the priest, I always see some people who cross the aisle to enter the queue of Friar Darcy. As if his hosts were more sacred than mine! But they don't do that if Seu Joel is in charge as minister of the Eucharist!'[67] In a CEB in Maranhão, a female leader recounted a similar experience. 'When I became minister of the Word, I could see the men staring off into space. You can see that, really.' Some observers suspect that as women became more common as ministers of the Word and Eucharist, male Church attendance declined.[68]

Women experience such disrespect in contradiction to their ascribed status, and this contradiction has pushed some of them towards a willingness to recognize their plight as being due to sexual discrimination. Dona Zenaide in Pôrto Alegre began to complain to her colleagues that men often became ministers of the Eucharist without being accompanied by their wives, but women who did the same became the subjects of gossip. 'What nonsense!' she said. 'They think that a woman can only accept the task when she's joined by her husband, because then you have a pair, a nice couple, and that a husband can only accept... and so on. But if he alone wants to go and she doesn't, it's no problem.'[69] Lusiane, from São Luis, was more explicit. 'The ministers should be treated equally. They have the same merits, I don't care if you are a man or woman. But many in the *comunidade* don't see it that way. That is a disgrace!' She suggested that, in fact, much gender inequality remained in the *comunidade*. Men who were separated from their spouses, for example, suffered no unusual treatment, but 'what do you think happens if a single mother or a separated woman wants to take on some task, like catechism? There still is that gossip for women, but not for men!'

Such resentment can, in some cases, bring about shifts in behaviour. In the CEB outside São Luis, a single mother recently wanted to become a catechist, but a male CEB director resisted the idea, arguing that CEB leaders had to serve as an example to the community's youth. Several women formed a delegation, led by Lusiane, and paid a visit to the director. Lusiane recounts what happened next:

> We said, 'Look, you want the leaders to be good examples? Then we should let Sr Antonio go tomorrow, because he is separated! And we should let you go tomorrow too, because you are separated.' We reasoned with him like this. And he saw that we were right, that it was wrong to keep women from becoming a catechist for this reason, since none of the men were excluded.

The policy changed after that. In this case, a decisive factor was the fact that the delegation was led by a woman who happened to be a minister of the Word. It thus appears that as women come to play higher-status roles in church, they increasingly enjoy the power to open up further spaces for other women, too. Such processes have only just begun.

Conclusion

In this chapter I have argued that the liberationist Catholic project, in the form of CEBs, stimulated women to expect and seek more equal treatment in their homes and in the Church. These processes have been quite widely acknowledged, even if not always closely scrutinized. In contrast, it has be generally assumed that the role of the Church, in both its progressive and non-progressive guises, has been to place strict ideological limits on discussion and action in relation to sexual violence and abortion. Whilst such limits are indeed present in the Church, the liberationist project has also catalysed ideological processes that have pressed on those limits and, in some cases, have stressed them to breaking-point. It is to these processes that I now turn.

Notes

1   Liesl Haas, 'Changing the System from Within? Feminist Participation in the Brazilian Workers' Party' in Victoria Gonzalez and Karen Kampwirth (eds.), *Radical Women in Latin America: Left and Right* (University Park, PA: Pennsylvania State University Press, 2001), 262–263; Sonia Alvarez, *Engendering Democracy in Brazil: Women's Movements in Transition Politics* (Princeton: Princeton University Press, 1990), 60–70; Sonia Alvarez, 'Women's Participation in the Brazilian "People's Church": A Critical Appraisal', *Feminist Studies*, 16 (Summer 1990), 381–408.
2   Elsa Tamez, *Through Her Eyes: Women's Theology from Latin America* (Maryknoll: Orbis, 1989); Elsa Tamez, The Amnesty of Grace (Nashville: Abingdon Press, 1993); Maria Pilar Aquino, *Our Cry for Life: Feminist Theology from Latin America* (New York: Orbis, 1993); Maria Pilar Aquino, 'Latin American Feminist Theology', *Journal of Feminist Studies in Religion*, 14 (Spring 1998), 89–107.
3   Leda Maria Vieira Machado, 'We Learned to Think Politically: The Influence of the Catholic Church and the Feminist Movement on the Emergence of the Health Movement of the Jardim Nordeste Area in São Paulo, Brazil' in Sarah A. Radcliffe and Sallie Westwood (eds.), *Viva! Women and Popular Protest in Latin America* (New York: Routledge, 1993), 88–111; Jennifer Schirmer, 'The Seeking of Truth and the Gendering of Consciousness: the Comadres of El Salvador and the Conavigua Widows of Guatemala' in Radcliffe and Westwood, *Viva!*, 30–64.
4   Elina Vuola, *Limits of Liberation: Praxis as Method in Latin American Theology and Feminist Theology* (Helsinki: Suomalainen, 1997).
5   As argued in Alvarez, *Engendering Democracy*.
6   See contributions to Barbara Boudewijnse, André Droogers and Frans Kamsteeg (eds.), *More Than Opium: An Anthropological Approach to Latin American and Caribbean Pentecostal Praxis* (Lanham, MD: Scarecrow Press, 1998); John Burdick, 'Gossip and Secrecy: The Articulation of Domestic Conflict in Three Religions of Urban Brazil', *Sociological Analysis*, 51, 2 (Summer 1990), 153–170; Cecilia Mariz and Maria das Dores Machado, 'Pentecostalismo e a redefinição do feminino', *Religião e Sociedade* 17, 1 (1996), 140–159.
7   Maria das Dores Machado, 'Family, Sexuality, and Family Planning: A Comparative Study of Pentecostals and Charismatic Catholics in Rio de Janeiro' in Boudewijnse, Droogers and Kamsteeg, *More Than Opium*; Maria das Dores Machado and Cecilia Mariz, 'Mulheres e Prática Religiosa nas Classes Populares', *Revista Brasileira de Ciências Sociais*, 12, 34 (1997), 71–87.
8   Pentecostal women frequently move in trans-household arenas: from door to door, in the open square, prisons and hospitals, neighbouring towns and cities. They travel away from home, in order to gain converts, teach the Bible, build membership, raise funds and lead groups of unrelated people in prayer. The Quadrangular Church began ordaining female ministers as early as the 1950s, and the Universal Church of the Kingdom of God now trains female pastors.
9   Maria Lucia Rocha-Couitinho, *Tecendo por Trás dos Panos: A mulher brasileira nas relações familiares* (Rio de Janeiro: Rocco, 1994), 114.

10 For a detailed description and analysis, see Helena Scarparo, *Cidadãs Brasileiras: o cotidiano de mulheres trabalhadoras* (Rio de Janeiro: Revara, 1996). This division of labour has been discussed for decades by Roberto Da Matta, most clearly in his *A Casa e a Rua* (Rio de Janeiro: Editora Guanabara, 1987).
11 Maria Izabel Magalhães, 'A Critical Discourse Analysis of Gender Relations in Brazil', *Journal of Pragmatics*, 23, 2 (February 1995), 183–197.
12 M. J. F. Rosado Nuñez, 'Women, Family, and Catholicism in Brazil: The Issue of Power' in Sharon Houseknecht and Jerry G. Pankhurst (eds.), *Family, Religion, and Social Change in Diverse Societies* (New York: Oxford University Press, 2000).
13 For example, Kevin Neuhouser, 'If I Had Abandoned My Children: Community Mobilization and Commitment to the Identity of Mother in Northeast Brazil', *Social Forces*, 77, 1 (September 1998), 331–358.
14 Carol Ann Drogus, *Women, Religion, and Social Change in Brazil's Popular Church* (Notre Dame: University of Notre Dame Press, 1997); Frances B. O'Connor and Becky Drury, *The Female Face of Patriarchy: Oppression as Culture* (East Lansing: Michigan State University Press, 1999); John Burdick, *Looking for God in Brazil: The Progressive Church in Urban Brazil's Religious Arena* (Berkeley: University of California Press, 1993), 95; Sonia Alvarez, 'Latin American Feminisms "Go Global": Trends of the 1990s and Challenges for the New Millennium' in Sonia E. Alvarez, Evelina Dagnino and Arturo Escobar (eds.), *Cultures of Politics, Politics of Cultures: Re-Visioning Latin American Social Movements* (Boulder: Westview Press, 1998), 299; Nikkie Craske, *Women and Politics in Latin America* (New Brunswick: Rutgers University Press, 1999), 200; Vuola, *Limits of Liberation*, 188; W. E. Hewitt, 'The Political Dimensions of Women's Participation in Brazil's Base Christian Communities (CEBs): A Longitudinal Case Study from São Paulo', *Women and Politics*, 21, 3 (2000), 1–25.
15 Ivone Gebara and Maria Clara Bingemer, *Mary, Mother of God, Mother of the Poor* (Maryknoll: Orbis, 1989), 169.
16 *Mães Unidas: Voz da Libertação*, July 1987, cited by Els Jacobs, 'The Feminine Way/ "O Jeito Feminino": Religion, Power and Identity in South-Brazilian Base Communities', PhD dissertation, (University of Utrecht, 2001), 65. A corollary of this image is that women have a natural affinity for communing with the Earth, and so must take the lead in bringing an end to a disharmonious relationship with nature. See, for example, José Comblin, *Called for Freedom: The Changing Context of Liberation Theology* (Maryknoll: Orbis, 1998); Leonardo Boff, *Tempo de Transcendência: O Ser Humano como um Projeto Infinito* (Rio de Janeiro: Editora Sextante, 2000); Ivone Gebara, *Longing for Running Water: Ecofeminism and Liberation* (Minneapolis: Fortress Press, 1999).
17 As cited in Lynn Stephen, *Women and Social Movements in Latin America* (Austin: University of Texas Press, 1997), 216–217.
18 Els Jacobs, 'The Feminine Way', 76.
19 Cf. Drogus, *Women, Religion, and Social Change*, 175.
20 Gebara's recent writings yield no overt reference to the gendered division of labour in the household. See for example, Ivone Gebara, 'A Feminist Perspective on Enigmas and Ambiguities in Religious Interpretation' in Thomas Bamat and Jean-Paul Wiest (eds.), *Popular Catholicism in a World Church* (Maryknoll: Orbis, 1999), 256–264; Ivone Gebara, 'Brazilian Women's Movements and Feminist Theologies', *Ecotheology* no. 4 (January 1998), 83–85.
21 Carol Ann Drogus, 'Liberation Theology and the Liberation of Women in Santo Antonio, Brazil' in John Burdick and W. E. Hewitt (eds.), *The Church at the Grassroots in Latin America* (Westport: Praeger, 2000), 98.
22 Machado, 'We Learned to Think Politically', 100.
23 Ibid., 100–101.

24 See Andrew Chesnut, *Born Again in Brazil* (New Brunswick: Rutgers, 1997); and his comparative argument developed in Chesnut, *Competitive Spirits: Latin America's New Religious Economy* (New York: Oxford University Press, 2003).
25 Paroquia Nossa Senhora das Graças, 'Como Escolher um Conselho Comunitário', mimeographed pamphlet, 1987.
26 The CEB-based women's rate of participation in secular social change organizations is higher than the rate of participation of women in society at large, or of evangelicals in general. See Rubem Cesar Fernandes *et al.*, *Novo Nascimento* (Rio de Janeiro: Mauad, 1998), 198.
27 Carol Ann Drogus, 'Religious Change and Women's Status in Latin America', Kellogg Working Paper, no. 205 (March 1994); Hewitt, 'The Political Dimensions of Women's Participation'.
28 Marjo De Theije, *All that is God is Good: An Anthropology of Liberationist Catholicism in Garanhuns, Brazil* (Utrecht: CERES, 1997), 112.
29 Jacobs, 'The Feminine Way'.
30 Drogus, 'Religious Change', 12; cf. Daniel Levine, *Popular Voices in Latin American Catholicism* (Princeton: Princeton University Press, 1992), 293–294.
31 Jacobs, 'The Feminine Way', 79.
32 De Theije, *All that is God*, 114.
33 Ibid., 117.
34 Jacobs, 'The Feminine Way', 142.
35 See the cases cited in Goetz Ottman, 'Symbolic Contestation: Genesis, Death and Resurrection of the Liberationist Project in the Bairros of São Paulo', PhD dissertation (Australian National University, 1999), 90.
36 Machado, 'We Learned to Think Politically', 100.
37 Teresa Caldeira, 'Women, Daily Life and Politics,' in Elizabeth Jelin (ed.), *Women and Social Change in Latin America* (Atlantic Highlands: Zed, 1990), 65.
38 De Theije, *All that is God*, 112.
39 Drogus, 'Liberation Theology', 99.
40 Drogus, *Women, Religion and Social Change*, 163; cf. Ottman, 'Symbolic Contestation', 90.
41 De Theije, *All that is God*, 113.
42 Drogus, *Women, Religion and Social Change*, 163.
43 Ottman, 'Symbolic Contestation', 91.
44 Caldeira, 'Women, Daily Life and Politics', 65.
45 Drogus, *Women, Religion and Social Change*, 163.
46 Jacobs, 'The Feminine Way', 96.
47 Caldeira, 'Women, Daily Life and Politics', 66.
48 Jacobs, 'The Feminine Way', 79.
49 Ibid.
50 See also Drogus's argument in *Women, Religion and Social Change*, 172, where she suggests that some CEB women have begun to call for equality in division of domestic labour.
51 Cf. Christine Eber, 'Seeking Our Own Food: Indigenous Women's Power and Autonomy in San Pedro Chenalho, Chiapas (1980–1998)', *Latin American Perspectives* 26, 3 (May 1999), 6–36.
52 Ottman, 'Symbolic Contestation', 91.
53 Caldeira, 'Women, Daily Life and Politics'.
54 Ibid.
55 Jacobs, 'The Feminine Way', 94. The minister of the Word enjoys the greatest prestige in the CEB, for he has the right to address the full congregation and interpret the Bible; the minister of the Eucharist, who distributes the host, also enjoys high status. The ministries of baptism, marriage, and liturgy deal with the more routine aspects of church life, and so are ranked lower.

56 Lucia Ribeiro, 'Comunidades de Irmãs e Irmãos: A questão do gênero nas CEBs', in José Oscar Beozzo et al. (coord.), *CEBs: Povo de Deus, 2000 Anos de Caminhada, texto-base* (Paulo Afonso: Fonte Viva, 2000), 152–177.
57 Jacobs, 'The Feminine Way', 141.
58 Alvarez, *Engendering Democracy*, 68.
59 Alvarez, *Engendering Democracy*.
60 Ibid.
61 Faustino Luiz Couto Teixeira, *Os Encontros Intereclesias de CEBs no Brasil* (São Paulo: Paulinas, 1996).
62 Ribeiro, 'Comunidades', 163; Teixeira, *Os Encontros*, 74.
63 Teixeira, *Os Encontros*.
64 Jacobs, 'The Feminine Way', 94.
65 Ribeiro, 'Comunidades', 166.
66 Jacobs, 'The Feminine Way', 94.
67 Ibid.
68 N. Patrick Peritore, 'Socialism, Communism, and Liberation Theology in Brazil,' *Latin America Series*, No. 15 (Athens, Ohio: Center for International Studies, Ohio University, 1990), 168; see also Frances B. O'Connor, *Like Bread, Their Voices Rise* (Notre Dame: Ave Maria Press, 1993), and Francis P. O'Connor and Becky Drury, *The Female Face of Patriarchy: Oppression as Culture* (East Lansing: State University of Michigan Press, 1999).
69 Jacobs, 'The Feminine Way', 95.

Chapter 4

The Progressive Church, Domestic Violence and Abortion

The Church and Domestic Violence

Despite 20 years of struggle by women's and human rights groups, domestic violence remains arguably one of the greatest threats to the health and well-being of Brazilian women today. In October 2001 the Perseu Abramo Foundation coordinated a nationwide study in which researchers interviewed 2500 women from all across the country. They found that nearly half of their sample had, at some time in their lives, been the victim of an act of domestic violence, including beating, rape and forced incest, at the hands of a spouse or other male of the household. This report concludes that a Brazilian woman is beaten in her home every 15 seconds, and many more suffer spousal rape, forced sex and other forms of domestic violence.[1] Violence within the home, writes Maria Aboim, 'is a constant threat in her life. Spousal abuse, rape and incest are common occurrences in the lives of Brazilian women of all classes: seventy percent of the crimes against women are committed inside the household.'[2] Furthermore, these are only the most recent statistics. There is good reason to believe that the frequency of domestic violence has been high through the whole post-Second World War period, though usually disguised behind the awful phrase 'crimes of passion'.[3]

One might assume that the progressive Catholic Church would concern itself with a situation that is so gravely unjust. Yet, from the 1960s through the 1990s, dealing with violence against women in the home was not a high priority for the progressive Church. This lack of concern was illustrated in the early 1980s when progressives in the São Paulo archdiocese of Dom Paulo Evaristo Arns conducted a 'campaign against violence'. What they meant by 'violence', it turns out, was state, police, street and interpersonal violence; the campaign left sexual violence entirely unaddressed.[4] In 1983, when the national Brotherhood Campaign focused on violence, violence against women was never mentioned. In 1990, when the Campaign focused specifically on women, domestic violence was touched upon only in the most cursory and oblique way; and in 1994, when the Campaign focused specifically on the family, the topic of domestic violence remained fuzzy and in the background.[5] Throughout the 1980s and 1990s, the national inter-ecclesial meetings of CEBs never once named sexual violence as an issue, nor placed it on the national agenda.[6] A survey of CEBs throughout Brazil, published in 1997, also failed to broach the issue.[7] Most recently, a detailed overview of 'women and CEBs', in the base-text of the tenth inter-ecclesial meeting of CEBs in 2000, allows sexual and physical violence against women to go unmentioned.[8]

It is important to note that women in CEBs have periodically sought to articulate and reflect on the problem of gender violence, usually with the assistance of the national feminist network known as Rede Mulher ('Women's Network'), which has worked assiduously since the early 1980s to place this issue along with many others on the agenda of female activists in the CEBs. The fate of such initiatives, however, has long been to be forced out of the Catholic space. In 1988 several women from CEBs of São Miguel Paulista, in the periphery of São Paulo, wanted to form a women-only group to work on women's issues, including domestic violence. They sought help from Rede Mulher, and also thought that the progressive bishop would be supportive. But Dom Bernardino, a well-known liberationist, 'did not want to give space to a group that represented "only" women'.[9] The group thus had no choice but to meet in non-Church spaces, and fund itself separately from the Church.

To some extent, this avoidance of the issue simply reflects the mother Church's doctrine on the sanctity of family, its taboo against dealing frankly with sex in any guise, and its prohibition of divorce. In addition, CEBs have not been good contexts for the articulation of domestic conflict of any kind, partly because of the conceptualization of domestic conflict as secondary to the issues of class and poverty.[10]

There is, however, one institution of the Church – the Pastoral of Marginalized Women (*Pastoral da Mulher Marginalizada*, or PMM) – which, inspired and shaped by progressive Catholic ideas (rather than by groups such as Rede Mulher), has made it its business to break the taboo not only on domestic violence, but also on rape and the sexual double standard. If these issues are radioactive in Brazilian society, they are doubly so in a Catholic context, where the mere mention of the word 'sexual' violates longstanding norms of propriety. To manage this violation, as well as to express fully its commitment to progressive Catholic values, the Pastoral links such sensitive issues with a broader critique of class oppression.

Originally conceived in the 1960s as an evangelizing mission to rid society of prostitution, the PMM earned official status as a Church-endorsed pastoral in the early 1970s,[11] and soon established several dozen centres nationwide to provide food, shelter, medical care, daycare, counselling, legal assistance and vocational training for women who were involved in prostitution, or who had recently left it.[12] Although the core activity of the PMM has always remained the running of these centres,[13] in the late 1970s leaders and agents of PMM came to regard their primary objective no longer as putting an end to prostitution, but rather to ending all forms of violence against women – of which prostitution was but one kind. By the mid-1980s the PMM had come to articulate a critique of domestic violence and the sexual double standard within the home. By the early 1990s its publications and study-guides addressed the issue of violence against women in general, on the street and at home. By the end of the same decade the PMM, with about 100 pastoral agents nationwide, had become the only official Catholic space where participants were urged to reflect about matters ranging from the sexual double standard applied to males and females before marriage, to the sexual abuse suffered from relatives, partners and spouses.

The key force that pushed the PMM to see prostitution as part of the larger probem of gender violence and inequality was liberation theology. Without that theology and its accompanying values, it is doubtful whether the PMM could have developed and sustained a mission beyond that of evangelizing prostitutes. Guided by liberationist ideas and methods, and strengthened by the institutional resources of the Church, the PMM has become an important participant in Brazil's widespread movement against gender violence. Through intensive small-group consciousness-raising work, a monthly national publication and outreach to secular feminist organizations, the PMM has forged a vibrant network of Catholic women deeply committed to the struggle against gender violence.

When it was founded in the early 1960s, the PMM was motivated by the view that prostitutes were 'fallen women' in need of evangelical love and salvation.[14] Then, towards the end of the decade, the Pastoral came under the influence of clergy committed to the preferential option for the poor.[15] These clergy helped develop the position that 'abject poverty, not individual immorality, causes prostitution', and that therefore ridding society of prostitution required ridding it of economic and social injustice.[16]

Agents of the PMM thus began to insist on symmetrical, respectful relationships with sex workers, rather than trying to bring salvation to 'fallen' women. In keeping with the liberationist spirit of 'living alongside' (*convivendo*) the wretched of the earth, pastoral agents entered the streets, brothels, sex motels, and red-light districts where prostitutes could be found. And in conformity with the progressive Church's commitment to the Freirian methodology of 'listening to the poor' and reflecting with them in intense, small groups, the PMM agents began to hear stories to which they might otherwise have been deaf. Margarida, a long-time participant in the PMM, recalled:

> At first, we went to meet the sex workers to tell them what they needed – information, and legal protection, and medicine. But little by little a surprising thing happened. We had this practice of going around the room, and asking the women to tell us their stories. And this practice, this little thing – or really, it was not such a little thing, it was a big thing – this really changed our perspective.

Listening can be an unsettling experience. At small-group meetings, when prostitutes spoke of their lives, pastoral agents found it increasingly difficult to squeeze their testimony into the simple explanatory box of economic oppression. The accounts were, rather, complex, troubling tales of young women thrown out of homes for having lost their virginity; of girls subjected to sexual assault by fathers and brothers; and (most upsetting for pastoral agents) women suffering under heavy loads of Church-induced guilt. The message borne by these accounts was considerably more knotty than 'poverty causes prostitution'. As Iolanda, a leader of the PMM, explained, hearing these stories 'made us reflect a great deal on our condition as women engaged in the search for solidarity with the most excluded of all women'.[17]

The idea that the turn to sex work might be a function of more than economic need, that one might have to consider as factors familial sexual violence and sexist double standards, took time for PMM's agents to assimilate. It was only by the third national meeting of the PMM, in 1978, that the Pastoral's leaders articulated for the first time the view that prostitution was rooted not just in poverty, but in sexism. 'The power of the masculine sex', declared the final document of the 1978 meeting, 'is arbitrary and its will is without restrictions: "women" and "objects" are goods over which, in similar ways, one exercises unlimited power.'[18] Ever since, the PMM has placed the everyday, 'private' sexism of the family – reflected in differential treatment of sons and daughters, in intra-familial sexual abuse and rape, and domestic violence – at the centre of its analysis.

To some extent, this expanded analysis has raised exactly the kinds of questions that the Church fears most. After hearing prostitutes' stories of sexual abuse at the hands of fathers and the guilt they felt because of their Catholic upbringing, some pastoral agents have begun to question values which they had previously regarded as sacrosanct. After hearing one such story from a woman named Cida, the pastoral agent found that 'I had to revisit all my assumptions, beliefs, values, profession. My whole ethical edifice fell down, it would have to be rebuilt, but it would be hard to use the debris. That hurt.' What had 'fallen down' for the pastoral agent was her trust in the inevitable goodness of family and the value placed on premarital chastity. Suddenly she realized that 'what I thought were beautiful things were not'. Cida's family was, it had turned out, a place not of safety but of danger and of searing, terrifying silence. The Catholic-instilled ethic of chastity had, this pastoral agent finally understood, led Cida to hate herself, while leaving her father emotionally unscathed. The Church's morality was, in practice, a morality enforced only on women. 'Because the guilt it created was not distributed equally', the PMM agent reflected, 'Cida's father felt no guilt. Only the daughter, the girl, from whom chastity is expected – but why? And at what cost?'[19]

This type of searching question has arisen wherever liberationist-minded PMM agents come into sustained, intense, face-to-face contact with prostitutes. Because of such contacts, the PMM has come to articulate a critique of familial sexual politics, and to express solidarity with all women subjected to them. As a PMM militant explained:

> It was listening to so many Cidas that I learned that the most important thing is not returning to that lost ethic, but the creation of nests of solidarity where women who have lost their home (home?!), their house, their family (family?!), their job, their place in school, their respect, their reputation, their self-esteem, can rest from so many discriminations and can reeducate us. We must become their pupils, recognize our complicity, that we have accepted a double morality, that we maintain and reproduce patriarchy.[20]

The inverted commas around 'home' and 'family' betray a denaturalizing, even revolutionary, attitude toward these institutions starkly uncharacteristic of any other niche within the Church. As another PMM activist declared, listening to the prostitutes' stories 'demands reflection and radical change. Solidarity requires courage! Courage to accept that, to the extent that we have contributed to the production of the feeling of guilt in women, we are agents of gender discrimination.'[21] Clearly, once the issue had been framed this way, it could no longer be limited to understanding prostitution. The Church had broached the issue of domestic sexual violence in general. 'This was not supposed to happen in the family,' said a PMM activist. 'This is not what we had been taught. So I was very upset, very angry to learn about this happening.'

By the early 1990s the PMM's publications and study-guides directly addressed the issue of sexual violence not just against women who ended up as prostitutes, but against women in general. In fact, the PMM was the first Catholic institution in Brazil to articulate the issue in a clear, sustained fashion. By the late 1990s it was only in the pages of *Mulher libertação* that one could find a clearly radical Catholic perspective on domestic violence. 'We know', stated one such article, 'that most cases of violence against women and girls take place within the home, between the four walls, invisible, silenced by the victim, by the family, and by society ... . Long before it becomes a police case, we know that women's fear silences them. Their self-confidence, their self-respect are sick and they hardly have the strength to ask for help.'[22] In contrast to the euphemistic language of the CNBB, the PMM has been explicit in its treatment of the topic. A typical PMM article states:

> It is a crime to oblige a person (either male or female) to have anal or oral sex, to place any kind of object into an intimate part against her will. This crime is very common inside the family, against children and adolescents. Pretending to be offering affection, many fathers, stepfathers, brothers, uncles, or friends of the family, seek sexual pleasure this way, without the other adults in the family suspecting anything about the depraved intent.[23]

Inspired by what they have learned, many pastoral agents have organized under the PMM banner to fight gender violence in a variety of ways, including proposing curricular changes at elementary schools to alter sexist language, marching to protest the legal defence of 'crimes of passion' for which men still receive desultory sentences, and working in coalition with other women's organizations to challenge the national penal code's discriminatory treatment of women. Declares a PMM activist:

> The code contains antiquated expressions that complicate the conception of women as a human being and citizen. There is the expression 'honest woman', for example, although there is no corresponding expression 'honest man', which already suggests civil discrimination. 'Honest woman', in any event, is an undefined term, used to characterize the personal, intimate life of women, but not of men.[24]

PMM agents continue to be prominent in lobbying efforts to see included in the revised national penal code the crime of family sexual violence; the same agents have been involved in joining other women's groups to call for changing rape from a crime against custom to one against the person.[25]

As an organ of the Church, it is not surprising that the PMM has encountered strong resistance. The PMM's language and agenda have met with resistance from the clergy, including the progressive clergy, worried about fomenting 'anti-male' sentiment. As one progressive priest explained:

> Of course we must fight against domestic violence, which is an offence against God. But we must be careful not to conclude from this that the family itself is bankrupt ... . And this is a danger some people see we run if we go too far. So yes, there is some concern there.

It is precisely because of this concern that one can detect limits on how far the PMM has been able to push its issues within the Church. In 1997 the PMM was able to articulate the need for the Church to develop a national campaign against domestic violence. As a PMM leader told me, 'we lobbied hard for this, arguing that the Church, as long as it stands for peace, and against violence, must also stand for peace in the family. And so if there is violence there, it must stand up against that.' The CNBB finally signed on to the idea, but insisted it was doing so as part of its mainstream commitment to fight 'violence in society', and, in its documents, it proclaimed that the campaign was in 'the name of the family'. A leading Church moderate in the Rio de Janeiro region explained that 'we are clearly supportive of any measures that can help bring greater peace and tranquillity to families, and so reduce separation, divorce, and the breakdown of the family'. As part and parcel of this position, the CNBB studiously refrained from framing the campaign as a defence of women's rights.

The family frame had consequences. When agents and prostitutes associated with the PMM urged the 1998 campaign to devote more discussions to the issues of rape and abuse within marriages, the CNBB baulked. Instead, the national campaign, as orchestrated by the CNBB, came to emphasize the abuse of children rather than violence against women. In some of the campaign literature, the issue of male violence against women faded almost entirely. 'Domestic violence', explained one pamphlet, 'is one of the main causes of the suffering of children.'[26] Progressive male clergy silently acquiesced in this framing of the campaign. When I interviewed progressive clergy in the North about the campaign, they spoke spontaneously about the defence of children, but only when I raised the issue of violence against women did they acknowledge that this, too, was a problem. Apparently the issue had not been troubling them enough for them to demand that more attention be paid to it in the campaign. One priest was candid about this. 'Look,' he said, 'we have had already many headaches with the CNBB, about our theology, about our radicalism, our support for the MST .... So, yes, we are a bit hesitant to take on another fight.' Overall, perhaps the best that can be said is that the PMM was instrumental in pushing the CNBB to endorse the national anti-domestic violence campaign, and having at least pushed some progressive clerics to realize that such violence includes violence against women. Prising open even this much space for the articulation of the issue is certainly no small accomplishment.

The difficulty faced by the PMM in moving progressive clergy to embrace explicitly the domestic abuse frame illustrates a core paradox in the liberationist Church: it is liberationist, but also Church. In other words, although it can inspire people to take up causes and proclaim them in radical ways, the liberationist Church itself cannot always fully accept these causes and proclamations. This paradox reared its head in the 1970s, we saw, when Catholic women sought to organize women-only groups to articulate gender issues, only to be scolded by progressive clergy for being divisive and self-indulgent. But it also reveals itself today in the limits placed on discourse within an institutional Catholic context. Thus, although PMM has gone further than any other official Catholic institution in articulating the issue of gender violence, being an organ of the Church makes it impossible for its members to examine closely a variety of related issues. Contraception and abortion, for instance, have yet to be confronted head-on by the PMM. The few articles in *Mulher libertação* that mention these topics touch on them obliquely and timidly. Further, the PMM has yet to promote thoughtful discussion of women's own sexuality or erotic desire; and nothing can be found in the work of PMM that deals with lesbianism and homosexuality.[27] Clearly, within the confines of an officially Church-linked organization, there are limits to how far the envelope can be pushed.

Once outside those confines, Catholic women are freer to pursue a broader range of gender-based agendas. Earlier I referred to the case of women in São Paulo who had sought to speak of gender issues within the Church. Excluded from using Church resources, these women founded the Associação de Mulheres da Zona Leste (AMZOL) in 1988. Though originating in the Catholic Church, once AMZOL established institutional autonomy, it could deal with any issue its members wanted. Because of this independence, AMZOL's members explored, in its early years, a variety of issues which the Church could not accommodate, including sexuality, erotic desire and contraception.[28]

And yet, structural independence from the Church does not imply immunity from its influence. Far from it. AMZOL remained strongly Catholic in style and membership: most of the women involved continued to be recruited from, and active in, their neighbourhoods' *comunidades*;[29] at organizational meetings, members routinely identified themselves by their *comunidade*,[30] and Catholic nuns and missionaries continued to work closely with the group, offering advice, designing workshops and seminars, and helping to represent the organization to outsiders. (Two such missionaries designed a course on women's spirituality in the early 1990s that continues to influence group members to this day.[31]) All told, AMZOL continued very much in a Catholic mould, its members steeped in the values of the Church.

It should therefore come as no surprise that AMZOL's experiments with talk about sexuality and pleasure did not last long. The influence of traditional Catholic norms and the progressives' insistence that exploring pleasure is self-indulgent as long as there is misery in the world, led members to abandon talk of physical pleasure for talk of physical brutality against women. In the 1990s AMZOL threw its energies into the struggle against sexual violence and founded, in 1996, the Maria Miguel Battered Women's Counselling Centre, to provide legal assistance to battered women.[32]

In general, it is difficult to understand either PMM and AMZOL without grasping that they are both legacies of the liberationist Church. It is not just that the language used by both is filled with a familiar vocabulary – 'liberation', 'Kingdom of God', '*caminhada*', '*estrada*', 'struggle', 'injustice', '*Povo*', 'brotherhood', 'leading out of slavery'. More important, for both of them, is that although their leaders ardently seek freedom and equality for women, in the end they imagine this liberation to be a means to the larger goal of gaining justice for all the oppressed.[33] AMZOL's founding statute identifies its goals as '1) to encourage the organization of women, and 2) to promote solidarity with social movements and support popular struggles'.[34] 'This is what we want,' proclaimed a leader of AMZOL. 'For women to have the freedom to enter the struggle for a better society for us and for all; in our demands for daycare, schools, housing and political parties, in our struggles for health and liberation and all popular movements.'[35] In one of its pamphlets, the organization declares:

We must be ready to transform the world. We say that we women must leave the private world and enter the public one, in order to bring about transformative actions; promote communal values; demonstrate an appreciation and reverence for the human body, for our planet and our universe .... What are our struggles today? We reply: health, daycare, education, asphalt, housing, health centers, hospitals. For this, we women must be prophets, we must denounce, announce, and celebrate, like Miriam, Deborah, and others![36]

Similarly, the publication *Mulher libertação*, of the PMM, is filled with articles on human rights, trade union and anti-globalization issues. As one of the magazine's contributors explained, 'We are for the liberation of women, of course, but this is not all. Because women are human beings too, they are and can be leaders of the human race. Our struggle for women is one part of our larger struggle: for the liberation of all the oppressed creatures of the earth.'

Abortion Rights

While the period since the 1980s has seen some advances in Brazil's legal treatment of abortion, women's access to the procedure remains severely limited. A 1940 law allowing abortions in cases of rape or threat to the life of the mother remained a dead letter for almost 50 years, until the Workers' Party won mayoral elections in São Paulo and Pôrto Alegre in 1988. In the following years, the municipal governments of these cities made legal abortion available in public hospitals, such that by 2000 there were over 20 hospitals providing the service.[37] Nevertheless, abortion rights in Brazil remain extremely limited in practice. Between 1989 and 2000, only 500 of the operations were performed legally in Brazil. All the hospitals providing the service are located in São Paulo and Pôrto Alegre, leaving women in the rest of the country without support. Bills seeking to further liberalize Brazil's regressive abortion law have languished in congress.

The main obstacles to making safe abortion more widely available are no doubt the widespread view that it is against the will of God, and the Catholic Church's deep-seated opposition to the practice. Faced with these powerful cultural constraints, various national feminist organizations, such as the Centro Feminista de Estudos a Assessoria (CFEMEA) – a major feminist NGO based in Brasilia – have teamed up with health-centred NGOs such as Rede Saude to dedicate themselves to educating the public about the issue, publicizing it in the mass media, and working to raise awareness in smaller meetings and seminars. A key player here has been Brazil's chapter of the international advocacy NGO, Catholics for a Free Choice (CFC). Because it has begun working directly with sympathetic priests and religious, CFC has a fighting chance to speak more directly to the bases on the matter. Who are these allies? How did they come to develop their pro-choice views, while still identifying themselves as servants of the vehemently anti-choice pope? The answer, we shall see, has everything to do with the perspective on social action and the world peculiar to the liberationist tendency of the Church. When it comes to the issue of abortion, the dominant position of the liberationist Church, in conformity with the Mother Church, is resolutely conservative.[38] The rejection of abortion by progressive Catholics, however, is due not only to Catholic absolutism about 'life', but also to the view that abortion reinforces social injustice. Some theologians of liberation have argued that abortion is an expression of the view that the powerful have an inherent right to dominate the weak.[39] 'The liberty of abortion', writes Himmelkraut, 'is nothing else than the liberty to treat unborn human life in the same way as the life of already born human beings is being treated ... [letting] the unborn die in the same way as it preaches the letting to die and killing of the poor.'[40] Others claim that abortion is complicit in the hegemonic system of capitalism that uses sex to distract the poor and oppressed from the struggle for social justice. 'As long as sex is one of the idols of the masses,' writes Antônio Moser, 'nothing very profound can succeed in terms of the re-structuring of society.'[41] Still others make the case that abortion is one more symptom of individualism run amok.[42] And in perhaps the most interesting argument, several liberationist Catholic writers say the pro-choice position provides aid and comfort to Northern propaganda that the 'demographic explosion', rather than exploitation, is the ultimate cause of poverty in the South.[43] According to this interpretation, Latin America faces a kind of 'contraceptive imperialism' in which abortion is a tool of imperial domination.[44]

While such arguments partly explain why progressive Catholics are opposed to abortion, much of that opposition must still be attributed to their more traditional Catholic reluctance even to broach the topics of sex or reproductive practices – let alone allow the opportunity, through discussion, to move beyond doctrinally rigid positions.[45] 'Certain themes,' observes Rosado Nunes, 'such as sexuality, the burden of unshared motherhood, the high rate of mortality due to clandestine abortion, among others, are not part of the "reality" to be "reflected on" in the communities.'[46] The progressive Church has not moved much beyond the view expressed by a liberationist priest in the early 1980s when a group of CEB women in Rio requested the use of a Church meeting space for a discussion about sexuality: 'That is not a proper topic of discussion for the Church,' he said, and simply refused to discuss it further.[47] In 1994 the Workers' Party, to accommodate the sensitivities of its many Catholic supporters, dropped abortion from its official platform.[48]

And yet, since the mid-1990s a small but growing handful of progressive Catholics has begun to talk about abortion in other than purely condemnatory terms. Progressive Catholic categories have provided them a way of thinking about abortion, not as a means to maximize women's freedom, but to defend the poor against institutionalized violence.

The development of this view has been a long time in gestation. As early as the 1970s some women in the CEBs began to seek venues for the articulation and discussion of reproductive issues. From the outset, they understood there would be a clear limit to what could be said within the confines of the Church. Throughout the 1980s, although even progressive clergy refused to allow discussion of reproductive issues within the space of the Church, some Catholic mothers' clubs began meeting in local schools and gyms to hear speakers and conduct seminars about these topics. Mariz and Machado found that in the neighbourhoods they studied, 'the women involved in the mothers' clubs decided to begin meeting independently in order to discuss sexuality and birth control – matters of particular interest to them but practically prohibited as topics for discussion within the church.'[49] While these rumblings continued, at the level of the progressive Catholic elite – clergy, nuns, and theologians – the issue remained stuck deeply in a conservative rut.

Until 1993, that is. It was in that year that a Catholic liberationist thinker publicly articulated a pro-choice position for the first time. Augustinian nun Ivone Gebara's views on abortion burst on to Brazil's national stage late in the year, when the news magazine *Veja* published an interview with her, in which she reflected on how her work among the poor had affected her. Witnessing poor women's lack of basic amenities, their fear of being unable to feed their children and their subjection to men who would not take 'no' for an answer, Gebara found herself feeling sympathy for those among them who had ended unwanted pregnancies. She was, at the same time, outraged that while wealthy women could, for a price, enjoy safe access to abortion, poor women died every day from the procedure. 'Catholic morality', she noted, 'does not reach rich women. They abort, having the economic resources to guarantee a surgical intervention under humane conditions.' Meanwhile, she reported, 'abortion is today the fifth cause of female mortality in Brazil. Those who die are the poorest women.'

This stark reality moved her, she announced, to reject the Church's official position on abortion. 'The law which the Church defends', she declared, 'is detrimental to poor women. Abortion must be decriminalized and legalized.'[50]

The ink was barely dry on these words when Recife's archbishop called upon Gebara to issue a retraction. She refused, and instead published a long article clarifying her views in the international eco-feminist journal *Conspirando*. This article became the first detailed statement linking abortion to liberation theology's reflection 'from the experience of the poor'. Gebara wrote:

> Living in a neighborhood on the periphery of the city and having contact with sufferings of hundreds of women, especially poor women living under tremendous stress, due to their personal problems as well as problems of survival, gives me the necessary backing for some of the affirmations that in

> conscience I must make. I treat the question more from the perspective of poor women because they are the greatest victims of this tragic situation.

These experiences had led her to the solemn conclusion that '[t]oday I am in favor of decriminalizing and legalizing abortion as one means of lessening the violence against life'.

Gebara then placed the issue into the framework of the liberationist dream of building a socially just society.

> Legalizing abortion is merely one of the important aspects of the broader process of struggle against a society that condones the social abortion of its sons and daughters. A society which does not provide the conditions of adequate employment, health, housing and schools is an abortive society. A society which obliges women to choose between keeping their jobs and terminating a pregnancy is an abortive society. A society which continues to permit pregnancy testing as a requirement for hiring women is abortive. A society which is silent about the responsibility of men and blames only women, disrespects their bodies and their history and is [a] exclusive, sexist, and abortive society.
>
> Decriminalizing abortion ... becomes a way of diminishing the violence against women and society in general.
>
> For me as a Christian, to defend decriminalizing and regulating abortion does not mean to negate the traditional teachings of the Gospel of Jesus and the Church, but rather to enter more deeply into these given the paradox of our human history, a way of actually diminishing the violence against life.[51]

Gebara suffered the consequences of speaking out. She was silenced by the Augustinian order in June 1994, and sent into exile in France for two years of 're-education'. Since her return to Brazil in 1996, she has avoided writing about abortion, turning her attention to developing eco-feminist Christian thought.[52]

But the words she had published in 1993 did not disappear into the ether. They provided a compelling justification for abortion for any Catholic liberationist who chose to take up the banner. And beginning in 1994, a small, growing number of progressive Catholic writers, inspired by Gebara, did just that. Among the first to broach the issue was Frei Betto, who brought to the task his prestige as a founder of Brazilian liberation theology. Seizing upon key liberationism-inspired features of Gebara's statement – the 'defense of life', the option for the poor, the struggle against institutionalized violence – Betto stated that:

> ... it is the defense of the sacred gift of life that raises the question of whether it is acceptable to keep abortion illegal, placing thereby at risk the lives of innumerable poor women who, lacking resources, try to provoke abortion by teas, poisons, needles, or the help of amateurs, under precarious hygienic and therapeutic conditions. It is possible that a law in favor of life will make this human problem emerge from the shadows, to be adequately treated in the light of law, morality, and the social responsibility of the public authority.[53]

Like Gebara, and true to the Catholic parameters of his thought, Betto made no connection between his acceptance of abortion under some circumstances and a woman's right to pursue a life not centred on motherhood and family, much less her right to make purely 'autonomous' decisions about her body. For him, the legalization of abortion was above all a way of ensuring that poor women would have the same right to survival as rich women already enjoyed. In a preface to a sociologist's publication about birth control practices in Christian base communities, Betto wrote approvingly that the women interviewed for the study

> ... are not moved by any banner of 'sexual revolution'. Rooted in a religious ethic, they wish to live out their sexual and reproductive lives inside the family, establish stable relations and follow the teachings of the Church. At the same time, they have their feet firmly planted on the ground, in contrast to certain pastoral agents – sisters and priests – who avoid touching on these subjects.'[54]

Statements such as Betto's helped to alter the climate in progressive Catholic circles around the abortion issue. It was this climate that allowed some Catholic-influenced grassroots women's groups to become more open to the issue. Consider the Movimento de Mulheres Trabalhadoras Rurais (MMTR – Movement of Women Rural Workers), founded in 1989 by the women's sector of the Catholic Church's Comissão da Pastoral da Terra (CPT). Given the official position of the CPT's women's sector against abortion and given that a large proportion of the women involved in MMTR were Catholics, the MMTR avoided broaching the topic of abortion for years after its founding. Yet the daily problems of survival and family size could not be swept under the carpet forever. At the start of the 1990s, the MMTR began tentatively to deal with reproductive issues under the guise of 'maternal health'.[55] Then, in 1994, the group began to refer openly to 'family planning' and, though still refraining from endorsing abortion, created opportunities for the frank discussion of the procedure. 'Our discussion', said a leader of the MMTR, 'is just that. It's not a question of the movement saying that we are in favor of abortion. In our understanding, abortion is a question that should be discussed today as a part of women's health. People should know the consequences and causes of abortion.'[56]

The turning point came in 1995, as the issue of women's reproductive rights and the Church's stance towards them made international headlines before and after the United Nations conference in Beijing. Some feminist liberation theologians, long hesitant to broach the topic, finally felt they could write – gingerly – about it. Theologian Tânia Mara V. Sampaio, for instance, who enjoyed national stature, came out for the legalization of abortion. Later that year, though not quite prepared to go as far as Gebara, Betto or Sampaio, other progressive Catholics began to entertain the possibility that under some circumstances certain 'medical interventions' might be acceptable.

The most influential of these was Cardinal Evaristo Arns, one of Brazil's leading progressive clerics. In late 1995 he became the highest-ranked Catholic to defend a rape victim's right to seek 'immediate medical intervention' to prevent a pregnancy. In a widely-cited newspaper interview, Arns tiptoed to the edge of heterodoxy by remarking that 'a woman who has suffered rape should at once go to a doctor, because she will thereby prevent internal suffering of her own and also for a child that could otherwise be born'.[57] Although criticized by the CNBB, Arns' statement had tangible political effects. Direct quotations from it were soon adopted into pro-choice pamphlets across Brazil and even found their way into the halls of Congress. José Genoino, the Workers' Party federal deputy for São Paulo, invoked the cardinal's words while arguing for a liberalized abortion law. 'Let me take note', he said, 'of the typically courageous recent statement by the Archbishop of São Paulo, Cardinal Arns, admitting the possibility of an abortion in a case of rape.'[58]

It is in this evolving ideological context that we may better appreciate the increasing importance in the late 1990s of the non-Church-based Católicas pelo Direito de Decidir (CDD) – 'Catholics for a Free Choice', which continued in a non-Church setting to refine a view of abortion shaped by liberationist thinking. Adopting classic liberationist 'see–judge–act' methodology, a pamphlet used to lead CDD discussion groups begins by calling on its readers simply to see the daily reality faced by poor women 'One finds Catholic women', the pamphlet begins, 'of all social classes, but mainly of the poorer layers of the population, confronting the reality of abortion on a daily basis.'[59] 'You see,' the pamphlet states, 'the reality of abortion is a daily reality, we live with it and with its consequences in the lives of women and families. In Brazil there are approximately one and a half million abortions every year! At a world level, nearly one hundred and fifty thousand women die each year because of clandestine abortions.'

Readers are then asked to 'judge' this harsh reality. For the poor, according to liberationist logic, are as entitled as the rich to a good life. 'The Bible does not speak of abortion, but rather of Life, of life in abundance …. What does it mean to "have life in abundance"? How many children come into the world only to suffer and to make others suffer! Can it be that God wishes this?'[60] The pamphlet goes on to answer its own question: 'The reasons why women decide to interrupt a pregnancy are not mere egotism or social convenience. Generally we are dealing with poor women, who objectively and subjectively do not have the ability to take on a child at that time.' In this context, is the decision to abort a sin? The answer comes in the form of taking action in support of women who seek abortions. 'It is true that life comes from God,' declares the pamphlet, 'but it is we who live and take care of it. And this life of ours does not occur in the clouds …. Sometimes, to defend life, it is necessary to decide.'[61]

While it might be assumed that the CEB rank and file would reject such views, opinion at the grassroots is in fact somewhat divided on the issue. In the *comunidades* studied by Ribeiro and Luçan, the rate of abortions among regularly practising Catholic women is comparable to the rate of abortions in the female Catholic population as a whole (about 20 per cent), and the rate of tolerance of abortions under the conditions of rape, risk to mother's health or economic necessity is comparable to the rate of such tolerance among Catholics more generally (40 per cent).[62] In fact, Ribeiro and Luçan found that women who were more active in their base community tended to be more open to justifications of abortion based on economic necessity. Another study found that female interviewees in a CEB tended to think of abortion not in purely moralistic terms, but rather in relation to constraints imposed by poverty. 'This is a very difficult question,' said one interviewee, 'and really it is only a question for the person who is going through it. And really, I think: one more person, with a husband who is unemployed, they live in the slum, five kids, and all of a sudden one more, I think that it is hard to recriminate with the woman if she decides to have an abortion.'[63] Another interviewee looked at the matter in terms that could only be qualified as 'structural'. 'It's a real snowball, isn't it?' she said.

> It's the financial question, it's the situation that we are living through as a country because of this misery, this lack of information, everything. It's machismo, the laying of all responsibility on the shoulders of the woman: 'it's your problem, you handle it', that kind of thing. So when the time comes, well, no one does that because they want to, no one does it with a tranquil heart.[64]

The pattern among the interviewees was typified by the following statement from a woman: 'The sin is not going to get that operation. I think the sin is filling up with kids and then letting them suffer in the street.'[65]

I discovered a similar pattern in my interviews with Catholic women in the *comunidades* in Rio de Janeiro and São Luis. Although most of the women I spoke with said that abortion was against the will of God, several questioned Church doctrine on grounds that could only be characterized as liberationist. Sonia, a long-time activist in the CEB, put the matter thus:

> I don't know, I have to say that all of these men in their robes telling women what to do makes me wonder [laughs]. No, I'm sorry, I think all of this has to be looked at closely. Because a poor woman with so many kids, of course she should be on the pill, or controlling things better. But her life is here and now. Are we going to sit by and let that be sacrificed?

That women in CEBs can hold such views has led some researchers to infer that the progressive Church has a greater capacity than the traditional Church to make women feel comfortable with moderate claims to reproductive rights. Ribeiro and Luçan infer that the values instilled by the CEB guide women's attitudes, encouraging them to think in social-contextual rather than moralizing terms, and stimulating them to have confidence in their own views rather than in official Church prohibitions.[66] When women in CEBs are compared with women in the Charismatic Renewal,[67] this inference gains credibility. Machado and Mariz found that Charismatic women tended to be more concerned than their counterparts in the CEB to follow to the letter Catholic doctrine on contraception.[68] Charismatic women tended to rely more on natural than artificial methods of birth control, while women in the CEB used artificial contraceptives without scruple. Charismatic women relied as often as CEB women on tubal ligation, but, in contrast to the women in the CEB, they sought out clerical guidance on this and reported feeling guilty about it. Overall, women in the CEB tended to be less concerned about the official doctrine of the Church on contraception and, by extension, less rigid in their denunciations of abortion.[69]

If this analysis is correct, CEB women may, when they think of abortion, have a greater tendency than do other Catholic women to bring to bear on their judgement two values that are central to the liberationist creed: first that all moral judgements must be made against the backdrop of the realities of poverty and inequality; and, second, that the authority to make such judgements lies primarily in the conscience of the believer, rather than in the priestly hierarchy. This hypothesis is strengthened when we consider that a few women within CEBs have worked out their views to what many might regard as a heterodox extreme, yet still insist on identifying themselves as faithful Catholics. Of the 265 women interviewed for Ribeiro's and Luçan's study (all of whom identified themselves as observant Catholics), 5 per cent said they regarded abortion as a 'right'. As Ribeiro and Luçan have concluded, such women

> ... do not feel they are 'unfaithful' in relation to the Church: the experience of the *comunidades* has made them become conscious of fundamental Christian values: justice, love, the dignity of the person, the value of life – that are concretized differently in the lives of each individual.[70]

Our conclusion that the liberationist Church has left as part of its legacy habits of mind that encourage receptivity to the message of Católicas pelo Direito de Decidir seems already to have been intuited by the movement. The organization has now announced its intention to enhance its 'links with some segments of the Catholic Church, in particular the sectors of the hierarchy that have a progressive outlook and are least dogmatic and most open to dialogue'. The organization maintains a strong relationship with Dominican clergy who belong to the Community for Solidarity and with the Dominican community in São Paulo. (In fact, one of the members of CDD's advisory council is a Dominican monk.) It further affirms that it 'maintains relationships with various pastorates, parishes and movements that turn to the group for advice, lectures and materials. These contacts with Catholic priests and communities are a part of the daily work of CDD.'[71] The long, hard process of building bridges to the women in the base communities, a key step in expanding Brazil's Catholic pro-choice movement, is already underway. And there is reason to believe that the process may bear the fruit the CDD hopes for.

Conclusion

I have, in this chapter and the last, sought to explore not only the intentional, direct impacts of the Catholic liberationist project on women's struggles for better treatment and equality, but also the subtler, indirect, and sometimes unintended outcomes of that project for these struggles. While I argued in Chapter 3 that the liberationist project stimulated women in the CEBs to seek more equal treatment in their homes and in the Church, in this chapter I argued that the liberationist Church nurtured the emergence of Church-linked (PMM) and non-Church-linked (AMZOL) organizations that articulated powerful challenges to gender violence. I also argued that the progressive Church unwittingly generated an ideological framework for the legalization of abortion that is so coherent that it has produced a small but growing Catholic pro-choice movement.

But taking now a more global view, we can ask: is it reasonable to expect liberationist Catholics to continue to play a role in the articulation of women's issues in Brazil? On the one hand, there is preliminary evidence that women may be distancing themselves from the liberationist Church at rates that are slightly higher than those of men.[72] The reasons for this trend are no doubt complex: some have to do with women's heavier work burden in the neo-liberal age;[73] and some probably have to do with women's continued frustration with the liberationist Church's reluctance to provide the kind of intense spiritual succour available from other churches in dealing with everyday struggles.[74]

However, I want to suggest that it would be premature to presume that the liberationist Church is on a path to exhausting its capacity to satisfy women who want assistance in dealing with the special, gender-based indignities they face every day on a daily basis. This chapter and the last have documented a variety of ways in which Catholics with a progressive outlook are currently responding to, and addressing, those indignities. While the overall numbers of women in Church-based political activism may be declining, most scholars agree that the women who have remained involved in such activism have become all the more committed and ideologically dynamic.[75] Indeed, the 'women's delegation' to the inter-ecclesial meetings of CEBs has only grown more articulate and robust in recent years.[76] But perhaps most intriguingly, it is important to point out that the last detailed, in-depth research on women's participation in CEBs followed a timeline only to 1993. Consequently, the current trend in women's participation in liberationist Catholicism is not fully known. Might it be possible that, as the liberationist Church increases its attention to issues of concern to women, as I suggest here it has begun to do in earnest, it will win back some of the women it has been losing?

Notes

1 To read the report, go to http://www.fpabramo.org.br/.
2 http://endabuse.org/programs/display.php3?DocID=96. For a review of the statistics on gender violence in Brazil and the women's movement's response, see Heleieth Saffioti, 'Contribuições feministas para o estudo da violência de gênero', *Cadernos pagu*, 16 (2001), 115–136.
3 See Miriam Grossi, 'Novas/velhas violências contra a mulher no Brasil', *Estudos feministas*, 2, 2 (1994), 473–483. For an excellent historical overview, see Maria Santos, 'The State, Feminism, and Gendered Citizenship: Constructing Rights in Women's Police Stations in São Paulo', PhD dissertation in political sociology (Berkeley: University of California, 1999).
4 Sonia Alvarez, *Engendering Democracy in Brazil: Women's Movements in Transition Politics* (Princeton: Princeton University Press, 1990), 66–67.
5 See http://www.oneworld.org/sejup/118.htm.
6 Faustino Luiz Couto Teixeira, *Os Encontros Intereclesiais de CEBs no Brazil* (São Paulo: Paulinas, 1996).
7 Clodovis Boff et al., *As Comunidades de base em questão* (São Paulo: Paulinas, 1997).
8 Lucia Ribeiro, 'Comunidades de Irmãs e Innãos: A questão do gênero nas CEBs' in Jose Oscar Beozzo et al. (cord.), *CEBs: Povo de Deus, 2000 Anos de Cominhada, texto-base* (Paulo Afonso: Fonte Viva, 2000), 152–173.
9 Carol Drogus, 'No Land of Milk and Honey: Women CEB Activists in Posttransition Brazil', *Journal of Interamerican Studies and World Affairs*, 41, 4 (Winter 1999), 43.
10 John Burdick, 'Gossip and Secrecy: The Articulation of Domestic Conflict in Three Religions of Urban Brazil', *Sociological Analysis*, 51, 2 (Summer 1990), 153–170; John Burdick, *Looking for God in Brazil* (Barkeley: University of California Press, 1993).
11 Margaret Eletta Guider, *Daughters of Rahab: Prostitution and the Church of Liberation in Brazil* (Minneapolis: Fortress Press, 1995); Teodoro Rohner, *Atendimento Pastoral as Prostitutas* (São Paulo: Edições Paulinas, 1987).
12 *Mulher libertação*, 54 (1999), 2.
13 Ibid.
14 Rohner, *Atendimento Pastoral as Prostitutas*, 8–10.
15 Guider, *Daughters of Rahab*, 82.
16 Ibid, 87, 175.
17 *Mulher libertação*, 53 (1998), 19.
18 *Serviço de Documentação*, 17 (1985), 783; Guider, *Daughters of Rahab*, 183.
19 *Mulher libertação*, 53 (1998), 21.
20 *Mulher libertação*, 54 (1999).
21 Ibid., 19–20.
22 Ibid., 24.
23 Ibid., 25.
24 Ibid., 5.
25 *Mulher libertação*, 55 (2000), 6.
26 CNBB, 1998, 11.
27 It is also striking that despite the PMM's examination of gender inequality and the commodification of women in Brazil's patriarchal culture, the organization never broached the question of the ordination of women.

28 Drogus, 'No Land of Milk and Honey', 43.
29 AMZOL, personal communication, October 2001.
30 AMZOL, 'Curso de Espiritualidade' (1991), 39.
31 AMZOL, personal communication, October 2001.
32 Carol Drogus and Hannah Stewart-Gambino, unpublished ms., November 2001.
33 Ibid.
34 AMZOL, 'Estatuto de Fundação', 1988, ms.
35 AMZOL, 'Curso de Espiritualidade', 1991, 65.
36 AMZOL pamphlet, 2000.
37 Wilza Willela, 'Making Legal Abortion Available in Brazil', *Reproductive Health Matters*, 8, 16 (2000), 77–82.
38 Elina Vuola, *Limits of Liberation: Praxis as Method in Latin American Theology and Feminist Theology* (Helsinki: Suomalainen, 1997), 182–197.
39 Ibid., 190; Pablo Richard, 'A Theology of Life: Rebuilding Hope from the Perspective of the South' in K. C. Abraham and Bernadette Mbuy-Beya (eds.), *Spirituality of the Third World: A Cry for Life* (Maryknoll: Orbis, 1994), 100.
40 Franz Himmelkraut, 'La teologia del imperio', *Pasos*, 15 (January/February 1988), 27.
41 Antonio Moser, 'Sexualidad' in Ignacio Ellacuria and Jon Sobrino (eds.), *Mysterium Liberationis*, II (San Salvador: UCA Editores, 1991), 122.
42 José Comblin, *Call for Freedom: The Changing Context of Liberation Theology* (Maryknoll: Orbis, 1998), 182; Enrique Dussel, *Filosofía Ética de la Liberacion*. Vol III (Buenos Aires: Ediciones La Aurora, 1988), 118.
43 Antonio Moser and Bernardino Leers, *Moral Theology: Dead Ends and Alternatives* (New York: Orbis 1990), 121; Vuola, *Limits of Liberation*, 184.
44 Pablo Richard, *Fuerza espiriual de la Iglesia de los pobres* (San José: Editorial DEI 1987), 16; Carol Ann Drogus, *Women, Religion, and Social Change in Brasil's Popular Church* (Notre Dame: University of Notre Dame Press, 1997), 156.
45 Ribeiro, 'Comunidades'.
46 Maria Jose Rosado Nunes, 'Autonomia das Mulheres vs. Contrôle da Igreja: Uma Questão Insolúvel?' (Trabalho apresentado na XXIII Conferencia da SISR, Quebec, 1994), 13.
47 This case comes from my own fieldnotes. But there are similar cases reported in the literature, such as Teresa Caldeira, 'Woman, Daily Life and Politics' in Elizabeth Jelin (ed.), *Women and Social Change in Latin America* (Atlantic Highlands: Zed, 1990); Alvarez, *Engendering Democrcay*.
48 Liesl Haas, 'Changing the System from Within: Feminist Participation in the Brazilian Workers' Party' in Victoria Gonzalez and Karen Kampwirth (eds.), *Radical Women in Latin America: Left and Right* (University Park, PA: Pennsylvania State University Press, 2001), 263. Since then, the PT has gone on record as supporting abortion in cases of rape and threat to the mother's life, and has supported the 1998 national regulation allowing abortion in such cases. Still, Lula has avoided politicizing the issue through national statements. Lula, 'A Nova Mulher brasileira', 10 March, 2002. (http://www.pt.org.br/). The party is aware that its base in the Catholic Church could weaken were they to heighten the visibility of their stand on abortion.
49 Maria das Dores Machado and Cecilia Mariz, 'Progressistas e Católicas Carismaticas: uma Analise de Discurso de Mulheres de Comunidade de Base na Atualidade Brasileira', *Estudos de Politica e Teoria Social*, 2, 3 (2000).
50 Jaije Nanne and Monica Bergamo, 'Entrevista a Ivone Gebara: "El aborto no es pecado"', *Revista Conspirando*, 6 (December 1993); Vuola, *Limits of Liberation*, 192–93.
51 Full text available at http://www.oneworld.org/sejup/104.htm.
52 Gebara, *Longing for Running Water: Ecofeminism and Liberation* (Minneapolis: Fortress Press, 1999).

53	Quoted in Maria Jose F. Rosado Nunes, 'The Treatment of Abortion by the Catholic Church', *Estudos Feministas*, 5, 2 (1997), 413–417.
54	Lucia Ribeiro and Solange Luçan, *Entre (In)certezas e Contradições: Práticas Reprodutivas entre Mulheres das Comunidades Eclesias de Base da Igreja Católica: O caso de Nova Iguaçu* (Rio de Janeiro: Editora Nau, 1997), 9; See also idem, 'Reprodução e Comunidades de Base: Dúvidas e Certezas' in R. S. Oliveira and F. Caneiro (eds.), *Corpo: Meu bem, meu mal* (Rio de Janeiro: ISER, 1995).
55	Lynn Stephen, *Women and Social Movements in Latin America* (Austin: University of Texas Press, 1997), 227.
56	Ibid., 228.
57	*Folha de S. Paulo* (22 December, 1995), section 1, p. 9.
58	*O Estado de S. Paulo* (13 January, 1996), p. A2.
59	Maria Jose F. Rosado Nunes and Myriam Aldana Santin, *Aborto: Conversando a gente se Entende* (São Paulo: CDD, 1997), 1–2.
60	Ibid., 8.
61	Ibid., 25.
62	Ribeiro and Luçan, *Entre (In)certezas*, 34.
63	Maria Jose F. Rosado Nunes, 'Autonomia das Mulheres e Controle da Igreja: Uma Questão Insoluvel?', presentation at 23rd Conference of SISR, 1995.
64	Ibid.
65	Ibid.
66	Ribeiro and Luçan, *Entre (In)certezas*, conclusion.
67	Charismatic Renewal is the devotionalist movement in the Church that calls for a return to basic orthodoxy.
68	Maria das Dores Machado and Cecilia Mariz, 'Mulheres e Prática Religiosa nas Classes Populares (The Body and Sexual Morality in Religious Groups)', *Estudos Feministas*, 7, special issue (1999), 38–54.
69	Maria das Dores Machado, 'Family, Sexuality, and Family Planning: A Comparative Study of Pentecostals and Charismatic Catholics in Rio de Janeiro' in André Droogers and Frans Kamsteeg (eds.) *More Than Opium: An Anthropological Approach to Latin American and Caribbean Praxis* (Lanham: Scarecrow Press, 1998), 190.
70	Ribeiro and Luçan, *Entre (In)Certezas*, 128.
71	http://www.cddbr.cjb.net/.
72	W. E. Hewitt, 'The Political Dimensions of Women's Participation in Brazil's Base Christian Communities (CEBs): A Longitudinal Case Study from São Paulo', *Women and Politics*, 2, 3 (2000), 1–25; Drogus, 'No Land of Milk and Honey'.
73	Drogus, 'No Land of Milk and Honey'.
74	Manuel Vasquez, *The Brazilian Popular Church and the Crisis of Modernity* (Cambridge: Cambridge University Press, 1998).
75	Drogus, 'No Land of Milk and Honey'.
76	Teixeira, *Os Encontros*; Ribeiro, 'Comunidade'.

Chapter 5

Searching for the Promised Land: Progressive Catholicism and the Shaping of MST Leadership

The blazing mid-morning sun had brought out a sheen of sweat on my face, as I trudged alongside Marcia over a path muddied from a night-time rain. The broad cheeks of this twentyish woman were dry, shaded under the brim of her fiery red baseball cap, and her step was brisk and cheerful. A medallion sporting a small portrait of Che dangled from her neck. 'These are our lettuces,' Marcia said, almost in a coo, as if introducing me to a child. 'See how cute they are? How green?' Yes, I said, the lettuces were cute. I wiped my brow and awkwardly grasped the lettuce tray. 'Careful,' she said. 'Those are the future of our community.'

Marcia was giving me the grand tour of Chaquara,[1] a collective farm of flat rice fields worked by 49 families on the great flat plains south of Pôrto Alegre in the southern state of Rio Grande do Sul. This farm happened to be one of the first settlements obtained through life-risking struggle by the Movimento dos Trabalhadores Sem Terra (MST), the Landless Workers' Movement, in the early 1980s.[2] Since its appearance on the national scene around that time, the MST has mobilized hundreds of thousands of landless workers in almost all the states of Brazil, to erect tarp-covered encampments (*acampamentos*), occupy the land, establish institutions of self-governance, endure threats from police and organize the production of food. A period of tense negotiation with the authorities usually ensues, sometimes leading nowhere other than to violent expulsion; sometimes talks end more felicitously, leading to the squatters gaining title to the land. In this event, the encampment officially becomes a settlement (*assentamento*) and the federal land authority (INCRA) issues title to the squatters, in many cases as private, individual holdings, but also in the form of collective tenure.[3]

This process has in general been resoundingly successful. Since its early stirrings in the late 1970s, and its official founding in 1984, the MST has secured a whopping 15 million acres of land for no fewer than a quarter of a million families. It has created hundreds of food cooperatives and small agricultural industries, a nationwide literacy programme, and a network of over 1000 primary schools serving over 50 000 children. No wonder that by the late 1990s, the MST could claim to be 'the largest social movement in

Latin America',[4] as well as, according to some observers, one of the most remarkable examples in the world of a concrete alternative to neo-liberalism.[5]

Chaquara is filled with 'collective spirit'. The resident families are allowed to enter the communal gardens at any time to pick what they need; neighbours join each other in preparing meals; plenary meetings of all member families occur regularly, at which matters of general concern are submitted to public discussion. At one of these, in Chaquara's whitewashed brick community centre, in the shadow of a huge mural depicting joyous work teams in the fields, I had earlier witnessed settlers participating in a boisterous debate about the consequences for Brazilian agriculture of the Free Trade Agreement of the Americas.

But right now there were only Marcia and me, chatting quietly amid the baby lettuces. Our conversation had turned to the reason for my visit.

'So you have come here to find out about our agricultural model?'

'Well,' I replied, 'not really. Actually, no.'

'You want to talk about MST's relation to the Workers' Party?'

'No, not really either.'

Marcia shot me a puzzled look. These were the topics researchers usually wanted to talk about. 'Well what do you want to talk about, then?'

'Religion.'

Marcia paused.

'Religion?'

'Yes.'

A smile slowly spread across her face. 'No one comes here to talk about religion.'

I began to feel disappointed. Then she added, 'This is important. There is much to say.'

Marcia was right. Religion – that is, the Catholic Church – continues today to play a key role in the MST's ongoing dynamism and survival. Yet Marcia is also right in her feeling that there has been a certain inattention to the current MST–Church relationship. Surprisingly, few scholarly researchers or MST leaders have had much to say about how the relationship between the Church and the movement has evolved in the years since the mid-1980s. Amid an outpouring of scholarship on the MST, one can count on one hand the writings that address the role of Catholicism in the movement for the period since 1985.[6] Ask an analyst of the MST about the movement's relations with the Church, and he will usually gravitate back to the halcyon years, to the time capsule of 1979–85.[7]

At first I assumed that the scarcity of commentary on post-1985 Catholic–MST relations was simply an indicator of the decline in Catholic influence over the MST. Yet as I interviewed activists and the rank and file, I was gradually disabused of this assumption. Through interviewing it became clear to me that, although the first half of the 1980s saw the most direct support by the Church to the MST, the influences of progressive Catholicism on the MST continued long afterwards, and that today they are pervasive, subtle and profound. The fact that most researchers have not concentrated on these influences is due in part to the widespread notion that the heyday of Catholic influence on the MST is pretty much over and done with.[8] This notion is widespread precisely because it encases a kernel of truth. It is quite true that, throughout most states in Brazil, the institutional influence of the CPT over the MST declined considerably after the early 1980s: the number of CPT activists directly involved in the MST shrank, the CPT ceased to initiate, organize or coordinate MST meetings, it gave up trying to offer the MST advice on land occupation strategy, and it no longer participated directly in the movement's national decision-making bodies. Thus, quite understandably, researchers with a nose for the 'big story' have seen little that would inspire them to focus on the relation between the MST and the Church. Most recent research on the MST has been conducted by sociologists and political scientists interested more in the highly visible political and economic aspects of the movement, not in its more submerged, less visible religious aspects.[9]

Whatever the causes of this scholarly neglect, making up for it is long overdue. This chapter and the next seek to take a preliminary step in this direction. I will argue in these two chapters that the Catholic dimension of the MST is in fact quite central to an understanding of the movement, not only as it unfolded in the past, but as it unfolds today. In particular I will argue that liberationist Catholic ideas continue to shape the thinking of key leadership and rank-and-file groups involved with the movement.

After describing the early phase of the MST and analysing the causes for the growing distance between the MST and CPT after the mid-1980s, I turn to the contemporary period and analyse the processes through which MST leaders continue to be formed inside the progressive Church. In the following chapter I turn to an analysis of the interactions between the leaders and the rank and file. That chapter examines, first, the nature of the work that CPT activists currently undertake with the MST leaders and the rank and file (in two states), and, second, analyses the world-views of the MST rank and file. Throughout, I document the pervasive influence of liberationist perspectives at both the leadership and rank-and-file levels.

The Early CPT–MST Relationship: From Dependence to Distance

In a major break from its long history of alignment with the country's landed elites, Brazil's Catholic Church began, in the 1950s, to support improved living conditions for the rural poor, adult education in the countryside and the organization of rural workers into labour unions.[10] Although such activities may have been novel for the Church, the motives for them were quite traditional: to ward off godless communism, to preserve the purity of a virtuous peasantry and to stave off the social degeneration caused by the exodus of peasants to the cities.[11]

In the 1960s, however, the Church underwent a further sea-change, and the motives behind its actions to support the rural poor became rather less traditional. Inspired by the winds of Vatican II and Medellin, young clergy flocked to rural parishes, no longer to keep them safe from communism, but to be on the side of the poor as they engaged in a historic struggle for justice.[12] It was this generation that laid the foundation for the Comissão da Pastoral da Terra (CPT) leading to its establishment in 1975.[13] The Comissão quickly became the moral centre of the People's Church, the home of its best-known prophets and martyrs.[14] Throughout the following decade, the CPT leapt to the forefront of struggles to organize rural workers in the Brazilian countryside, to defend the rights of smallholders, push for land reform and socialize a generation of rural grassroots leaders.[15] A typical roster of CPT activities in the 1970s included marching to raise public consciousness about land issues, stationing pastoral agents in areas of land conflict, building legal cases for the regularizing of land titles, conducting literacy campaigns and, somewhat later, leading health workshops and teaching agricultural extension courses. Through it all, the core of the CPT's message was that the rural poor were a latter-day Chosen People whose struggle was favoured by God; that it was the will of God that the rural poor should live and work collectively, in love, equality and harmony; and that, because of the greed of social and political elites, the only way to realize God's will for humanity's relationship to land was through struggle, sacrifice and martyrdom.[16]

Given its history and ideology, it is not surprising that at the end of the 1970s, the CPT became a major player in the early history of the Landless Workers' Movement. By providing strategic information, material infrastructure, access to power-holders, an extensive communication network and a compelling biblical interpretation of land struggle, the CPT helped to ensure that what started out as a set of local initiatives would, by the mid-1980s, be woven into a major national social movement.[17]

The story of the MST has been told often and in many different ways, but we may start it in 1966, when Brazil's military regime allowed several hundred non-Indian families to settle on the Kaingang Indian reservation in the state of Rio Grande do Sul. In the late 1970s, in the context of growing Indian demands for land, the Kaingang expelled non-Indian families from their reserve. In 1978, quite suddenly, the several hundred non-Indian families found themselves with nowhere to go. Desperate, they erected a temporary camp on a stretch of public land, located within sight of a large unused estate. Some of the families spoke of invading the estate, but the fear of reprisals stayed their hands.

Then, in a turn of events that has become legendary, João Pedro Stédile, at the time a mid-level bureaucrat in Rio Grande do Sul's ministry of agriculture, joined Father Arnildo Frietzen and several others in informing the squatters that they had discovered something significant in the land records: the title to this unused estate belonged to the federal government. With lightning speed, over 200 families gathered up their belongings and occupied the estate.[18] The military police arrived within hours in a show of force, but this only inflamed the squatters. Joined by a rapidly growing number of arrivals from elsewhere in the country, the occupiers fended off efforts to destroy their encampment. In the Encruzilhada Natalino camp, between 1979 and 1981, hundreds of occupiers learned lessons in organization and solidarity, and became a model for other squatters to emulate. The Landless Workers' Movement had been born.

The survival of Encruzilhada Natalino, its ability to move others to action by its example and its eventual success in regularizing land title for its occupants were a string of successes all deeply indebted to the CPT, both as an institution and as a carrier of liberationist theology. To begin with, the CPT had at its disposal a national network of well-informed people – pastoral agents, allies within the state, lawyers and researchers – connected by what in the early 1980s was the scarcest of resources: telephones. The CPT was able to offer land occupiers detailed information about what was happening elsewhere in the state and country. When, for example, the government offered land parcels in the Amazon to the occupiers, the CPT rapidly prepared a report, based on documentary materials requested over the phone, showing that, without credit or infrastructure, such parcels would be unsustainable. Armed with the report, the occupiers turned down the government's offer. The CPT's network of experts played a key role again in getting occupiers favourable land settlements, by coming up with a feasible plan in which the government purchased lands upon which to settle encamped families.[19] And the fact that the CPT was equipped not only with telephones, but also with meeting places and international funding for travel, lodging and meals, meant that it was able to call and host the basic organizing meetings of the fledging movement.[20]

In those early years the CPT was crucial in mobilizing the resources needed to keep land occupiers' bodies and souls together. At the most basic level, this meant involvement in negotiations to ensure their access to land – any land – to tide them over until they could secure a legal settlement. In 1982, for example, when the police increased pressure on encampments in Rio Grande do Sul, the CPT helped broker the agreement that transferred 150 landless families to Church-owned land,[21] and succeeded, with the support of regional politicians, in getting the national bishops' conference to buy land for encamped families.[22] In other contexts, especially later in the 1980s, the CPT provided more direct material support – for example in the form of a trucking network that made it possible for already established, productive MST settlements to donate a part of their harvests to more recent occupiers.[23]

At a more complex political level, the CPT often served as a legitimizing bridge between the fledgling movement and the state. While the movement received growing support from officials and candidates in opposition parties, especially after 1982, there were numerous occasions throughout the decade when the involvement of men of the cloth helped open the doors of governors and legislatures.[24] In 1980, when land occupiers in Rio Grande do Sul sought an audience with the governor, he refused, saying he would consider their grievances only through the offices of the Catholic Church. Several years later, when MST leaders sought an audience with José Sarney, then president of the Republic, he declared that he would only accept messages from them when delivered to him by a delegation of bishops.[25] Also in the mid-1980s, when land occupiers killed a gunman who had attacked their settlement, the MST turned for political cover from the only institution that they knew could soften the inevitable governmental blow – the CPT.[26]

If one major resource of the Church was its political legitimacy, another was its ability to tap into a network of clergy who could, at short notice, pack buses with peaceful, hymn-singing demonstrators. This ability, and its impact on the negotiating process, was suggested in June 1981, when no fewer than 6000 people from Christian base communities converged at Encruzilhada Natalino, media in tow, thrusting the landless movement into the national spotlight. It was also dramatized by the mobilization of tens of thousands of people in the famous *romarias da terra* ('pilgrimages for the land').[27] These mobilizations impressed not only the government, but also a growing contingent of politically moderate bishops. Because the *romarias* were religious gatherings, they were generally immune from repression, and so helped spread the message about land injustice and build a momentum of popular support.[28] The CNBB's willingness to purchase land for occupiers in 1981 cannot, in all likelihood, be separated from the fact that bishops had seen over 20 000 people peacefully marching in the *romaria da terra*, displaying the faithfulness and integrity of the landless workers for all the world to see.

In addition to such political and material resources, the CPT provided the land occupiers of the emerging landless movement with a powerful interpretation of their experience. The story of Moses had long been a favourite of the liberationist Church, embodying as it did the values of resistance, solidarity and liberation. It thus comes as no surprise that, in the late 1970s, Moses' march towards the Promised Land was increasingly referred to as holding the spiritual key to the land occupations.[29] We can see the key turning in the lock during the very first land occupation. Families afraid to join an early encampment at Macali in Rio Grande do Sul had, so the story goes, showed up at the door of Father Arnildo Frietzen, a pastoral agent of the CPT. As the families crowded into his living room, Father Arnildo read aloud from Exodus. Later, the same families called on the Father again to discuss the story of Exodus; and soon thereafter joined the encampment.[30] The families involved described the march towards the land they were now occupying as a 'wandering in the desert'. Verses from the book of Exodus were read and glossed as an inspiration for the landless in search of land upon which to live in peace. Comparable scenes were played out in other states across the country in the early 1980s.[31]

While this early period is regarded by many as the Golden Age of CPT–MST collaboration, in the mid-1980s a number of forces began to generate tensions between the two organizations. Despite many regional variants, throughout Brazil the MST was concerned, soon after establishing itself officially in 1984, to affirm its political autonomy both from secular parties and from the Church. As early as a 1982 regional meeting of the MST in Goiânia, a declaration of intent was passed stating the importance of creating a directorate independent of the CPT.[32] 'The Church is accustomed to being the mother of the popular movement,' observed one landless activist in the mid-1980s. 'A mother who doesn't accept it when her child grows up and wants to leave home.'[33] Throughout the late 1980s and into the early 1990s, MST activists made a point of insisting upon their gratitude for all the CPT had done for them, but also upon the fact that they were no longer dependent on the CPT and could get along quite well without it.[34] This attitude is still occasionally in evidence today. I was told by leaders of the CPT in Maranhão that an MST leader had recently interrupted the singing of a CPT-inspired hymn at an MST-led meeting because it was 'too much from the Church'. An MST leader in the region confirmed that this had probably occurred, and added his own insistence that 'we are after all, different entities. It is important to keep ourselves distinct.' Although today the general attitude that characterizes MST–CPT relations is one of cordiality and mutual respect, such comments reveal an enduring emphasis on the part of the MST on avoiding any hint of institutional conflation.

Once MST leaders were no longer under the direct control of the Church, many of them came increasingly to embrace a discourse more radical and less spiritual than liberation theology. By the end of the 1980s many top MST leaders identified themselves as Marxist–Leninist. This identification had two main effects. First, the MST grew impatient with the progressive Church's criticisms of what the latter regarded as risky and confrontational tactics. CPT activists always viewed the occupations as a necessary condition for the longer process of petitioning for title through the courts;[35] yet while supporting land occupations, progressive Catholic clergy were known to criticize the MST for its insensitivity to the risk they were asking the poor to run by making land occupation a priority.[36]

Stung by such criticism, the MST's leadership began in some places to plan occupations without heeding the views of the CPT.[37] For example, when in 1988 the MST initiated an occupation in Paraiba, the CPT warned against it, but the MST went ahead anyway. CPT leaders fulminated that the MST did not understand the risks they were calling on this vulnerable Northeastern population to assume; the MST counter-charged that the Church feared a loss of influence, and that it was the MST, not the Church, that had the rural poor's interests really at heart. Such tensions multiplied in the late 1980s, as the MST, to the CPT's chagrin, increasingly acted without consulting it.[38] Indeed, throughout the following decade, such 'authoritarianism' estranged many pastoral agents.[39] By 2002 a CPT agent in Maranhão said that 'I think it is harder than ever these days really to work with the MST. They think they are the "owners of truth", so what are we supposed to do?'

Second, the institutional Church's reduction of support for progressive clergy since the mid-1980s has made the MST wary of becoming too cosy again with the Church. Several MST leaders said they could no longer rely on the CPT as an ally because of what they perceived as the vulnerability of progressive clergy. Usually such comments were prefaced by expressions of gratitude for the 'early period', followed by clear-eyed realism about the limits of the Church today. As Edilton, an activist in the MST in Maranhão, explained:

> You know, since that time in the 80s, the Church has changed. It is no longer as much in the struggle as it once was. Even the CPT itself. It is a shame that today the CPT is no longer like it was in the 1980s. In Tocantins, in the south of Maranhão, boy, what the CPT was like back then! Today, I don't see much of the leadership of the CPT connected to the issue of land as they used to be. They are still involved, but it's not like it was before! Like Padre Jósimo, he organized the people, he didn't wait for permission to organize the people. The CPT used to have a lot of that. But not today ... Historically in the 80s, the Church was different from what it is today. It was at the height of its involvement in social struggles. But then there was a backward movement in this question. Today you see very few pastorals that are really committed to the struggle.

Long-time analyst of the CPT, César Goes, explained that:

> The leadership of the MST does not believe that the CPT has an important future role to play. Inside the church, the CPT has lost strength throughout the 1990s. As with the other social pastorals, it has become surrounded on all sides, and so has tended toward reformism, leaving its radicalism behind.

By the 1990s, then, while institutional influence of the CPT on the MST had declined significantly, Catholic liberationist perspectives continued to exert a strong influence on the minds and motivations of both the leaders and rank and file of the MST. The numbers of CPT activists directly involved with the MST may be lower than they were in the glory days of the early 1980s, but the influence of the liberationist Church remains as central to the MST as ever. However, because it has become so deeply embedded in the movement, it requires a bit of cutting beneath the surface to see it clearly. Let us take one first cut by examining the stories of several MST leaders.

The Backgrounds of MST Leaders

It is widely acknowledged that the majority of the MST's *liderancas históricas* – the 'historic' leaders involved in the movement during the 1980s – began their activist lives in the bosom of the progressive Church. 'The majority of the best prepared militants,' João Pedro Stédile, the MST's national leader, has written, 'received their progressive training in the seminars of the Church.'[40] The list of national-level leaders who began their careers in Catholic youth pastorals, Christian base communities, and the CPT is a long one, and includes José Rainha and Stédile himself.[41] Regional leaders, too, emerged from the Church, migrating from Catholic youth groups and the CPT to the MST.[42] An MST leader in São Paulo compared this organizational migration to climbing a ladder: 'The Church is the first step, the MST is the last.'[43]

Whilst most observers recognize this pattern for the first generation of MST's leaders, they have generally left the matter there, neglecting to pose further questions about the phenomenon. They have assumed what the organization claims: that it is now a secular organization which produces its own leaders through its own system of internal training.[44] Yet important questions need to be posed about current MST leaders' Catholic backgrounds. To what extent does the Church still serve today as a reservoir and proving ground for the MST's leaders? In what specific ways does such a background affect the perspective and behaviour of an MST leader?

Let us begin with the first question. I had assumed that as the Church has grown more politically cautious, and as the MST has separated from the Church, the trend has been to replace the Church by other groups in civil society – including other social movements, universities and the MST itself – as sources of MST leadership. It is thus noteworthy that my informants, both in the MST and CPT, insisted that a significant cluster of the MST's leaders continues to emerge from the Catholic youth pastorals and the CPT and that, in some regions, whole cohorts of leaders continue to originate from these sources. Since 1997, for example, in the Santa Ana region northwest of São Luis, no fewer than 15 people in their twenties left the Catholic youth pastoral, took the requisite six-month MST leadership training and became full-time MST cadres.[45] A priest working with the CPT in São Luis believed that almost all new MST leaders in the region had come out of Catholic youth pastorals. 'I know lots of young people', noted Idiomar, a 21-year old CPT activist in São Luis, 'who are leaving the youth pastorals, and who are heading to the MST ... . They say, "Ah, I'm leaving the *pastoral da juventude*, and going to the MST." That is common.'

Meanwhile, in the southern state of Rio Grande do Sul, there is good evidence that there are still MST leaders flowing out of the Church. Frei Sergio Gorgen, one of the most respected observers of the MST in the region, wrote that base communities continue to serve as a 'genuine leadership school', and that 'the majority of the leaders and militants come from this group'.[46] The leader of a major MST settlement near Pôrto Alegre affirmed that 'most of the leaders in this state come out of the experience of the [Catholic] *comunidades*'. And according to a longstanding CPT leader with broad experience throughout the state of Rio Grande do Sul, over half the MST settlements are led by activists under the age of 35 who received their initial stimulus to activism in the youth pastorals and CPT.[47]

Thus it appears that the youth pastorals, CEBs and CPT can still generate considerable enthusiasm for activism around the issue of landlessness. Many activists who came of age in the 1990s credit the Church with having pushed them into intense everyday contact with the poor, with exposing them to misery, nurturing their thirst for social justice and awakening their sense of themselves as able to change the world 'from the bottom up and inside out', as one of them put it. Consider Edu, now in his early twenties, a CPT activist preparing to enter the MST, who became aware of the plight of rural workers in 'the pastoral of youth, when I was fifteen years old. That was the big impulse for engagement, and so I got involved in all the visits of the youth pastoral.' What moved him was the combination of suffering he saw, and 'the lessons I learned in the Church, that God does not want people to suffer; that suffering is the result of human sin and exploitation, not God's will'. He went on to become a coordinator of the youth pastoral at the diocesan level, an experience which gave him a sense of the potential of a wider movement. 'That experience was really important', he said. 'because it started at the base, feeling that *convivência* [intimacy through co-residence] with youth in the community. But then, all the [Catholic youth] assemblies at the level of Maranhão were very important. You realize that it is not just you who are in the struggle – at those meetings, you see all the others!'

Involvement in a Catholic youth organization was also crucial in the political education of Almyr, now in his twenties and a specialist in land economics with the MST in Maranhão. 'I was active in the *comunidades*,' he said, 'and a large part of my education was within the Church ... . The part of the Church that always attracted me was the side that was more about struggle, not so much about purely spiritual things.' Active in the youth pastoral, and coming from a rural family himself, in the 1990s Almyr found himself travelling to remote rural areas to lead reflection groups with local youths. That is when he witnessed for the first time the raw exploitation of landless rural workers. So moved was he that he considered making a lifetime commitment to the cloth because 'I thought that [being a priest] would be the only way I could be close to the workers, listening to their situation.'

A similar process took hold for Marcia, in her twenties now and a leader of a major *assentamento* outside Pôrto Alegre. She had grown up in a traditional third-generation Italian Catholic family, the daughter of a small landholder and had gone through the typical early experiences of Catholic youth groups, becoming the neighbourhood catechist. Then, in the early 1990s, she saw her family lose its land to a wealthy land-grabber, and she was exposed to the teaching that God was on the side of the poor. 'That was very important for me,' she explained, 'to learn that God was by my side, right here and now, not just waiting for me in the next life, that He was on the side of all of us who suffered and struggled.' Inspired, Marcia threw herself into raising the consciousness of rural youth, spending weekends in remote areas and, increasingly, on the settlements of the MST. But she had not yet decided on her ultimate vocation. Her mother, good Italian smallholder that she was, hoped that her daughter would become a nun; Marcia did, in fact, seriously consider the cloth for a time as a way of working more intensively among the poor.

But if progressive Catholic youth pastorals catalysed these people's activism, they could never fully contain it. For while the pastorals initiated them into the universe of social struggles, it did not satisfy their thirst for deeper immersion in them. As they strove to become more involved in the tense world of rural land conflict, their consciousness-raising activities in the youth pastoral began to pale by comparison. 'I started to think,' said Almyr, 'that what I was doing in the pastoral was too, you know, "light": it wasn't like actually struggling directly for the land. It was all preparation for others ... it was all mainly reflection and discussion, in meetings, assemblies, kids praying.'

At this point in their trajectories, young leaders often moved from the youth pastoral to the CPT. 'The CPT is stronger, this was a real entry into struggle,' explained Edu. 'In the reflection groups, it was more "see" than "act". In the CPT at least you get to start acting more.' Thus, too, Benedito, an MST leader in rural Rio de Janeiro, moved up the 'ladder' of activism in the mid-1990s. Already active as a youth leader at the CEB level, he was recruited by his parish priest to work for the CPT. 'I started in the pastoral of land ... . So, there were some land occupations, and we went to give our support ... . We slept there. Then there were some seminars of the CPT, in Rio, we were there two days. I just started getting interested in the land question.'[48]

But although the CPT offered greater opportunities for direct involvement in land struggle, this was not enough for these restless, idealistic youths. 'It's like, you begin to feel that the activism in the Church is good,' explained Edu, 'but it still stands on the outside looking in; and I wanted to be on the inside, to really participate directly in this, to help make decisions.' Almyr, meanwhile, found his growing commitment to activism hamstrung by the need to coexist with conservative laity and clergy. 'I saw that some people in Church still said, "God wants people to be poor!" And I felt it would be hard to be in an institution where people still hold those kinds of views.' He finally dropped out of seminary, left the CPT and entered the MST when he realized that if 'my mission in life is really to help liberate the workers, then I need to be free of the Church, which can slow or stop work by a change in bishops'.

Almyr's story suggests that, for some young people, moving from Church-based to MST-based activism was part of a process of deciding on a different kind of 'mission' through which they could realize the values they had learned in the progressive Church, devote their lives to the poor, yet avoid a life of the cloth. This was clear in Marcia's case, in which she faced not only her own, but her mother's hopes:

> I thought for a while that I would be a nun because I saw nuns working with the poor … . But I realized that I was being influenced by my mother. So I decided instead to enter the MST, that was my mission in life. I was very excited about this, and I told my mother, but she didn't understand, she said, 'Struggle for land? Why? You're a woman. The thing to do is either be a nun or get married. It's up to your husband to struggle for land!'

Marcia smiled ruefully as she recounted:

> But I saw what I had to say to her: I explained that really I was becoming a kind of missionary, that I was going on a mission to do what the Church taught, to help others, to help them live the life that really God wanted for them. And that made her happy … she didn't question my option again.

While most MST leaders have ceased to participate in the Church-based organizations that started them on their activist paths, still they carry into their MST activism modes of thought and action inherited from their involvement in the Church. For them, these have become second nature, their transmission to the MST more a matter of unconscious habit than a deliberate effort to spread the word of Catholic liberationism. And yet these modes have had far-reaching effects on the everyday practices of the MST.

First, MST leaders who cut their political eye teeth in the progressive Church tend, in general, to adopt a more 'culturally aware' approach towards the rank and file than do leaders with other, non-Church, backgrounds. To grasp what this means, recall that the model of activism used in the CEB, youth pastorals and CPT is predicated on immersion in the local community.[49] Church-originated leaders consequently tend to have a richer experience of *convivência* ('co-living', or long-term intimacy) with the poor before arriving at the MST than have leaders recruited from university or political parties. Cristiane, an MST leader with years of experience in the Catholic pastorals, explained:

> People who come to the movement from some other organization don't have the experience we do at the base, they just don't. Because the church gets us really to interact at the base with the poor … . To live with them, eat with them, celebrate with them, share everything with them. That makes a difference. Some of these other people, they come from the university, they simply don't have the

convivência we have. The ones who have not lived with the people, they have more difficulty really connecting.

Thus, too, Marlene, a 25-year old MST activist in Mato Grosso, testified that 'Before I even stepped into the MST I had years of participating in the Church to know the reality of our communities, which were very poor. That militancy was very good. It was a stage of great apprenticeship for us.'[50]

This 'apprenticeship' includes learning how to use music, symbols, theatre and ritual to connect emotionally with popular constituencies. Edu affirmed that:

> ... the ones from the church have a special feeling for the 'charisma' of the people. They feel these things more in their bones. The ones who come from the CEBs: that is *festa* and dance that animated people. They already have that habit with the people. And not always do those who come from the other side [the secular activist] have that talent [*jeito*].

This talent is the foundation of a set of practices often pointed to as a distinguishing feature of the MST's political culture: *mística*, the use of symbol-rich public performances to inspire and mobilize through touching people's 'spirits'.

During the 1980s progressive pastoral agents already used the term *mística* to refer to any faith-based stimulus to social action. In the CEBs I came to know during that period the symbolic use of locally meaningful objects – tools, garden implements, fruits of the earth, work uniforms – was routinely referred to as *mística*. In the pamphlets of the time, the term was common. '*Mística*', proclaims a rural youth pastoral pamphlet in 1985, 'is that interior force that impels and animates the *caminhada* of the person and groups; it is a mysterious force that shores up and solidifies deeper and more permanent commitments and helps in overcoming momentary setbacks.'[51] The later discussion of *mística* in liberation theology systematized what had already become everyday discourse of the CEBs.[52] More recently, the term has been used to refer to the training of 'animators' of CEBs,[53] and to the importance of nurturing 'the *mística* of Mother Earth'.[54]

It is therefore quite logical to infer that the MST's interest in *mística* was rooted in the Church. Father Flavio, leader of São Luis' CPT, had no doubt that the MST-style *mística* derived from the Church. 'Look,' he said, 'the Left does not have this tradition on its own. Where else did the MST get it? Only the MST has such a large number of leaders from the Church ... . If you go to a meeting of the CUT [the main organization of the labour movement] or even the PT [the Workers' Party], you will not see anything like the MST's *mística*. Because those groups don't have the roots in the Church that the MST does.' Frei Orestes was equally insistent. 'The whole notion of *mística*,' he said, 'that is very Catholic! Where does that come from? It only comes from these leaders' roots in the Church.'

It is not just the term that comes from the Church; it is its content as well. References to *mística* by MST leaders are filled with near-religious tone. 'Labor is an act of prayer,' said one MST leader in 1995, 'just as prayer is an act of labor. Both are interconnected [and] help develop our spirituality ... and strengthen militancy.'[55] It is no accident that the MST's *místicas* bear a close resemblance to the liturgies of the People's Church. In each *mística* (which precede and follow important meetings), while everyone sings the MST anthem, objects with strong local meanings – seeds, farm implements, farm clothing, jars of water, vegetables, grains – are paraded and displayed. Then, in the sombre style of biblical dramatizations, a mini-drama is performed, in which the players act out allegorical roles. In one *mística*, a group of ten children enacted, with sweeping arm gestures and slow, deliberate steps, the confrontation between Uncle Sam and the countries of Latin America. In another, a group of adults realized a scene in which landowners and police threatened resisting landless peasants. In still another, locals embodied the roles of martyrs, including Zumbi, Padre Jósimo, and the people felled at Eldorado de Carajás. At the end of such *místicas* the audience stands in a circle and, in a gesture drawn directly from the moment of fraternization made popular by the progressive Church, join hands above their heads.[56]

The leaders of the MST have created *místicas* which look and sound unmistakeably like the Eucharist. Towards the end of one *mística* popular in the north-east, a leader walks around the circle with a jug, pouring wine into small cups held reverentially by each participant, and declaring it to symbolize the blood spilt by landless workers in the struggle for justice. 'When the Church uses wine', explained an MST leader, 'it is the blood of Christ. For us, the wine symbolizes the blood of the workers who died in the struggle for the land.' It is an emotionally powerful moment in which participants are called upon to remember the violent deaths of their comrades, and to interpret those deaths as blood shed to ensure the welfare of the living. 'It is', said an MST leader, 'like we are taking on the power, the spirit, the courage of those who died.' Little wonder that some MST activists feel their *mística* is equally, if not more, compelling than the CPT's own texts and homilies.[57]

The MST has also instituted *místicas* which involve the breaking of bread. Usually this occurs at centrally located meetings, when people from different settlements are present. A loaf of bread is passed around, each person tearing off a small piece, as the leader declares, 'We share with you the fruits of our labour, the fruits of our struggle.' Alternatively, in some settlements, a dish made with collectively grown crops is passed, each person helping him- or herself. In still another *mística*, a young woman entered the room carrying a bowl weighted with the 'fruits of the land', fruit candy and homemade biscuits. In a gesture modelled directly on the Catholic afro liturgy's placement of food near the altar, she placed the bowl on a table in the centre of the room, covered with a white cloth, and surrounded by carefully arranged gourds, flowers and vegetables. Everyone approached and took a piece of the offering. The ritual's goal, I was told, was to celebrate the energy of the living in bringing forth the fruits of the earth, and to remind those present of the importance of community in creating the abundance necessary for all to live. In the classic meaning of communion, as one participant observed, 'by eating the sweet there, we were becoming even more a part of the community'.

The influence of liberationist thinking is also evident in MST leaders' talk about their mission in helping to bring about not only structural change but personal transformation too. As I spoke with MST leaders I could detect the tone and language of near-religious conversion. Edu spoke quite clearly in this spirit. 'To bring people around to a new vision is no easy task,' he explained. 'It is a journey [*caminhada*]. But at the end what do you have? Is it the old person? No, what we find is that someone who has travelled with us through this process, has become a new person altogether.' It is no wonder, given this commitment to creating 'new men' and 'new women', that the MST has dedicated many of its resources to pedagogy and education. The aim is not just to increase the skills and knowledge of the rank and file, but to realize the dream of Paulo Freire – to nurture and empower a new consciousness in which individualism has been replaced by the ethos of collectivism.[58]

Further evidence of the ideological influence of the liberationist Church may be found in the ways in which many MST leaders invest land itself with a special sacred quality. The Catholic liberationist version of the story of Exodus was central to the early development of the MST, and it is still important in mobilizing land occupations. In the minds of MST activists, this version lives two lives: the politico-instrumental and the personal. 'Whenever I can,' says Marcia, 'during moments of celebration, even in conversations with others in the settlement, I bring up Exodus. It's just part of the way I think now, about our mission – not just to conquer, but to build the Promised Land.' Edilton, the MST organizer in Maranhão, said that 'there is a moment when we use religious language more: working with the base, to conquer the land, we use a little bit of that: you know, the "Promised Land" ... They themselves already think in these terms, about the struggle being for the Promised Land, at the start when we first occupy the land.' Although one can often hear MST leaders justify occupation of land as a fundamental secular right,[59] in some contexts, especially with members of the CPT or MST rank and file present, they are capable of justifying occupation as a defence of a 'divine gift'. In such situations, a common refrain among MST leaders is that 'land is a gift from God to all people'.[60] 'The sacred significance of land as a condition of life for all', said an MST activist, 'placed a fundamental imprint of fraternity and solidarity in the search for its conquest.'[61]

In general, the story of Exodus possesses deep personal resonance for many MST leaders. In the early phase of their involvement in the movement, current leaders say they thought frequently about Exodus. As Marcia explained:

> When we were engaged in the occupation, Exodus came up for me all the time, that was certainly a big part of my *mística*. Very central, because you are living it. The priests would draw the connections, and that was very reassuring. Because you think: 'Well, God was on the side of the landless then, so he will be on our side now.'

Conclusion

In this chapter I have argued that, despite the institutional independence of the liberationist Church and the MST, the former continues to exert a deep, submerged, influence within the latter. I have illustrated this influence at the level of the MST leadership who were formed by, and emerged out of the matrices of the liberationist Church, especially the rural youth pastorals and the CPT. However, the focus on MST leaders leaves two important questions about liberationist influence on the movement unanswered. First, to what extent does the CPT continue today to exert *direct* influence within the MST settlements? And, second, to what extent is it possible to see traces of liberationist influence among the rank and file at the grassroots within the settlements? Only when we have answered these questions will we have a fuller picture of the nature and extent of liberationist Catholic influence on the MST. It is to these two questions that I now turn.

Notes

1. The names of settlements have been changed to protect the confidentiality of informants.
2. The most complete and up-to-date account of the MST is currently Bernardo Fernandes, *A Formação do MST no Brasil* (Petrópolis: Vozes, 2000). Recent sources in English on the history of the MST include Sue Branford and Jan Rocha, *Cutting the Wire: The Story of the Landless Movement in Brazil* (London: Latin American Bureau, 2002); Miguel Carter, 'Ideal Interest Mobilization: Explaining the Formation of Brazil's Landless Social Movement', PhD dissertation (Columbia University, 2002); Henry Veltmeyer and James Petras, 'The Social Dynamics of Brazil's Rural Landless Workers' Movement: Ten Hypotheses on Successful Leadership', *La Revue Canadienne de Sociologie et d'Anthropologie*, 39, 1 (February 2002), 79–96; Wilder Robles, 'The Landless Rural Workers' Movement (MST) in Brazil', *The Journal of Peasant Studies*, 28, 2 (January 2001), 146–161; John L. Hammond, 'Law and Disorder: The Brazilian Landless Farmworkers' Movement' *Bulletin of Latin American Research*, 18, 4 (October 1999), 469–489.
3. There is great regional variation with regard to how land is allocated between individual and collective tenure, and these allocations have altered significantly in settlements over time. Currently, Manuel Carter has suggested that most MST settlements are based on individual rather than collective holdings, and this is also suggested by the move in the

1990s toward the 'family farm' model for MST settlements. Miguel Carter, personal communication, May 2003.
4   Recent statistics on land occupations may be found at http://www.mst.org.br/. See also the recent analysis by Maurilio de Lima Galdino, 'The Return of Radicalism in the Brazilian Countryside', unpublished ms.
5   As argued by, among others, Lucio Flavio Almeida, *et al.*, 'The Landless Workers' Movement and Social Struggles against Neoliberalism', *Latin American Perspectives*, 27, 5(114) (September 2000), 11–32; James Petras and Henry Veltmeyer, 'Are Latin American Peasant Movements Still a Force for Change? Some New Paradigms Revisited', *The Journal of Peasant Studies*, 28, 2 (January 2001), 83–118.
6   The few analyses of current Church–MST relations include Leandro Sidinei Nuñes Hoffman, 'A Cruz e a bandeira: A construção do Imaginário dos sem Terra', master's thesis, Universidade Federal do Rio Grande do Sul, 1997 and John Cunha Comerford, *Fazendo a Luta: Sociabilidade, Falas e Rituais na Construção de Organizaçaões Camponesas* (Rio de Janeiro: Relumé Dumará, 1999). Others will be cited below.
7   This includes commentary from MST leaders such as João Pedro Stédile. See Maria Pinassi *et al.*, 'An Interview with João Pedro Stédile', *Latin American Perspectives*, 27, 5(114) (September 2000), 46–62. The early role of the Church is also avowed in the historical section of the movement's website, as well as in the many histories of the movement published by the MST, such as MST, *O Movimento dos Trabalhadores Rurais Sem Terra: Uma Introdução* (São Paulo: MST, 1995), and MST, *Breve Histórico da Luta Pela Terra no Brasil* (Pôrto Alegre: MST, 1996).
8   Virtually all historical accounts of the movement include a description of how in the early 1980s the CPT provided leadership, resources and political protection for the fledgling movement, but then leave the matter there, floating somewhere in the doldrums of the mid-1980s. A good review of this scholarship is provided by César Hamilton Brito Goes, 'A Comissão Pastoral da Terra: História e Ambivalência da Ação da Igreja no Rio Grande do Sul'; Masters thesis (Mestrado: UFRG, 1997). See also Elisete Schwade, 'A Luta Não Faz Parte da Vida: O Projeto Politico-Religioso de um Assentamento no Oeste Catarinense', Masters thesis (Mestrado, UFSC, 1993).
9   Zander Navarro, personal communication, June 2002. There has been a distinct lack of research on the MST by sociologists of religion, for example. Another reason for the lack of research into post-1985 Church–MST relations may have to do with the MST's political image. Since the mid-1980s an important part of that image has been of institutional autonomy, the ability to define by itself the movement's own goals, mission and strategy. Precisely because of its early dependence on the Church, it is now a point of honour for most MST leaders to emphasize their independence from it. This kind of public talk has very likely shaped the perceptions of researchers and their research agendas.
10 Vanilda Paiva, 'A Igreja Moderna no Brazil' in Vanilda Paiva *et al.* (eds.), *Igreja e a Questão Agraria* (São Paulo: Edições Loyola, 1985), 15.
11 Regina Novaes, *De Corpo e Alma* (Rio de Janeiro: Graphia, 1997); Abdias Vilar de Carvalho, 'A Igreja Católica e a questão agraria' in Paiva, *A Igreja e a Questão Agrária*, 68–75.
12 Ivo Poletto, 'A CPT, A Igreja e os camponeses', in Comissão Pastoral da Terra, *Conquistar a terra, Reconstruir a Vida* (Petrópolis: Vozes, 1985), 29-85; Claudio Perani, 'O Início da Comissão Pastoral da Terra' in Ivo Poletto and Antônio Canuto (eds.), *Nas Pegadas do Povo da Terra* (São Paulo: Loyola, 2002), 47–53.
13 Ivo Poletto, 'A Terra e a Vida em Tempos Neoliberais' in Secretariado Nacional da CPT, *A Luta pela Terra: A Comissão Pastoral da Terra 20 Anos Depois* (São Paulo: Paulus, 1996), 21–69; José de Souza Martins, 'O significado da criação da Comissão Pastoral da Terra na história social e contemporânea do Brasil', in ibid., 70–78.
14 Such as Ricardo Rezende, Dom Pedro Casaldáliga, and Padre Josimo. See the Secretariado Nacional da CPT, *A Luta pela Terra*.

15 Such as João Canuto, of the northern state of Pará, who, encouraged by the CPT, became a leader of the Union of Rural Workers, and was eventually murdered. See Ricardo Rezende, *Song of the Earth* (Maryknoll: Orbis, 1994), 4.
16 See the analyses in Poletto and Canuto, *Nas Pegadas do Povo da Terra*.
17 Fernandes, *A Formação do MST*, 10.
18 Ibid., 17–18.
19 Ibid., 60.
20 Christine de Alencar Chaves, *A Marcha Nacional dos Sem Terra* (Rio de Janeiro: Relumé Dumará, 2000), 160; Peter Houtzager, 'Social Movements amidst Democratic Transitions: Lessons from the Brazilian Countryside' *Journal of Development Studies*, 36, 5 (June 2000), 59.
21 Fernandes, *A formação do MST*, 22.
22 Ibid., 60. Miguel Carter's blow-by-blow analysis of this period is essential to grasping that each region of Brazil was very different with regard to the conduct of police, politicians, and the Church. See Carter, 'Ideal Interest Mobilization'. After 1982 the CPT tended to work alongside oppositional parties for landless workers' rights. In regions where opposition parties were winning local and federal office after 1982 (as in Rio Grande do Sul) more political space was open for the landless movement, which was seen as a potential political constituency. In contrast, where the party in power remained that of the military, as in Tocantins, the landless movement had fewer allies and political space remained highly restricted. There, the landless movement emerged separately from the CPT.
23 Ibid., 64.
24 See the analysis of this function of the Church by Houtzager in 'Social Movements', and in Peter Houtzager, 'Collective Action and Political Authority: Rural Workers, Church, and State in Brazil', *Theory and Society*, 30, 1 (February 2001), 1–45.
25 Fernandes, *A formação do MST*, 128.
26 Ibid., 124.
27 I will have a good deal more to say about these pilgrimages later.
28 Miguel Carter, personal communication, May 2003.
29 João Paulo Lajus Strapazzon, *E o verbo se fez terra* (Chapecó: Grifos, 1998), 45. 'The book of Exodus', writes João Pedro Stédile, 'was one of the references to help the workers better understand their own histories. In the communities, during the biblical studies, an analogy was made between the Hebrew exodus and the exodus experienced by the rural workers' (Fernandes, *A formação do MST*, 74).
30 Fernandes, *A formacao do MST*, 52.
31 In Bahia the landless 'studied the Book of Exodus and had as a reference the *caminhada* of the People of God in the direction of the promised land' (Fernandes, *A formação do MST*, 98). See also Sergio Gorgen, 'O MST e a religião' in João Pedro Stédile et al. (eds.), *A reforma agrária e a luta do MST* (Petrópolis: Vozes, 1997), 282. In 1982 occupations in Paraná were organized by agents who 'compared the locals' experience with that of the Hebrews' and distributed a pamphlet that announced: 'The People of God was weak, for many years lived oppressed and enslaved in Egypt. The lack of freedom was total and their oppression was so great that they were hardly able to pray to their God. But despite this situation, God placed Himself by the side of this enslaved people. God called and sent Moses to pull this people out of slavery and lead them to a land of milk and honey, that is, the land of liberty … . The Pharaoh was king of Egypt. God saw how much the people of Israel suffered at the hands of Pharaoh. God punished Egypt and its king with the plagues' (Strapanzon. *E o verbo*).
32 Fernandes, *A formação do MST*, 79–80.
33 Chaves, *A Marcha Nacional*, 125.
34 Strapazzon, *E o verbo, passim*.
35 Ibid., 63.

36 For example, in the north, the CPT had warned against an especially risky occupation in the forest and, when the MST refused to heed the warning, the clergy complained that '500 of the 900 peasants who were settling turned back. They are human beings, they are also afraid of entering the deep jungle and to live in the midst of nothing.' Quoted in Daniela Issa, 'What is the Role of the Catholic Church in the Mobilization of the Landless Rural Workers' Movement (MST) in Pará, Brazil in the 1990s?', MA thesis, (University of South Florida, 1999), 77.
37 Fernandes, *A formação do MST*, 120.
38 Ibid., 111, 133.
39 See the debate between Zander Navarro and Guimarães, in *Conjuntura Politica* (May–June 2000); and Strapazzon, *E o verbo*, 95.
40 João Pedro Stédile and Bernardo Fernades, *Brava Gente* (São Paulo: Perseu Abramo, 1999), 59.
41 Chaves, *A Marcha Nacional*, n. 158, 161; Houtzager, 'Social Movements, 59.
42 Issa, 'What is the role ... ?', 93–94.
43 Chaves, *A Marcha Nacional*, n. 30, 143.
44 Zander Navarro, personal communication, May 2002; Roseli Caldart, *Pedagogia do Movimento dos Sem Terra* (Petrópolis: Vozes, 2000).
45 Interview with CPT leaders in São Luis, June 2002.
46 Gorgen, 'O MST e a religião', 287.
47 Interview with Frei Orestes, CPT/MST activist, May 2002.
48 Andréa Paula dos Santos, Suzana Ribeiro, José Carlos Sebe Bom Meihy, *Vozes da Marcha pela Terra* (São Paulo: Loyola, 1998), 194.
49 This approach has been called *basista*. See David Lehmann, *Struggle for the Spirit* (London: Polity, 1996).
50 Santos et al., *Vozes da Marcha*.
51 Coordenação Estadual do Pastoral da Juventude Rural, *Pastoral da Juventude Rural* (Petrópolis: Vozes, 1985), 58–59.
52 Leonardo Boff, *Mística e espiritualidade* (2nd edn, Rio de Janeiro: Rocco, 1994). Important in this connection is Boff's fascination with Meister Eckhart, whose mystical works he helped to translate and edit in the early 1980s. See Leonardo Boff, *Mestre Eckhart: a mística de ser e de não ter* (Petrópolis, RJ, Brasil: Vozes, 1983).
53 Grupo Tao, *A mística do animador popular* (São Paulo: Editora Atica, 1996).
54 Pastoral da Juventude Rural do Brasil, *Crédito para a Juventude Rural* (PJRB, Pôrto Alegre, 2001), 3.
55 Antonia Chiareli, 'The Forging of "Political Resource Communities": The Landless Rural Workers' Movement and the Political Construction of Rural Cooperatives in Southern Brazil', PhD dissertation (Northwestern University 2000), 284.
56 The hand gesture is common, and was commented upon to me as a direct borrowing from the People's Church by CPT agents in São Luis.
57 As Flavio, a CPT agent in Sao Luis, said: 'in fact, when the MST comes to participate in our rites, of the CPT, they often complain that the mystical element is very weak, it doesn't have the power to mobilize or affect consciousness like their own rites do!' Radical priests in their masses may sometimes refer to the blood of the workers being 'mixed in' to the holy chalice in which wine is transformed into the blood of Christ; but such talk is rare.
58 First Congress of the CPT, *Terra, Agua, Direitos: Luzes e Perspectivas* (Pôrto Alegre: CPT, 2001), 9.
59 Chaves, *A Marcha Nacional*, 125.
60 Chiareli, 'The Forging of "Political Resource Communities"', 154.
61 Chaves, *A Marcha Nacional*, 123.

Chapter 6

Finding the Promised Land: Liberationism and MST Rank and File

In the last chapter I argued that at the level of the MST's leadership – both among the older, 'historic' leaders of the 1980s and among the newer generation from the 1990s – there exists a general sympathy for the ideas, goals, methods, and symbols of the liberationist Catholic Church. It remains to be seen just how this sympathy translates into more direct influence by the Church within the settlements, and the extent to which the MST's 'rank and file' – the non-leaders who till the soil every day and make up the demographic base of the movement – have made these ideas their own. In this chapter, then, I will begin by examining the work of CPT agents within the MST: the concrete contexts in which they enter the settlements and the religio-political messages they convey there. I will then describe and assess the ways in which liberationist Catholic ideas have, and have not, become part of the everyday commonsense of the MST rank and file.

The CPT Agents and MST Settlements

It is not surprising that MST leaders with liberationist Catholic roots keep the doors of the camps and settlements under their jurisdiction open to the pastoral agents of the CPT. More surprising – to me at least – is just how thick with CPT pastoral agents the settlements are. Despite the recent overall decline in the numbers of CPT agents in the countryside, they continue to be the strongest non-MST organizational presence in the MST camps and settlements. No rural union has as much access to MST camps and settlements as does the CPT.[1] Even the Workers' Party does not enjoy the preference shown the CPT. 'The PT would like to have a cell in each settlement,' a PT activist told me in Pôrto Alegre, 'but the MST is careful to keep us as outsiders, as visitors. I would say they welcome the CPT more than they do us.' In Rio Grande do Sul, about 30 religious agents regularly visit the 60 MST settlements in the state, for everything from liturgical preparation, to religious celebrations to house-to-house visits.[2] In some settlements the CPT has established permanent in-residence pastoral teams. In one of the MST's largest settlements in the south, a colony of Franciscans occupies a residence which they use as a base to disseminate CPT literature.[3]

The preferential welcome shown by MST leaders towards the CPT is quite logical. MST settlements are 90–95 per cent Catholic,[4] and many people among the rank and file regard the weekly Catholic *celebração* as essential to their religious lives. Indeed, from the earliest days of the settlements, there have usually been, in each one, a special committee, often made up of people with prior involvement in lay organizations, dedicated to organizing priests' visits, preparing the liturgy and seeing to the maintenance of the chapel (when the community has one). And while it is not surprising that members of such religion committees are eager to have the priest (or, where the priest is unavailable, a seminarian) come to their settlement to direct religious celebrations,[5] it is also important to appreciate the importance of such visits for MST leaders. Priests, they know, attract and inspire the rank and file. As an MST leader in São Luis, explained:

> We understand the need to work with the people's religiosity and we continue to say that the church is the only entity that has the power to really bring people together. We in the movement don't have that capacity, the church does, because the people are religious. The church can mobilize and really inspire.

Priests, in the MST leaders' view, provide the masses the right kind of inspiration. 'We see the visits of priests as essential', explained the leader, 'in helping the people to remember the great reasons they are in the struggle. That this is the will of God.' The Bible, then, becomes a way of overcoming the centrifugal tendencies within the settlements for many of these leaders. An MST leader in Pôrto Alegre, explained:

> You see, there are many tensions in the settlements between individualism and the values of communalism. So we encourage the visits of the priests, because they help people to think of each other as brothers. In a community where people come from all over, there is no local root – you need this! In communities where there is this spirituality, each one tries better to help their brother – in the others, you can see they try to cheat each other.

The Weekly Mass or Celebration

The first social context in which the CPT agents interact with MST rank and file is the Sunday celebration or, when a priest is present, mass. When neither an agent nor a priest can be present (which is much of the time), the celebrations are run by the lay religious leaders of the community.[6] But whenever and wherever they can, CPT agents, and sometimes priests, make their way to the MST settlements to participate in the Sunday ritual. And wherever possible, MST leaders encourage rank-and-file attendance at rituals presided over by the CPT. In the settlement studied by Chiareli in Rio Grande do Sul, for example, MST leadership treated these rituals as time for which workers were remunerated, or scheduled them to follow directly after the monthly general assembly meeting.[7] After the ceremony was over, many settlers would stay in order to receive blessings, converse, receive advice and invite the priest to their homes. CPT agents I interviewed in Rio Grande do Sul saw their task as helping locals plan the content of the celebrations. A priest affiliated with the CPT, explained:

> For all celebrations in the settlements we prepare so that these will be in light of the Kingdom, in this battle against the media and TV, which offer only consumerism and individualism. So our work in the *assentamentos* is crucial. There are conflicts in the *assentamentos*, but I am there once every two weeks, we all are, and we work hard in the *nucleos de familia*, the liturgy, to counteract these forces ... . Sometimes I arrive and people say to me, 'let's have a celebration', and I say 'no! We must first prepare it!' So much of my time, on the weekends I go, is spent in preparing the liturgy, reflecting with them about the symbols to use, and how to arrange things.

The celebrations are opportunities for consciousness-raising. In their sermons and homilies progressive clergy remind their listeners in the settlements that they, the poor, are the latter-day chosen of God. In this, the story of Exodus, according to one liberationist Catholic leader, is

> ... fundamental in our work. We work this very hard before, during, and after the encampments, so that when it comes time to be in the settlement, they can associate our work with that of the people of Israel, and so build a collective life within the *assentamento* ... . Whenever we do readings in the Bible, we always have as a backdrop this perspective of Exodus.[8]

A CPT agent in Rio Grande do Sul informed me of the content of his homily the week before at one of the settlements:

> My theme was the story of the Hebrews – which is a story we have the habit of telling over and over again in the encampments. So I said, 'Friends, you used to go to your fields every day, isn't that right? And you tilled the soil, and you scratched your livings out of the earth, just as the Hebrews did in days of old. That's because God had a plan for the Hebrews, just as He has a plan for you.'

The parallel to the Hebrews does not end there. In their sermons progressive Catholics visiting the settlements call upon the rank and file to recognize that land is a gift from God, not only to the Hebrews but to all men who seek to bring about the Kingdom of God. During a different homily, by a different priest in a different settlement, he preached that when the Bible says 'go forth and take possession of the earth, He did not intend people to think only about their own personal possession of it; He meant that all men should struggle together so that all men had land'.[9] In a pamphlet used widely to guide masses and celebrations in MST settlements, the authors announce that 'The followers of Jesus ... know that only collectively will they be able to live out God's plan for this world .... They continue to live communally and in equality, solidarity, and fraternity, joining their faith with their works.'[10]

Catechism

In contrast to religious services, which are directed to everyone in the settlement, catechism classes perform a more narrow educational function and are often directed mainly at youth. Since MST leaders see the formation of the next generation as central to their mission, any educational initiative not fully controlled by the MST is normally viewed as in competition with it. It is therefore not surprising that some MST leaders regard Catholic catechism classes with suspicion. 'We had difficulty introducing catechism courses in this region,' explained a CPT agent in Maranhão, 'because we sensed a certain resistance ... catechism is too close to education, which is the prerogative of the MST ... . It is not our role to missionize, and catechism is easily seen as mission.'

Yet in settlements in Rio Grande do Sul, catechism classes for youth have been warmly received by the MST leadership.[11] This reception has partly to do with the MST's longer and deeper history in the region, but it also results from leaders' worry that young people's commitment to the communal ideal is flagging. 'The MST and we agreed', explained an agent of the CPT, 'that the pressures on youth in the *assentamentos* is great. They are bombarded with consumerism, TV, all this pressure .... The leaders of the MST have been worried, and we too, that individualism is building in the *assentamentos*. The new catechism is our effort to counteract this.'

Accordingly, the CPT of Rio Grande do Sul recently developed an elaborate 37-session catechism course for youths in the MST settlements. Two agents worked full time writing and illustrating the course, with periodic consultations with leaders of the MST.[12] The agents began to teach the course in a half dozen settlements, in weekly hour-long sessions held in community centres.

This catechism is based upon telling the story of Exodus in precisely the same stages as the development of a typical MST settlement. As in the sermons, the suffering of the Hebrews is compared to the plight of the landless today. A text to be read during the first session of the 2002 CPT's catechism for rural youth, declares:

> The life of the Hebrew people of the Old Testament was full of suffering. They wandered from one place to the next like a dog without an owner. They worked for a master called Pharaoh, who owned all the land. The people paid high rents and taxes in order to plant on the land ... With the frequent droughts, they were

obliged to descend to the plains of Egypt looking for better conditions .... Our life today is very similar to that![13]

As Pharaoh demanded increased agricultural production, so too do landowners today; as the law of Egypt exploited the Hebrews, so too 'today the capitalist system exploits the poor, helped by law'.[14]

God, however, does not wish that such suffering last indefinitely, and so works through the rational minds of His chosen. As a growing number of Hebrews felt the injustice of their plight, so too 'people started to realize that it was unfair for some people to work to enrich others'.[15] The 'organization' of the Hebrews against Pharaoh foreshadows, in the catechism, the uprising of the MST, pictured as a man standing before a burning bush.[16]

The climax of the story, when God ensures the Hebrews' escape from Egypt, has remained a key to CPT preaching, catechism, and pilgrimage. A CPT leader explained his primary mission when working with squatters who were contemplating a possible land occupation:

> Naturally, when they are thinking of occupying the land, they are afraid, they are worried about the police, they are worried about whether this is wise, will it succeed? ... But that is when I work the point that in the Old Testament, God too organized his people to leave the enslavement of Egypt, that he stood by them, promised them land, that He never breaks His promises, and that these oppressed creatures took the land of the Canaanites, Pharisees! And that He is doing it again!

In its catechism for rural youth, the CPT affirms that just as God helped the Hebrews in their flight across the Red Sea, so too does He today help the landless flee the master's land into MST encampments.[17] A priest in a settlement in Rio Grande do Sul catechized:

> [J]ust as you lead Joshua, the successor of Moses, to conquer the Promised Land, no one will be able to stand up against you all the days of your life. As I was with Moses, so will I be with you; I will never leave you nor forsake you. Be strong and courageous, because I will lead these people to inherit the land ... Do not be terrified; do not be discouraged, for the Lord your God will be with you wherever you go.[18]

Yet for the catechism, as for the sermons, this is only the first phase of the story. For while they are eager to remind their students that God is on their side, that His loving hand will help them through the dangers of land occupation, CPT catechists' message is that God's favour hinges upon the fulfilment of the Covenant: that if the newly-landed wish to retain their rights in the Promised Land, they must live in fraternity, harmony and equality. To do this, they must remember that no one owns the land other than God, that it is a gift for which they must be forever grateful; and that they must live out the creed of Jesus, the quintessential landless man. Although the struggle is hard and strewn with temptations, the CPT insists that the poor can resist them. As the Hebrews were distracted by their idolatry of a god of gold, say the pastoral agents, so the landless today are distracted by money and television; as the Hebrews fell into the sin of individualism, so too the landless slip today. But just as the Hebrews learned through 40 years of wandering how to be an egalitarian community, so too, 'today in the encampment do we learn the values of community and equality'.[19] Just as the Hebrews found in the promise of the land of milk and honey the courage they needed to prevail, so too today must the vision of a Promised Land in which all shall live in equality and justice fill the landless 'with the same hope as at that time'.[20] And just as the ultimate remedy for the Hebrews' sins was Moses' proclamation of the ten commandments, so today 'we have the rules of the MST, cooperatives, associations, and other groups so that we can live and work in an orderly way'.[21]

Pilgrimages

Whilst sermons and catechism take place routinely in the settlements, pilgrimages are less common. Because they activate the whole person across time and space, and are able to create collective experiences of intense (if temporary) egalitarianism, pilgrimages are often more emotionally charged than catechism or even the mass.[22] Inspired by the tradition of pilgrimage to the shrines of saints and martyrs, the CPT initiated the practice of 'pilgrimages for land' (*romarias da terra*) in the late 1970s, and soon discovered they had found an enormously popular ritual practice. Christian pilgrimages evoke both the Exodus narrative of wandering and the procession of Jesus to Calvary.[23] In their structure they condense the key themes of the faith: identification with suffering, purification from sin through sacrifice, and the triumph through arrival in the Promised Land and the attainment of salvation.

No one, however, foresaw just how popular the land pilgrimages would become. In their first year, 1978, 400 faithful congregated for the march to São Gabriel, in Rio Grande do Sul, at a site sanctified by the massacre two centuries earlier of a large group of Indians who had dared defend their land.[24] Word spread rapidly, and by the early 1980s, an average of over 12000 people were appearing each year for the march. Soon the annual march to key sites of martyrdom became a permanent part of the CPT's identity. In the 20 years that followed, in almost every state of the nation, hundreds of thousands of pilgrims have made an annual gesture of penance and solidarity with the struggle for land.[25]

The MST rank and file, meanwhile, have marched in the *romarias* since the early 1980s.[26] From the point of view of both the CPT and MST leaders, the *romaria* offered an ideal opportunity to publicize the plight of the landless workers' struggle, and to counteract anti-MST propaganda. As an

MST leader explained, 'The *romarias da terra* have been very important ... by getting traditional churchgoers to think in a new way, more sympathetic toward the MST, toward the issue of land. So they won't believe as much the prejudice that the media makes against the MST ... . The *romaria* creates an atmosphere of acceptance of the MST.'[27]

CPT–MST cooperation eventually led the Landless Workers' Movement to adopt the pilgrimage ritual for its own purposes. By the mid- to late 1980s, the MST was organizing its own marches and *caminhadas*. The elements of the march – a long walk, followed by an assembly – were patterned after the CPT's *romarias*, and paralleled the steps from encampment to settlement.

Rarely was the modelling of the MST march after the CPT, or the CPT's continued presence among the MST, more visible than during the Landless Workers' Movement's national march to Brasilia in February to April 1997, to honour the memory of 19 landless workers massacred in 1996.

From the very start, the march was indebted to the forms and language established for nearly 20 years by the CPT in its *romarias*. Not only was the idea itself of a long march to commemorate martyrs an echo of the *romaria da terra*; throughout the march secular speeches were interspersed with spiritual ones and the event culminated in a great 'ecumenical' rite of communion and thanksgiving.

The narrative of Exodus, once again, is a motif of powerful oratory at both *romarias da terra* and at MST-sponsored marches. During the 1997 march to Brasilia, Bishop Dom Luiz of São Paulo proclaimed that the great flux of people toward Brasilia 'reminds us of the exit of the people of God from slavery in Egypt in search of the promised land', and CPT agent Nelson Ferreira announced that the landless were 'going to Brasilia to meet with Pharaoh and cry out for him to return the stolen lands'.[28] But again, too, just as in the sermons and catechism, the message during the pilgrimages is a visionary one in which God wishes land to be held collectively. A priest who spoke at the final celebration of the MST's 1997 march to Brasilia, declared before the throng that 'land belongs to God, and God has walked with us'.[29] Dom Bernardino, also speaking at the march, declared that 'the earth, with all its beauty, is a gift of God and the struggle for land to belong to all, the struggle of the MST, is marked by the presence of God'.[30] He went on:

> We understand that the land already belongs, by the loving will of God, to all those who need it, even if human laws do not yet give them access to it. We know that the land, that God has already given by rights of inheritance to all of his children, was robbed by the powerful and ill-distributed by those who can make the laws. That is why the poor and weak children of God must unite to reconquer the land.

But in this 'reconquest', the poor must not reproduce the sins of the powerful; they must instead be inspired by Jesus. And as Dom Pedro

Casaldáliga proclaimed to the MST marchers, 'You of the MST are a vein unobstructed by greed or egotism, who are bringing new blood to the heart of Brazil. And this blood must infect the whole social fabric of our country, bringing a revolution. You are a sign of hope, a sign of the Kingdom of God.'[31] Until the arrival of the Kingdom, however, the wretched of the earth would have to prepare themselves for struggle and martyrdom. For in the struggle to reach the Promised Land, there was no choice but the path of sacrifice. Thus, a priest at the final celebration of the 1997 march reminded his listeners that:

> ... with us today are present all the martyrs of the struggle for land. Present are the nineteen landless of Eldorado do Carajás, who one year ago today bathed the Brazilian land with their blood. Present are the martyrs of Corumbiara, present are the assassinated Indians, workers, youths, housewives, all the brothers and sisters, we are heirs of their blood. They are the companions who have been faithful to Jesus, companions of struggle for life and life in abundance. Our martyrs march taking with them a new history, with them we march, liberating the future.[32]

The Rank and File

I now have to describe how MST leaders assimilated liberationist practices and ideas into their everyday routines, and how CPT activists have striven to introduce a liberationist theology of land into MST routines through sermons, homilies, catechism and pilgrimages. The time has come for us to consider the impact of these routines on the rank and file of the Landless Workers' Movement. To what extent, and in what ways, have these routines connected experientially and intellectually with the landless workers at the base?

No single, simple pattern emerges – at least, not from my limited sample. The rank-and-file participants I got to know sometimes accepted, sometimes rejected and sometimes arranged in new syntheses the elements of liberationism purveyed by CPT and MST leaders. I will describe three religious fields in which the rank and file developed such syntheses: the story of Exodus, the meanings of the Cross and the meanings of saints.

The Rank and File's Response to the Exodus Story

I have already described the liberationist version of Exodus disseminated by pastoral agents and MST leaders. But have the settlers been listening? What is the evidence that the story of Exodus is for at least some of them an important part of the land struggle?

The short answer is that the evidence of this connection is substantial. I found numerous indications that invoking the story of Moses when landless workers are contemplating joining a land occupation provides sustenance to those willing to brave the attendant risks and sacrifices. Gearing up to join others in an illegal land occupation is obviously a frightening prospect, especially in a social environment in which police violence is an everyday reality. As Matilde, now an MST settler in Maranhão, told me:

> Before you go into the occupation, your heart is beating very fast. It is a scary thing. You can plan an occupation for months, but – will the police come in and wipe it out, maybe killing people? ... And you feel afraid, because according to the oppressors' laws, it is against the law. Is this the right thing to do? There are lots of fears and doubts before an occupation.

Enter the Moses story in its liberationist version. Margarida, a settler in Rio Grande do Sul, recalled that on the eve of a land occupation, she heard a priest tell the story of Exodus:

> Everyone was afraid, well, some said, 'I'm not afraid', but I was afraid. Frei Orestes arrived here and gave a word, to say that God was marching alongside us, just as He had marched alongside Moses ... And that just as Moses had found the Promised Land, we shouldn't doubt God would now lead us to the Promised Land ... . And when I heard that, I thought: 'Ah, God is good! God is good. If the people of Israel were not afraid, God opened up the Red Sea for them, should I be afraid?'

Once in camp, a new period of uncertainty begins. As Edson, an MST leader in Maranhão, explained:

> Life in an MST camp is a hardship, a learning experience. It is the most life-transforming experience a worker has had ... . Above all, it is a period that calls upon the worker to have faith, because there is always the chance that a land title will not come through, that police will invade and throw the landless out. This period can go on for years.

And, indeed, during this uncertain period the Moses story can be crucial to maintaining morale. Said one settler named Carmen, in Rio Grande do Sul, recalling her time in camp, 'in the desert, they wandered for forty years there, that was no overnight stay! ... But then God rewarded them for their perseverance, and He led them into the Promised Land.'

For several of my informants, the Moses story introduced elements of oppositional consciousness that helped reshape their very identity.[33] Until joining an MST encampment, landlessness had been a source of shame for these informants, but the act of land occupation transformed it into one of pride.[34] Although some of this pride no doubt derived from the experience of occupation itself – that is, of reclaiming basic dignity through an act of defiance and self-help, a part of the pride also came from the feeling that one's actions were identical in some way with those of the people of God, as described in the Bible.[35] A female settler from the south told me:

> In the camp, we studied the Bible ... . And this changes the way you think, makes you see the whole thing very differently. Before that, I thought of myself as someone without land ... But I realized that the Hebrews had no land either! ... So today I say 'We are the new people of God in search of a promised land.' I say, 'We are today the new wandering people!'

Once the land is regularized and the immediate risk subsides, telling the Moses story becomes less urgent. Still, the emotional intensity of occupation, encampment, negotiation and regularization of title, ensure that references to the Hebrews will remain an undercurrent of MST settlers' identity and discourse. When I asked settlers why they were on the *assentamento*, they usually replied in quite practical terms about wanting land and a better life for themselves and their children.[36] But when I asked why they thought they had succeeded in getting the land, their voices turned reverent and they alluded to the favour God had shown them. Listen to Augusto, a young *assentado* in Maranhão:

> I think it is just as God worked in the Old Testament. He did not say: I'm going to give you this tomorrow, no. They had to wander for forty years! So they had to struggle together, just as we have, we have worked hard for this, it was not just given to us ... I think that this is what God wants for us – to realize that we only achieve our goals through sacrifice, through staying together.

So resilient are such accounts of the process of occupation and settlement that those MST leaders who seek to stimulate a more secular understanding find themselves faced with tough passive resistance. Gilcemar, an MST leader, commented:

> At first, we usually accept, no, encourage, references to Exodus. But then, frankly, some of us feel that it is time, particularly when we go from occupation to settlement, to start another discussion, to say that the comrade [*companheiro*] must have more confidence in his ability, along with those of his companions, to do what needs to be done, that it is not just God. But this is not easy. You see, when you start a work of *conscientização* [consciousness-raising] what you always hear from the farmers, is talk about how they are in the Promised Land.

The liberationist version of the Moses story thus lives on, embedded in the hearts and minds of the *assentados*, through its experiential and spiritual resonances. Listen to Bene, an *assentada* whose legs took her all the way from São Paulo to Brasilia in the 1997 march. 'The most important things', she said, 'that have happened on earth, that I've heard of, was the exodus of Moses from Egypt with the Hebrews ... and this march, in which I could participate!'[37] Or to Ojefferson, a young *assentado* who walked all the way from Bahia to Brasilia, and who wrote the following song, which won first place in the national Congress of Landless Youth:

> Sometimes I stand looking
> And my heart breaks
> To see the massacred bodies
> Tossed upon the ground
> All the workers
> Descendants of Moses
> Who struggled for the land
> To give to his faithful
> The people were persecuted
> Devoured by the lion
> Just because they wanted land
> Just because they wanted a bit of ground
> Moses eno
> Moses eno
> Crossed the Red Sea
> And conquered his land[38]

Ojefferson's comment on his lyric provides a summary of the emotional resonances of the Moses story for all *assentados*:

> Whatever happens up in front, whatever conflict, we are in this together! And we are there too, leading the people too. Like Moses, like the music says ... Moses, searching for the promised land: the people really stuck with him! It's the same thing with the leader, raising consciousness, and the people following him and conquering the land.[39]

The Cross: Heart of the People

After following Marcia for an hour through the fields and gardens of the settlement of Chaquara, I asked if I could see the community centre, which was located at the geographic centre, or heart, of the settlement. In front of the low wood and brick structure, in a clearing about 200 feet across, stood a simple cross made of sun-bleached wood, about five feet high. At its base in a circle lay 19 stones the size of soccer balls, painted red, symbolizing, I learned, the 19 landless workers killed by the police in 1996. Hanging from the arms of the cross hung half a dozen ribbons, half white and half black. When I asked Marcia about the cross, she smiled and said, 'Ah, that is our cross. You'll find, you go into any settlement anywhere in this country, and at the center, there is the cross.'

'Who planted it?'

'That is something that the leaders don't do anything about – the people themselves plant these.'

Rather than insist that such ritual innovations always originate spontaneously at the grassroots, or derive from the reflections of an organic leadership, it is preferable to think of such moments as dialogical, in which rank-and-file creativity interacts with the initiatives of liberationist leaders. It would be unwise to imagine that rank and file are always, or usually, at the receiving end of such interactions. When I asked Flávio, a leader of the CPT, if his organization had anything to do with the crosses, his response was categorical. 'No,' he replied. 'These are really the work of the settlers themselves. We sometimes use the crosses, perform *místicas* there, but no one needs to guide the people on these. The very first thing they do when they get to a camp or settlement is to erect a cross.' This opinion was shared by Daniela, a young *assentada* who told me that '[n]o one can take away the cross; it is the heart of the settlement. It is the heart of the people.'

No doubt there is some measure of ideological special pleading at work here. Yet again it would be naive to view the rank and file as mainly passive recipients of leaders' ritual actions. Indeed, there is considerable evidence to warrant the view that they are active participants in the construction of crosses' meanings. In contrast to their understandings of Moses, which follow closely the official liberationist version, *assentados* display creativity in their uses of the cross. What do these crosses mean to them? What meanings have these symbols accreted through the collective experience of struggle? To what extent can one discern in them the residues of liberationist Catholic meanings?

The first thing to note is the urgency and dispatch with which families plant crosses at the centres of newly occupied lands. In 1979, when over 100 families arrived by moonlight at the Fazenda Macali, the first thing they did before setting up tents or lighting a stove was to plant a cross. 'That is the very first thing,' said Frei Orestes. 'No matter what else happens, as soon as they arrive, the people want to plant a cross.' The action stands out because the immediate planting of a cross is not typical of land settlement in Brazil. Usually settlements emerge slowly, as people move into adjoining plots and gradually come to think of themselves as a community. The emerging landed identity is marked through the building of a chapel. In contrast, with MST occupations, the occupiers need an instant way of signalling that a territorial conquest has been made. In Brazil's history, the planting of crosses was the way in which a conquering army symbolized its new stake. As every Brazilian schoolchild learns, the very first act of Bernardo Cabral, discoverer of Brazil, upon setting foot on the new territory, was to plant a cross. An *assentado* told me, 'Like Cabral planted a cross, so we say, "This is ours, this is our territory now."'

The symbolism of territorial conquest may be part of the reason for cross-planting but, as the camp settles in, other associations emerge and become dominant. Once in place, the cross defines the encampment's central space where settlers gather for assemblies and where visitors are welcomed. The cross soon takes on the identity of the settlement as a whole, a token of the place and everyone in it. When settlers decide where to build their community centre, it is always near the cross. When settlers participated in the 1997 national march bringing together people from around the country, they brought with them their cross, emblazoned with the name of their settlement.[40]

By symbolizing the place, the cross carries a heavier burden than simply serving as signifier of a specific geographic locale. First is the experience of intense sacrifice and suffering connected to encampment, and the longing for these to be recompensed through collective triumph. In Christian iconography, the cross refers to the core mystery of the faith, the paradox that through Christ's suffering and death were realized redemption and resurrection. The cross for Christians has come to embody the individual soul's struggle against death, its triumph through faith. By analogy, the cross in the settlements has come to signify the struggle for land itself, as each settler faces the struggle's sacrifices and the promise of eventual triumph. 'When I look at the cross in our settlement,' said an *assentada*, 'I remember that Christ is on the side of those who sacrifice, and those who have faith in him.'

For the settlers I interviewed, the cross refers to all those who have suffered and sacrificed for the struggle. Here the inner logic of the cross seemed spontaneously to connect in the minds of settlers to the liberationist discourse swirling about them. In an important bit of religio-political creativity, in the camp of Encruzilhada Natalino in 1981–82, whenever a child died from disease or malnutrition, campers hung white ribbons on the cross, each one symbolizing one child.[41] 'This was to show that we would not be deterred,' said a settler with memory of the period. 'We knew that there would be suffering before the struggle was over, that others would die … . But we would win in the end … because the cross is the proof that we will win in the end.' The idea spread quickly, and soon other settlements hung ribbons on their crosses too. Later, in an extension of the symbol, settlers also began to hang black ribbons, as a reference to the adults who had died from police or death-squad violence.[42]

It was almost natural that the crosses should become sites for ritual. 'We started performing our *misticas* right at the cross', explained a CPT leader, 'because this was the most sacred place in the settlement.' It was also logical that, soon after the massacre at Eldorado in 1996, when the MST and CPT needed to create a rite to commemorate the martyrs of that day, they gravitated to the crosses. Throughout the country, stones or other objects were placed at the foot of the crosses, to remember the dead and keep them close to these sanctuaries of redemption.

It is important to appreciate the collective nature of this redemption. Crosses that appear inside church walls usually refer to the salvation of the individual soul. The outdoor crosses of MST settlements are self-consciously associated not with the fate of the individual but of the group as a whole. In Encruzilhado Natalino, when a small cross bearing the inscription 'Save your soul' was planted in the central square, it did not last long and was soon replaced by a large rustic wooden cross. When the settlement received contributions from a number of farmers', workers' and student unions,[43] buttresses bearing the name of each entity that had shown support were nailed to the cross. Thereafter, whenever there was a demonstration, the cross was held aloft by settlers who grasped its numerous flying buttresses, thereby reminding anyone who cared to be reminded of these external solidarities. Many other settlements have created similar buttressed crosses. Clearly, in these cases the cross's traditional meaning had been supplemented at the grassroots by a more liberationist one, in which collective redemption through struggle received greater emphasis than individual salvation.[44]

But in the popular imagination the cross is more than just a meeting of individual salvation and collective liberation. Given its multiple emotionally intense associations – conquest, place, community, redemption, struggle – it follows that some settlers believe that the crosses protect their settlements from evil. 'I feel safer with the cross nearby,' explained one *assentada*. 'It's as if the cross were keeping the whole settlement safe, protecting it.' The tradition of seeing the cross in this way may have emerged early in the history of the MST, in the aftermath of Encruzilhada Natalino's refusal to be removed to a colonization project in winter of 1981. When the government burned down several houses, the settlers fought back. When soldiers forcibly kept a human rights' delegation from entering the camp, the campers took up their cross and brandished it against the military barrier. The event, captured on national television, generated an outpouring of support for the occupiers, placed the government on the moral defensive and forced the withdrawal of the military. The encampment had won a crucial battle in which the symbol of the cross had been the central weapon. Given stories such as this, it was inevitable that, in some settlements, *assentados* would receive blessings in the shadow of the cross before heading to demonstrations or joining in occupations as supporters. 'Before I go to a demonstration', said an *assentada*, 'I feel more tranquil if I have visited the cross. I feel I am carrying an added amount of protection with me.'[45]

Here, then, we see the settlers themselves, with little input or guidance from leaders, seizing upon a symbol of the Christian faith and investing it with their own meanings. Whilst these meanings are, of course, convergent with those of Catholic liberationism, liberationists probably ought not take too much credit for this remarkable show of symbolic creativity. All that can be said is that, indirectly, the liberationist Church, in the form of priests accompanying the encampments, immediately embraced, endorsed and legitimated the crosses. To this extent, the Church helped carve out a space of freedom in which the MST settlers could experiment with religious icons.

The Saints

In the examples I have given, there is substantial overlap in the values of the leaders and settlers. But it is also possible for the rank and file to combine fairly conservative values with emancipatory ones. In such cases, the legacy of liberationism is not so much to counter the conservative stance, but rather to accrete new, more liberatory meanings to it. It is to such symbolic hybrids that I now turn.

Upon entering Chaquara's community centre, I noticed right away in a far corner, underneath an enormous mural depicting the triumph of cooperative farming, a two-foot high statue of Santa Luzia, patron saint of eyesight, palms upturned in benediction, base strewn with lilies and white roses. The mere presence of a saint in a settlement's community centre is no cause for surprise. Most settlements have a patron saint – often the personal protector of a key member of the settlement – and the saint's image ends up in the community centre. In the nine days leading up to the saint's day on the calendar, the image is circulated through the homes of the community, just as it would in non-MST communities.

The main difference, on the surface at least, is that it is against MST regulations to name settlements after a saint. The rationale, as an MST leader explained, is that 'we want locals to name the community after a hero, or martyr for the cause, or after a place where martyrs have fallen.' Thus, for example, there are settlements named Jósimo, the priest murdered in 1986 while fighting landowners; or Eldorado, the site of the 1996 massacre; of Zumbi; even of Che. Nowhere to be seen are Santo Antonios or São Mateuses or São Joãos.

Yet forbidding the naming of a community after a saint does not prevent settlers from identifying a saint as their patron – of having a special relationship to the place. Thus I learned of settlements with patron saints from Saint Francis to Saint Lucius to Saint Luzia. MST leaders are quick to say they tolerate, even celebrate, the practice. As one told me, 'we value this practice, because we feel that it strengthens the *assentamento* as a community. The movement does not interfere in this part – or in deciding what the saint will be! We feel that these choices are theirs, these do not interfere in the process of struggle.'

In the context of the MST settlement, saints carry all the traditional, even conservative, meanings they hold in other places: they are exemplary humans who have earned a special place in heaven, and so now act as intercessors for the living and as purveyors of divine blessing and healing. As a CPT leader explained, 'many of the settlers still have that traditional veneration for the saints, they make *promessas*, and everything'. As one *assentada* whom I asked about Saint Luzia confirmed, she held her in esteem because of her ability to heal the blind (she was going blind herself).

And yet the politicized atmosphere of the *assentamento* reshapes, for at least some settlers, the meanings of the saints. In this process both the MST and CPT leaders use a gentle, coaxing hand. The MST now urges settlements' religion teams to organize the nine days celebrating the patron saint, so that they include social and political themes. On each of the nights leading up to the saint's day, a different theme is highlighted, with guests invited to lead discussion and reflection. In one settlement near São Luis celebrating the feast days of Saint Francis, the religious team organized events dealing with youth, women and land reform; one night was devoted to 'the MST'. Regional activists were invited to speak, and one student recalled:

> I went, along with a girl in the church there, and we chose a reading during the *celebração*. And I worked the angle of struggle in it, for land. If I am going to do an activity inside a church that has a patron saint, and the saint has this aspect that I can compare with the issue of struggle, then I take it up! This community's saint was Saint Francis. So I took up everything that he did about defending the poor, the whole discussion around him. And everything that Saint Francis dreamed about.

Similarly, in Chaquara, one of the MST leaders made a concerted effort to refer to Saint Luzia in public speech: whenever she spoke in the community centre, she constructed for her listeners a thoroughly liberationist interpretation of the saint, explaining:

> Look, Santa Luzia is the saint of eyesight, right? So I work with that. When I speak of her, I say: 'Look, everyone, Santa Luzia is the saint of vision, she is the saint who teaches us the necessity of looking forward, of opening our eyes, of seeing through to what is behind things, OK? Like seeing the exploitation that TV and the media and everyone tries to keep covered up. The lies, to see the truth. But also to look forward, to see how things might be, to keep our vision large and hopeful. So I work the vision of Santa Luzia into this, and people nod their heads, and I think it makes sense, you know?

These kinds of interventions, added to the other politically charged meanings of Exodus and the cross, are having an effect – though not necessarily the effect activists expected. I interviewed a middle-aged woman in an *assentamento* for whom traditional and liberationist meanings of Saint Luzia combined in a kind of seamless web. For her, the saint was clearly a protector of the community. 'She is our patron saint, so I think of her as in heaven, looking down on us,' she smiled. 'And we pray to her, I pray, when we are passing through difficulties, I will say, "Ah, my Santa Luzia, have pity on us, Oh, my sweet Santa Luzia, we are passing through such difficulty, if only you could help us a little, we need your help."' She laughed again, embarrassed.

I remained quiet, and so did she. Then she added, 'I say, look, Santa Luzia, we have struggled so hard, we are still struggling. We have worked very hard to be a community, to live in community with each other, as brothers, to share what we have. But still things are hard. So please Santa Luzia, pray for us, give us the strength to confront these things we still need to do.'

Conclusion

In these last two chapters I have tried to show the ongoing centrality of liberationist ideas and practices to what is widely regarded as the largest, most important social movement in Latin America. I argued that these ideas and practices not only shaped, but continue to infuse the worldview and everyday habits of successive cohorts of MST's leaders. I also argued that CPT agents are actively present in many MST settlements, developing and applying thoroughgoing liberationist Catholic land theology. And I concluded by claiming that these ideas and practices had successfully filtered through the noise of everyday life and left their mark on the MST's rank and file.

By 'successfully filtered', however, I do not mean duplicated. Far from it. The landless workers I got to know had already inherited too much complex religious belief to have the liberationist version go down without alteration. While the Exodus story functioned for them pretty much as the CPT leaders hoped it would, we also saw the rank and file innovate practices – for example, their version of the cross and saints – unintended in liberation's philosophy.

Yet if liberationism had not dreamed these things, it certainly could appreciate them. The clergy I spoke with expressed unmixed praise and admiration for the rank and file's creativity, and their creation of these hybrid religious forms and practices. One evening in São Luiz, the sun filled the horizon with a deep, dark red – the red of blood – but not of blood spilled; rather, of blood of connection, the blood all humanity shared looking at that horizon. I was looking at it with Frei Waldemar, a Franciscan who had spent much time on MST settlements. He had just completed describing the innovations of saint veneration he had witnessed. On his face, reddened by the sunset's glow, there was a smile of satisfaction as he recounted a settler's promise to a saint that he would never plant alone, but only with others. Waldemar's smile, too, was a legacy of liberation.

Notes

1   As an MST leader remarked in the early 1990s, 'We don't have too much connection with the unions. If it weren't for this contribution of the priest, we wouldn't have survived and we would have given up.' See Daniela Issa, 'What is the role of the Catholic Church in the Mobilization of the Landless Rural Workers' Movement (MST) in Pará, Brazil in the 1990s?', MA Thesis (University of South Florida, 1999), 76.

2 Interview with Frei Orestes, Pôrto Alegre, May 2002. See also Antonio Chiareli, 'The Forging of "Political Resource Communities": The Landless Workers' Movement and the Political Construction of Rural Cooperatives in Southern Brazil", PhD dissertation (Northwestern University, 2000), 289.
3 Interview with Frei Orestes.
4 Gorgen, 'O MST e a religião', in João Pedro Stédile et al. (eds.), A reforma agrária e a luta do MST (Petrópolis: Vozes, 1997).
5 Interview with Wilson Dallagnol, CPT, Pôrto Alegre, May 2002.
6 While the ratio of ordained priests to baptized Catholics varies significantly depending on location and region, generally there still is in Brazil what may be characterized as a scarcity of priests. Masses are few and far between, and the task of coordinating weekly celebrations falls mainly to local lay leaders. On the organization of Catholic life in Brazil, see Goetz Frank Ottmann, Lost for Words? Brazilian Liberationism in the 1990s (Pittsburgh: University of Pittsburgh Press, 2002); for an earlier analysis, see Thomas Bruneau, The Church in Brazil (Austin: University of Texas Press, 1982). In a region such as the fourth district of Duque de Caxias, for example, in the urban periphery of Rio de Janeiro, three priests minister to 100 small towns and villages; logically, much of the everyday work of administering Catholic ritual life falls to the laity. My own treatment of the organization of local Catholic laity appears in John Burdick, Looking for God in Brazil (Berkeley: University of California Press, 1993).
7 Chiareli, 'The Forging of "Political Communities"', 283, 218.
8 Interview with Wilson Dallagnol, May 2002.
9 Gorgen, 'O MST e a religião', 291.
10 Paul Cerioli, Ensino Social da Igreja e o Direito de Organização dos Empobrecidos, vol. vi (Petrópolis: Vozes, 1994), 26; cited in Chiareli, 'The Forging of "Political Resource Communities"', 290.
11 Catequistas dos Assentamentos da Região do Pôrto Alegre, RS, Catequese em Mutirão (Pôrto Alegre: Comissão Pastoral da Terra, 2002).
12 Frei Orestes, personal communication, May 2002.
13 Comissão Pastoral da Terra, Catequese em Mutirão (Pôrto Alegre: CPT, 2002), 5.
14 Ibid., 7.
15 Ibid., 6.
16 Ibid., 11.
17 Ibid., 13.
18 Chiareli, 'The Forging of "Political Resource Communities"', 288.
19 CPT, Catequese, 15.
20 Ibid., 17.
21 Ibid., 20–23.
22 This claim is based on Turner's analysis of pilgrimage as built around the profoundly egalitarian experience of communitas. See Victor Turner, 'Pilgrimage and communitas', Studia missionalia, 23 (1974), 1–21. See also his 'The Center Out There: The Pilgrim's Goal', History of Religions, 12 (1973), 191–230.
23 Christine de Alencar Chaves, A Marcha Nacional dos Sem Terra (Rio de Janeiro, Relumé Dumará, 2000), 366.
24 Wilson Dallagnol, As Romarias da Terra no Rio Grande d Sul (Pôrto Alegre, CPT, 2001), 18.
25 Ibid., 51. In 1985, the romaria in Rio Grande do Sul reached its peak attendance, with 70 000 pilgrims.
26 Fernandes, A formação do MST no Brazil (Petrópolis: Vozes, 2000), 108. In December 1988, the CPT worked with the MST to bring about the First romaria da terra of Alagoas, when over 2000 families marched to the statue of Zumbi.
27 It should be pointed out that the names assigned to these pilgrimages vary considerably throughout Brazil. In Tocantins, the pilgrimage is named after the local martyr, Padre

Jósimo; in Amazônia, it is named '*Romaria das Aguas*'. Miguel Carter, personal communication, May 2003.
28 Chaves, *A Marcha Nacional*, 131.
29 Ibid., 362.
30 Ibid., 62.
31 Ibid,, 362.
32 Ibid., 363.
33 For a good discussion of the distinctions between oppositional consciousness and group identity, see Jane Mainsbridge, 'Complicating Oppositional Consciousness' in Jane Mainsbridge and Aldon Morris (eds.), *Oppositional Consciousness* (Chicago: University of Chicago Press, 2001), 238–264.
34 Padre Flavio, São Luis CPT, personal communication, June 2002.
35 Sergio Gorgen, *O Massacre da Fazenda Santa Elmira* (Petrópolis: Vozes, 1989), 96–97.
36 See also the testimonies in Andrea Paula dos Santos *et al.*, *Vozes da Marcha pela Terra* (São Paulo: Loyola, 1998), for similar accounts.
37 Ibid., 200.
38 Ibid., 75.
39 Ibid. Another indicator of this identity is that many settlers have been reinforced in their understanding of the land as a gift from God. Jonas, 29 years old, said that 'the land is not mine, the land is ours. Since God gave it to us. I think now only about struggling on this land for us' (ibid., 144). And an *assentada* said, 'Land is sacred and a God-given gift. But it also remains His ... the large landowners take this gift of land away from us and hold [it] from God.' (Chiareli, 'The Forging of "Political Resource Communities"', 289.) See also Miguel Carter, 'Ideal Interest Mobilization: Explaining the Formation of Brazil's Landless Social Movement', PhD dissertation (Columbia University, 2002), 285.
40 Chaves, *A Marcha Nacional*; see also the role of the cross in Luis Ignacio Germany Gaiger, *Agentes Religiosos e Camponeses Sem Terra no Sul do Brasil* (Petrópolis: Vozes, 1987), 41.
41 João Stédile and Bernardo Mancano Fernandes, *Brava Gente: A Trajetoria do MST e a Luta Pela Terra no Brazil* (São Paulo: Editora Fundação Perseu Abramo, 1999).
42 It is interesting to note that in some early camps, such as Annoni, there were heated debates about which colours to use. Miguel Carter, personal communication, May 2003.
43 Ibid.
44 Cf. Chaves, *A Marcha Nacional*, n. 165, p. 161.
45 Similarly, a woman in an encampment described by Chiareli commented that 'without the blessing of the friar before we join the demonstrations, we are unprotected from what could happen there' (Chiareli. 'The Forging of "Political Resource Communities"', 285). Originating in the camps and settlements, these symbolic associations now are carried by crosses wherever they are taken. The cross as a symbol of the struggle, sacrifice, and the promise of eventual triumph is central to the various pilgrimages of land organized by the MST, in conjunction with the CPT.

Conclusion

In the preceding pages I have argued that, despite its loss of high-profile visibility over the past decade, liberation Catholicism continues to exert a strong, even pervasive, influence on Brazilian society through the continuing interventions of social activists shaped by the progressive Church. To build this argument I focused on three arenas of social struggle in which activists touched by the Church have been deeply involved. I began by arguing that progressive Catholicism contributed fundamentally to the formation of the movement within the Church to struggle against anti-black racism. I argued that the progressive Church fostered this movement by recruiting non-white seminarians, legitimating a racial injustice frame, encouraging involvement in social movements, highlighting racially discriminatory behaviour and valuing personal identification with the oppressed. These orientations, I have argued, led young non-white seminarians to demand an increase in the number of clerical vocations for blacks, to call for black rights and dignity, to valorize the cultural heritage of Afro-Brazil, to embrace a new racial language and to build a network of people committed to preparing black and poor high school students to pass college entrance examinations. By the start of the twenty-first century, the Black Pastoral of the Catholic Church had become one of the handful of genuinely national networks of activists engaged in the struggle for racial justice in Brazil.

From the anti-racist struggle I turned to the struggle of women. In this arena I argued that despite its well-deserved reputation for insensitivity and indifference to women's issues, the progressive Church has in submerged, sometimes unintentional ways, offered women important new sources of authority, ideas for challenging traditional gender norms and opportunities to act upon these challenges. I argued that by drawing women into new social relations that hone their intellects and leadership skills, the Church unwittingly encouraged them to question the traditional division of authority in the household and to expect the end of gender discrimination in the Church. I further argued that by emphasizing socio-structural rather than individual–moral frames for understanding human action and by encouraging small-group reflection, Catholic liberationism catalysed among some Catholic women a critique of patriarchy and an unexpectedly radical analysis of gender violence. But perhaps the most surprising ideological consequence of progressive Catholicism is that its commitment to the poor has created a conceptual and value-based context within which an admittedly small, but growing, network of clerics have found themselves defending poor women's right to abortion.

The last field of progressive Catholic action I examined was that of the Landless Workers' Movement. I made the case that the progressive Church, despite experiencing significant ideological tensions with the movement, has over the past decade made the orientation of liberation theology an important presence in the thinking and action both of MST's leaders and rank and file. I have argued that the Pastoral Land Commission and the Youth Land Pastoral continue to this day to serve as training grounds for many MST leaders; I have also argued that progressive Catholic thought continues to strengthen in these leaders a thirst for social justice, an awakened sense of historic agency, a vision of Christian collectivism, a hope for personal transformation, an appreciation of the mystical in everyday life and a passion for key Catholic symbols. It is also clear that the Pastoral Land Commission still continues to lend intellectual stimulation and institutional support to liberationist consciousness among the rank and file of the MST, a consciousness built up around the Exodus story, and enriched and complemented by impressive syntheses of popular with theology-based ideas and beliefs.

In more general terms, I have sought in this book to enrich and extend the current discussion in the sociology of social movements about movement 'outcomes'.[1] That literature is marked by a strong preference for tracing the causal connections between social movement action and institutional, policy and legislative change.[2] Although such connections are clearly important, they in no way exhaust the ways in which social activists exert influence on culture and society. Doug McAdam and Donatella della Porta have recognized the need to conceptualize outcomes more broadly, in order to include, at the individual level, changed value orientations of activists and, at the collective level, new, emerging collective meanings that social movement activists articulate and disseminate.[3] The latter effect can be theorized as part of the process of collective articulation of modes of understanding that run counter to the modes authorized by socially powerful elites and institutions. Such articulations may be viewed as a step in the process of building an emergent counter-hegemonic point of view, thereby creating a reservoir of meanings available to a widening array of activists committed to challenging prevailing structures of power.[4] From this perspective, we may regard the ideas and interpretations developed by a cohort of activists as contributing to the growth of a kind of intellectual fund, to which current and future activists can turn when they need cognitive or moral guidance.[5]

This image of a 'fund' fairly describes what I have witnessed over the past decade as the everyday practice of the liberationist Catholic Church in Brazil. While limited in its ability to bring about major structural changes, and while often less attractive to its own targeted grassroots constituencies than are its apolitical religious rivals, one may still observe that the liberationist Church continues to inject values into activist and popular interpretations of the world, sustaining a kind of common 'fund' of ideas, in which placing the poor first, assigning a premium to the struggle for social justice and equality, and endorsing confrontational tactics as sometimes necessary, have all become solidified through the claim that these partake in the will of God and Christ for man. As long as these ideas are sustained by their divine status, the counter-hegemomy in Brazil and Latin America against the free rein of the neo-liberal state and corporate power remains that much richer, denser and durable.[6]

But it is not enough simply to point out that Catholic liberationism continues to add to Brazilian counter-hegemony. It is important to identify at least some of the key processes and channels through which this happens. Thus I wish to return here to my description of liberationism's legacy for Brazilian society with a more highly burnished analytical lens.

I note that, throughout this book, I have returned recurrently to three key processes. First, I have repeatedly stressed that involvement in Church-oriented movements has inspired and prepared individuals to become active in various fields of social struggle outside of the original institutional context of the Church itself. They have done this both through the self-conscious action of the Church, and through networks at odds with, or otherwise constrained by, the Church. As an example of the former, pastoral agents who had been involved in the Church's Black Pastoral eventually moved, with the Church's blessing, towards forming independent organizations such as Educafro to carry forth the anti-racist struggle. As an example of the latter, some networks of women whose consciousness had been raised within the Church eventually felt the need to create organizations imbued with an orientation at odds with their clerical superiors. In both cases, the ideology of the progressive Church had produced action – in one case deliberate, in the other not – that broke through the confines of the Church and became a presence on the Brazilian ideological scene.

Second, I have emphasized throughout the book that the Church does not form generic 'leaders', but rather leaders whose form of action and thought bear the mark of their progressive Catholic background. Activists in the MST who originated in the Youth Land Pastoral brought with them a specific set of sensitivities to local culture which make them especially effective grassroots organizers. Catholic women who have gone from the CEB to abortion-rights activism frame their appeal in terms of how best to read God's will for the poor, rather than for women. Church-originated leaders apply the lessons they learned in the CEB about working with popular culture, but also import to their MST activism their unconscious, habitual use of symbols, such as wine and bread, to embody martyrdom and communion. The leaders from the Church campaigning for affirmative action in college recruitment bring all the vocabulary of *caminhada* they have acquired through their religious training. And all this religious thought and language increases the likelihood of intensified resonance and connection with at least some of the extra-Church's movement's targeted constituencies.

This brings me to the last main process I have witnessed. I have insisted throughout this book that the perspectives and practices carried by leaders originating in the Church have in fact had an effect on the rank and file of those movements. Certainly in some cases, the liberationist perspective of leaders meets resistance at the grassroots, as when women felt irritated with liberationist devalorization of their concerns, or when others, especially the poor and illiterate, feel frustrated with liberationist theoretical abstractness. What I have endeavoured to document in this book are the various ways in which the liberationist vision has been reshaped and appropriated at the base to make it more compatible with local understandings and ideology. For example, despite the best efforts of Black Pastoral agents to convey an essentialist, rigid view of black–white identity and relations, locals resisted this essentialism and instead embraced the message of mutual tolerance, uniting it with local, more fluid understandings of religious and racial identity. But it remains true that without the original liberationist initiative, it is likely that locals would not have felt the need to develop a new set of institutions to stimulate, articulate and channel anti-racist sentiment. Similarly, although the CPT's liberationist versions of Exodus have filtered successfully to the grassroots, the emancipatory visions of the rank and file have not been limited to Exodus. Rather, landless locals have mixed top-down ideas about Exodus with their own bottom-up ideas about saints and crosses. The result is neither a purely Church-originated nor a grassroots-originated vision, but rather a hybrid that is nonetheless ineluctably marked by liberationist values and ideals.

Clearly, I believe that attention to the kinds of subtle effects I have described here – the formation of new leadership cohorts, the transmission of those cohorts' values and views to new social contexts, and the new perspectival inflections of popular consciousness that result – are all worthy of study in relation to other social movements, social-change groups and social practices in Brazil. In particular, the approach I have developed here would lend itself readily to an analysis of the Workers' Party, now enjoying state power in Brazil, as well as of the neighbourhood association movement, the indigenous rights' movement,[7] and the variegated environmentalist movement. Beyond Brazil, as elsewhere in Latin America, an assessment of the role of liberationist Catholicism's ongoing influence in the nooks and crannies of political life would repay study in connection to a host of contexts and struggles. Obvious candidates for a deeper analysis include the ongoing role of the Abejas movement and Catholic liberationism among the Zapatistas, as well as among indigenous rights' movements of Central America and elsewhere. Equally important would be an evaluation of liberationist contributions to afro-Latin struggles in Colombia, Ecuador and elsewhere. Whilst there have been numerous analyses of how progressive Catholicism contributed to the origin and early development of many of these struggles, few, if any, authors have delved into how elements of liberationist thought continue (or not) to influence and shape them.

At the most general level, paying attention to the kinds of processes of subtle influence and shaping that I have argued for here should push the analysis of social movement 'effects' to become more dialectical. In the literature on the 'effects' of social movements, the focus is almost always on the extent to which the movement has achieved its explicit, stated goals. This focus might be altered if we recognized that movements are really clusters of idea-positions, some of which are dominant at any one time, some of which are not. Too often scholars have limited themselves to observing whether a movement is accomplishing the movement's dominant objectives. But at any one time, the movement is also generating groups and networks whose views are not necessarily reducible to the claims of those who dominate the movement, and it is generating effects that are not necessarily anticipated by movement leadership. In order for a fuller, more realistic assessment – both of social movements' limits and potential for bringing about social and cultural change – it is as important to pay attention to their internally subversive projects and unanticipated effects as to their official positions and plans. Only then will we be able to resist the claims of those in power that the era of progressive social movements is over. Only then will we be able to say that it is in fact not over, but is rather just starting a new phase. In this phase there remain great possibilities for the most recent generation of social movements to ramify and coil their tendrils – of ideas, values, and practices – beneath the surface of the landscape, thus offering nutriment and roots, both to movements we know and to other movements as yet undreamed and unimagined. The era of social movement change has only just begun.

Notes

1   Jennifer Earl, 'Methods, Movements, and Outcomes: Methodological Difficulties in the Study of Extra-Movement Outcomes' in Patrick Coy (ed.), *Research in Social Movements, Conflicts and Change* (Stanford: JAI Press, 2000), 2–36.
2   Edwin Amenta and Michael P. Young, 'Making an Impact: Conceptual and Methodological Implications of the Collective Goods Criterion' in Marco Giugni *et al.*, (eds.), *How Social Movements Matter* (Minneapolis: University of Minnesota Press, 1999), 22–41.
3   See Doug McAdam, 'The Biographical Impact of Activism,' in Giugni *et al.*, *How Social Movements Matter*, 119–148; and Donatella della Porta, 'Protest, Protesters, and Protest Policing: Public Discourses in Italy and Germany from the 1960s to the 1980s' in ibid., 66–96.
4   The general theoretical framework for this view is of course Gramsci. See Antonio Gramsci, *Selections from the Prison Notebooks of Antonio Gramsci*, ed. and trans. Quintin Hoare and Geoffrey Nowell-Smith (New York: International Publishers, 1971).

The idea of 'emergent' views derives from Raymond Williams, *Marxism and Literature* (Oxford: Oxford University Press, 1977).

5 A useful, if slightly redundant and over-simplified, version of this argument is presented in Ron Eyerman and A. Jamison, *Social Movements: A Cognitive Approach* (University Park, PA: Pennsylvania State University Press, 1991). Thomas Rochon's view, set forth in his book *Culture Moves* (Chicago: Chicago University Press, 1999), is also suggestive in this regard, but may place too much emphasis on the role of intellectual elites, without paying attention to the development of alternative values at the non-elite grassroots level.

6 For a similar discussion, see Christian Smith, 'Correcting a Curious Neglect, or Bringing Religion Back In' in Christian Smith (ed.), *Disruptive Religion: the Force of fait in Social Movement Activism* (New York: Routledge, 1996), 1–28.

7 See Jonathan Warren, *Racial Revolutions* (Durham: Duke University Press, 2001).

Select Bibliography

Adriance, Madeleine, *Promised Land: Base Christian Communities and the Struggle for the Amazon*, Albany, NY: SUNY Press, 1995.

Adriance, Madeleine, 'Opting for the Poor: A Social-Historical Analysis of the Changing Brazilian Catholic Church', *Sociological Analysis*, 46, 2, Summer 1985, 131–146.

Akkari, Abdeljalil, 'The Construction of Mass Schooling in Brazil: A Two-Tiered Educational System Reference to Role of Education in Determining Class Status in Brazil', *Education and Society*, 17, 1, June 1999, 37–51.

Alexander, Robert, *Juscelino Kubitschek and the Development of Brazil*, Athens: Ohio University Center for International Studies, 1991.

Almeida, Lucio Flávio *et al.*, 'The Landless Workers' Movement and Social Struggles against Neoliberalism', *Latin American Perspectives*, 27, 5(114), September 2000, 11–32.

Altemeyer Jr, Fernando, 'A pastoral católica no ano de 1995'. *Tempo e Presença* 285, January–February 1996, 23–25.

Alvarez, Sonia, *Engendering Democracy in Brazil: Women's Movements in Transition Politics*, Princeton, NJ: Princeton University Press, 1990.

Alvarez, Sonia, 'Women's Participation in the Brazilian "People's Church": A Critical Appraisal.' *Feminist Studies*, 16, Summer 1990, 381–408.

Alvarez, Sonia, 'Latin American Feminisms "Go Global": Trends of the 1990s and Challenges for the New Millennium' in Sonia E. Alvarez, Evelina Dagnino and Arturo Escobar (eds.), *Cultures of Politics, Politics of Cultures: Re-Visioning Latin American Social Movements*, Boulder, CO: Westview Press, 1998.

Amenta, Edwin and Michael P. Young, 'Making an Impact: Conceptual and Methodological Implications of the Collective Goods Criterion' in Marco Giugni *et al.* (eds.), *How Social Movements Matter*, Minneapolis: University of Minnesota Press, 1999, 22–41.

Andrews, Reid, *Blacks and Whites in São Paulo, Brazil, 1888–1988*, Madison: University of Wisconsin Press, 1991.

Angrosino, Michael, 'The Culture Concept and the Mission of the Roman Catholic Church', *American Anthropologist*, 96, 4, 1994, 824–832.

Aquino, Maria Pilar, 'Latin American Feminist Theology', *Journal of Feminist Studies in Religion*, 14, Spring 1998, 89–10.

Aquino, Maria Pilar, *Our Cry for Life: Feminist Theology from Latin America*, New York: Orbis, 1993.

Bairros, Monica, 'Os APNS e a Luta Contra Raçismo na Igreja', unpublished ms, 1997.

Bell, Daniel M., *Liberation Theology After the End of History*, New York: Routledge, 2001.

Berryman, Philip, *Religion in the Magacity*, Maryknoll: Orbis, 1996.

Boff, Clodovis, 'CEBs: A que ponto Estão e aonde vão' in Clodovis Boff, Solange Rodrigues, *et al.* (eds.), *As Comunidades de Base em Questão*, São Paulo: Paulinas, 1997, 251–306.

Boff, Clodovis *et al.*, *As Comunidades de base em questão*, São Paulo: Paulinas, 1997.
Boff, Clodovis, 'Desafios atuais da pastoral popular', *Tempo e Presença*, 232, 1988, 30–32.
Boff, Clodovis, *Cristãos: Como Fazer Política*, Petrópolis: Vozes, 1987.
Boff, Leonardo, *Mestre Eckhart: a mística de ser e de não ter*. Petrópolis, RJ, Brasil: Vozes, 1983.
Boff, Leonardo, *Ecclesiogenesis: The Base Communities Reinvent the Church*, Maryknoll: Orbis, 1986.
Boff, Leonardo, *The New Evangelization: Good News to the Poor*, Maryknoll: Orbis, 1991.
Boff, Leonardo, *Mística e espiritualidade*, 2nd edn, Rio de Janeiro: Rocco, 1994.
Boff, Leonardo, *Ecology and Liberation: A New Paradigm*, trans. John Cumming, Maryknoll: Oribis, 1995.
Boff, Leonardo, 'Christian Liberation Toward the 21st Century', LADOC, 25 (March–April 1995), 1, 3.
Boff, Leonardo, *Tempo de Transcendência: O Ser Humano como um Projeto Infinito*, Rio de Janeiro: Editora Sextante, 2000.
Branford, Sue and Jan Rocha, *Cutting the Wire: The Story of the Landless Movement in Brazil*, London: Latin American Bureau, 2002.
Brooks, Sarah, 'Catholic Activism in the 1990s: New Strategies for the Neoliberal Age' in Christian Smith and Joshua Prokopy (eds.), *Latin American Religion in Motion*, New York: Routledge, 1999.
Bruneau, Thomas, *The Political Transformation of the Brazilian Catholic Church*, Cambridge: Cambridge University Press, 1974.
Bruneau, Thomas, *The Church in Brazil*, Austin: University of Texas Press, 1982.
Burdick, John, 'Gossip and Secrecy: The Articulation of Domestic Conflict in Three Religions of Urban Brazil', *Sociological Analysis*, 51, 2, Summer 1990, 153–170.
Burdick, John, 'Brazil's Black Consciousness Movement', *NACLA Report on the Americas*, 25, 4, 1992, 23–27.
Burdick, John, *Looking for God in Brazil*, Berkeley: University of California Press, 1993.
Burdick, John, *Blessed Anastacia: Women, Race, and Popular Christianity in Brazil*, New York: Routledge, 1998.
Burdick, John, 'The Lost Constituency of Brazil's Black Consciousness Movements', *Latin American Perspectives*, 98, 25, January 1998, 136–155.
Burdick, John, 'The Evolution of a Progressive Catholic Project: The Case of the Black Pastoral in Rio de Janeiro, Brazil' in John Burdick and W. E. Hewitt (eds.), *The Church at the Grassroots in Latin America: Perspectives on Thirty Years of Activism*, Westport, CA: Greenwood Press, 2000, 71–84.
Butler, Kim, *Freedoms Given, Freedoms Won*, New Brunswick: Rutgers University Press, 1998.
Caldart, Roseli, *Pedagogia do Movimento dos Sem Terra*, Petrópolis: Vozes, 2000.
Caldeira, Teresa, 'Women, Daily Life and Politics' in Elizabeth Jelin (ed.), *Women and Social Change in Latin America*, Atlantic Highlands: Zed, 1990.
Carter, Miguel. 'Ideal Interest Mobilization: Explaining the Formation of Brazil's Landless Social Movement', PhD dissertation, Columbia University, 2002.

Carvalho, Abdias Vilar de, 'A Igreja Católica e a questão agraria' in Vanilda Paiva (ed.), *A Igreja e a Questão Agraria*, São Paulo: Edições Loyota, 1985, 68–75.

Castro, Nadya Araújo and Antonio Sérgio Alfredo Guimarães, 'Racial Inequalities in the Labor Market' in Rebecca Reichmann (ed.), *Race in Contemporary Brazil*.

Catequistas dos Assentamentos da Região do Pôrto Alegre, RS, *Catequese em Mutirão*. Pôrto Alegre: Comissão Pastoral da Terra, 2002.

CELAM, *Medellin Conclusions*, Washington, DC: National Conference of Catholic Bishops, Secretariat for Latin America, 1979.

Cerioli, Paul, *Ensino Social da Igreja e o Direito de Organização dos Empobrecidos*, Petrópolis: Vozes, 1994.

Chaves, Christine de Alencar, *A Marcha Nacional dos Sem Terra*, Rio de Janeiro: Relumé Dumará, 2000.

Chesnut, Andrew, *Born Again in Brazil*, New Brunswick: Rutgers, 1997.

Chesnut, Andrew, *Competitive Spirits: Latin America's New Religious Economy*, New York: Oxford University Press, 2003.

Chiareli, Antonio, 'The Forging of "Political Resource Communities": The Landless Rural Workers' Movement and the Political Construction of Rural Cooperatives in Southern Brazil', PhD Dissertation, Northwestern University, 2000.

Cleary, Edward, *Crisis and Change: The Church in Latin America Today*, Maryknoll: Orbis, 1985.

Cleary, Edward, 'The Brazilian Catholic Church and Church–State Relations: Nation Building', *Journal of Church and State*, 39, 2, Spring 1997, 253–72.

Collins, Denis E., *Paulo Freire: His Life, Work, and Thought*, New York: Paulist Press, 1978.

Comblin, Jose, 'Algumas questões a partir da prática das comunidades eclesiais de base no nordeste', *Revista Eclesiástica Brasileira*, 50, 198, 1990, 335–381.

Comerford, John Cunha, *Fazendo a Luta: Sociabilidade, Falas e Rituais na Construção de Organizações Camponesas*, Rio de Janeiro: Relumé Dumará, 1999.

Comissão Pastoral da Terra, *Catequese em Mutirão*, Pôrto Alegre: CPT, 2002.

Coordenação Estadual de Pastoral da Juventude Rural, *Pastoral da Juventude Rural*, Petrópolis: Vozes, 1985.

Covin, David, 'Learning from Brazil's Unified Black Movement: Whither Goeth Black Nationalism?', *National Political Science Review*, 1999, 7, 84–95.

Covin, David, 'Narrative, Free Spaces, and Communities of Memory in the Brazilian Black Consciousness Movement', *The Western Journal of Black Studies*, 21, 4, Winter 1997, 272–279.

Cox, Harvey, *The Silencing of Leonardo Boff*, Pak Park: Meyer-Stone, 1988.

Cox, Harvey, 'Inculturation Reconsidered: Indigenization as Form of Continuing Oppression', *Christianity and Crisis*, 51, 13 May 1991, 140–142.

Cox, Harvey, 'Catholicity, Inculturation, and Liberation Theology: The Case of Leonardo Boff', In *Struggles for Solidarity*, Minneapolis: University of Minnesota Press, 1992, 105–113.

Craske, Nikkie, *Women and Politics in Latin America*, New Brunswick: Rutgers University Press, 1999.

Dallagnol, Wilson, *As Romarias da Terra no Rio Grande d Sul*, Pôrto Alegre, CPT, 2001.

Damasceno, Caetana et al., *Catálogo de entidades de movimento negro o Brasil*, Rio de Janeiro: ISER, 1988.
Damasceno, Caetana, 'Cantando para Subir', Master's thesis, Programa de Pos-Graduação de Antropologia Social, Universidade Federal de Rio de Janeiro, 1990.
Da Matta, Roberto, *A Casa e a Rua*, Rio de Janeiro: Editora Guanabara, 1987.
Dassin, Joan (ed.), *Torture in Brazil: A Report*, New York: Vintage, 1986.
Daudelin, Jean and W. E. Hewitt, 'Latin American Politics: Exit the Catholic Church?' in Sattya Pattnayak (ed.), *Organized Religion in the Political Transformation of Latin America*, New York: University Press of America, 1995.
Della Cava, Ralph, 'Catholicism and Society in Twentieth Century Brazil', *Latin American Research Review*, 11, 2, 1976: 7–50.
Della Cava, Ralph. 'The "People's Church", the Vatican, and *Abertura*' in Alfred Stepan (ed.), *Democratizing Brazil: Problems of Transition and Consolidation*, New York: Oxford University Press, 1989.
Della Porta, Donatella. 'Protest, Protesters, and Protest Policing: Public Discourses in Italy and Germany from the 1960s to the 1980s' in Marco Giugni and Doug McAdams (eds.), *How Social Movements Matter*, Minneapolis: University of Minnesota Press, 1999, 66–96.
Demerath, Nicholas, *Crossing the Gods*, New Brunswick: Rutgers, 2001.
De Theije, Marjo, *All that is God is Good: An Anthropology of Liberationist Catholicism in Garanhuns, Brazil*, Utrecht: CERES, 1997.
Doimo, Ana Maria, 'Social Movements and the Catholic Church in Vitoria, Brazil', in Scott Mainwaring and Alexander Wilde (eds.), *The Progressive Church in Latin America*, Notre Dame: University of Notre Dame Press, 1989.
Doimo, Ana Maria, *A Vez e a Voz do Popular*, Rio de Janeiro: Relumé Dumará, 1995.
Drogus, Carol Ann, 'Religious Change and Women's Status in Latin America', Kellogg Working Paper no. 205, March 1994.
Drogus, Carol Ann, *Women, Religion, and Social Change in Brazil's Popular Church*, Notre Dame: University of Notre Dame Press, 1997.
Drogus, Carol Ann, 'No Land of Milk and Honey: Women CEB Activists in Posttransition Brazil', *Journal of Interamerican Studies and World Affairs*, 41, 4, Winter 1999.
Drogus, Carol Ann, 'Liberation Theology and the Liberation of Women in Santo Antonio, Brazil', in John Burdick and W. E. Hewitt (eds.), *The Church at the Grassroots in Latin America*, Westport: Praeger, 2000.
Dussel, Enrique, *Filosofía Ética de la Liberacion*, Vol III, Buenos Aires: Ediciones La Aurora, 1988.
Earl, Jennifer, 'Methods, Movements, and Outcomes' in Patrick Coy (ed.), *Research in Social Movements, Conflicts and Change*, Stanford: JAI Press, 2000, 3–25.
Eber, Chrsitine, 'Seeking Our Own Food: Indigenous Women's Power and Autonomy in San Pedro Chenalho, Chiapas (1980-1998)', *Latin American Perspectives*, 26, 3 May 1999, 6–36.
Fernandes, Bernardo, *A Formação do MST no Brasil*, Petrópolis: Vozes, 2000.
Fernandes, Rubem Cesar et al., *Novo Nascimento*, Rio de Janeiro, Mauad, 1998.
Figueira, Vera Moreira, 'O preconceito racial na escola', *Estudos Afro-Asiáticos*, 18 1990, 63–71.

First Congress of the CPT, *Terra, Agua Direitos: Luzes e Perspectivas*, Pôrto Alegre: CPT, 2001.
Flynn, Peter, *Brazil: A Political Analysis*, Boulder, CO: Westview, 1978.
Fontaine, Pierre-Michel (ed.), *Race, Class and Power in Brazil*, Los Angeles: Center for Afro-American Studies, 1985.
Freire, Paulo, *The Pedagogy of the Oppressed*, trans. Myra Ramos, New York: Herder and Herder, 1970.
Gaiger, Luis Ignacio Germany, *Agentes Religiosos e Camponeses Sem Terra no Sul do Brasil*, Petrópolis: Vozes, 1987.
Gay, Robert, *Popular Organization and Democracy in Rio de Janeiro*, Philadelphia: Temple, 1994.
Gebara, Ivone, *Longing for Running Water: Ecofeminism and Liberation*, Minneapolis: Fortress Press, 1999.
Gebara, Ivone, 'A Feminist Perspective on Enigmas and Ambiguities in Religious Interpretation' in Thomas Bamat and Jean-Paul Wiest (eds.), *Popular Catholicism in a World Church*, Maryknoll: Orbis, 1999, 256–264.
Gebara, Ivone, 'Brazilian Women's Movements and Feminist Theologies', *Ecotheology*, 4, Jan 1998, 83–85.
Gebara, Ivone and Maria Clara Bingemer, *Mary, Mother of God, Mother of the Poor*, Maryknoll: Orbis, 1989.
Goes, Cesar Hamilton Brito, 'A Comissão Pastoral da Terra: História e Ambivalência da Ação da Igreja no Rio Grande do Sul', Mestrado, UFRG, 1997.
Goldman, Marcio, 'Segmentaridades e movimentos negros nas eleições de Ilhéus', *Mana*, 7, 2, October 2001, 57–93.
Goldman, Marcio and David Rogers, 'An Ethnographic Theory of Democracy. Politics from the Viewpoint of Ilhéus's Black Movement (Bahia, Brazil)', *Ethnos*, 66, 2, 2000, 157–180.
Goldstein, Donna M., *Laughter Out of Place: Race, Class, Violence and Sexuality in a Rio Shantytown*, Berkeley: University of California Press, 2003.
Gomes da Cunha, Olivia Maria, 'Black Movements and the Politics of Identity in Brazil' in Sonia Alvarez, Evelina Dagnino and Arturo Escobar (eds.), *Cultures of Politics, Politics of Cultures*, Boulder, CO: Westview, 1998, 220–251.
Gonzaga de Souza Lima, Luiz, *Evolução Política dos Católicos e da Igreja no Brasil*, Petrópolis: Vozes, 1979.
Gorgen, Sergio. 'O MST e a religião', in João Pedro Stédile et al. (eds.), *A reforma agrária e a luta do MST*, Petrópolis: Vozes, 1997.
Gorgen, Sergio. *O Massacre da Fazenda Santa Elmira*, Petrópolis: Vozes, 1989.
Gramsci, Antonio, *Selection from the Prison Notebooks of Antonio Gramsci*, ed. and trans. Quintin Hoare and Geoffrey Nowell-Smith, New York: International Publishers, 1971.
Grossi, Miriam, 'Novas/velhas violências contra a mulher no Brasil', *Estudos feministas*, 2, 2, 1994, 473–483.
Grupo Tao, *A mística do animador popular*, São Paulo: Editora Atica, 1996.
Guider, Margaret Eletta, *Daughters of Rahab: Prostitution and the Church of Liberation in Brazil*, Minneapolis: Fortress Press, 1995.
Guillebeau, Christopher, 'Affirmative Action in a Global Perspective: The Cases of South Africa and Brazil', *Sociological Spectrum*, 19, 4, October–December 1999, 443–465.

Guimarães, Antonio Sergio Alfredo, *Racismo e Anti-Racismo no Brasil*, São Paulo: Editora, 34, 1999.
Guimarães, Antonio Sergio Alfredo, *Classes, Raças, e Democracia*, São Paulo: Editora, 34, 2002.
Gutierrez, Gustavo, *Theology of Liberation*, Maryknoll: Orbis, 1973.
Gutierrez, Gustavo, *The Power of the Poor in History*, Maryknoll: Orbis, 1983.
Gutierrez, Gustavo, *Theology of Liberation*, Maryknoll: Orbis, 2nd edn, 1988.
Haas, Liesl, 'Changing the System from Within? Feminist Participation in the Brazilian Workers' Party' in Victoria Gonzalez and Karen Kampwirth (eds.), *Radical Women in Latin America: Left and Right*, University Park, PA: Pennsylvania State University Press, 2001.
Hammond, John L. 'Law and Disorder: The Brazilian Landless Farmworkers' Movement', *Bulletin of Latin American Research*, 18, 4, October 1999, 469–489.
Hanchard, Michael (ed.), *Orpheus and Power: The Movimento Negro of Rio de Janeiro and Sao Paulo, 1945–1988*, Princeton: Princeton University Press, 1994.
Hanchard, Michael (ed.), *Racial Politics in Contemporary Brazil*, Durham: Duke University Press, 1999.
Hasenbalg, Carlos and Nelson do Valle Silva, 'Raça e oportunidades sociais no Brasil' in Peggy Lovell (org.), *Desigualdade racial no Brasil contemporâneo*, Belo Horizonte, 1991: Centro de Desenvolvimento e Planejamento Regional (CEDEPLAR)/Universidade Federal de Minas Gerais (UFMG), 1991.
Hasenbalg, Carlos and Nelson do Valle Silva, 'Race and Educational Opportunity in Brazil' in Rebecca Reichmann (ed.), *Race in Contemporary Brazil: From Indifference to Inequality*, University Park, PA: Pennsylvania State University Press, 1999.
Hewitt, W. E., 'From Defenders of the People to Defenders of the Faith: A 1984–1993 Retrospective of CEB Activity in São Paulo', *Latin American Perspectives*, 25, 1, January 1998, 170–191.
Hewitt, W. E., 'The Political Dimensions of Women's Participation in Brazil's Base Christian Communities (CEBs): A Longitudinal Case Study from São Paulo', *Women and Politics*, 21, 3, 2000, 1–25.
Himmelkraut, Franz, 'La teologia del imperio', *Pasos*, 15, January–February 1988.
Houtzager, Peter, 'Social Movements Amidst Democratic Transitions: Lessons from the Brazilian Countryside', *Journal of Development Studies*, 35, 5, June 2000.
Houtzager, Peter, 'Collective Action and Political Authority: Rural Workers, Church, and State in Brazil', *Theory and Society*, 30, 1, February 2001, 1–45.
Irarrazavel, Diego, *Inculturation: New Dawn of the Church in Latin America*, Maryknoll: Orbis, 2000.
Issa, Daniela. 'What is the Role of the Catholic Church in the Mobilization of the Landless Rural Workers' Movement (MST) in Pará, Brazil in the 1990's?', MA thesis, University of South Florida, 1999.
Jacobs, Els, 'The Feminine Way/O Jeito Feminino': Religion, Power and Identity in South-Brazilian Base Communities', PhD dissertation, University of Utrecht, 2001.
Keck, Margaret, *The Workers Party and Democratization in Brazil*, New Haven: Yale University Press, 1992.
Kozak, David, 'Ecumenical Indianism: The Tekakwitha Movement as a Discursive Field of Faith and Power' in Elizabeth Brusco and Laura Klein (eds.), *The*

Message in the Missionary: Local Interpretations of Religious Ideology and Missionary Personality, Williamsburg: Studies in Third World Societies, 1994, 1–114.

Krischke, Paulo and Scott Mainwaring (eds.), *A Igreja nas Bases em Tempo de Transição*, Pôrto Alegre: CEDEC, 1986.

Lehmann, David, *Struggle for the Spirit: Religious Transformation and Popular Culture in Brazil*, Cambridge: Polity, 1996.

Lesbaupin, Ivo, Carlos Steil and Clodovis Boff, *Para Entender a Conjuntura Atual*, Petrópolis: Vozes, 1996.

Levine, Daniel, *Popular Voices in Latin American Catholicism*, Princeton: Princeton University Press, 1992.

Levine, Robert, *The History of Brazil*, Westport: Greenwood, 1999.

Levy, Charmain, 'CEBs in Crisis: Leadership Structures in the São Paulo Area' in Burdick and W. E. Hewitt, *The Church at the Grassroots in Latin America: Perspectives on Thirty Years of Activism*, Westport, CA: Greenwood Press, 2000, 167–182.

Libânio, João Batista, *Igreja Contemporânea: Encontro com a Modernidade*, São Paulo: Edições Loyola, 2000.

Libânio, João Batista, *Cenários da igreja*, São Paulo: Loyola, 2000.

Lima, Delcio, *Os Demônios Descem do Norte*, Rio de Janeiro: Alves, 1987.

Löwy, Michel, 'The French Sources of Liberation Christianity in Brazil', *Archives de sciences sociales des religions*, 42, 97, January–March 1997, 9–32.

Lyons, Barry, 'Religion, Authority, and Identity: Intergenerational Politics, Ethnic Resurgence, and Respect in Chimborazo, Ecuador', *Latin American Research Review*, 36, 1, 2001, 7–48.

McAdam, Doug, 'The Biographical Impact of Activism', in Marco Giugni *et al.* (eds.), *How Social Movements Matter*, Minneapolis: University of Minnesota Press, 1999, 119–146.

Machado, Maria das Dores, 'Family, Sexuality, and Family Planning: A Comparative Study of Pentecostals and Charismatic Catholics in Rio de Janeiro' in Barbara Boudewijnse, André Droogers and Frans Kamsteeg (eds.), *More than Opium: An Anthropological Approach to Latin American and Caribbean Pentecostal Praxis*, Lanham, MD: Scarecrow Press, 1998.

Machado, Maria das Dores and Cecilia Mariz. 'Mulheres e Prática Religiosa nas Classes Populares', *Revista Brasileira de Ciências Sociais*, 12, 34, 1997, 71–87.

Machado, Maria das Dores and Cecilia Mariz, 'The Body and Sexual Morality in Religious Groups', *Estudos Feministas*, 1999.

Machado, Maria das Danes and Cecilia Mariz, 'Progressistas e Calólicas Carismaticas: Uma Análise de Discurso de Mulheres de Comunidade de Base na Atualidade Brasileira', *Estudos de Politica e Teoria Social*, 2, 3, 2000.

Maclean, Iaian, *Opting for Democracy: Liberation Theology and the Struggle for Democracy in Brazil*, New York: Peter Lang, 1999.

Mafra, Clara, *Os Evangélicos*, Rio de Janeiro: Zahar, 2001.

Magalhães, Maria Izabel, 'A Critical Discourse Analysis of Gender Relations in Brazil', *Journal of Pragmatics*, 23, 2, February 1995, 183–197.

Maggie, Yvonne, 'Os novos bacharéis. A experiência do pré-vestibular para negros e carentes', *Novos Estudos CEBRAP*, 59, March 2001, 193–202.

Maggie, Yvonne and Claudia Barcellos Rezende (eds.), *Raça como Retórica: A Construção sa Diferença*, Rio de Janeiro: Civilização Brasileira, 2002.

Mainsbridge, Jane, 'Complicating Oppositional Consciousness' in Jane Mainsbridge and Aldon Morris (eds.), *Oppositional Consciousness*, Chicago: University of Chicago Press, 2001 238–264.

Mainwaring, Scott, 'Grass-roots Catholic Groups and Politics in Brazil' in Scott Mainwaring and Alexander Wilde (eds.), *The Progressive Catholic Church in Latin America*, Notre Dame: University of Notre Dame Press, 1989, 151–192.

Mainwaring, Scott, *The Catholic Church and Politics in Brazil, 1916–1985*, Stanford: Stanford University Press, 1986.

Mariz, Cecilia and Maria das Dores Machado, 'Pentecostalismo e a redefinição do feminino', *Religião e Sociedade*, 17, 1, 1996, 140–159.

Mesters, Carlos. *A Bíblia Como Memória dos Pobres*, Petrópolis: Vozes, 1983.

Meyer, David S. and Nancy Whittier, 'Social Movement Spillover', *Social Problems*, 41, 1994, 277–298.

Mosconi, Luis, *Santas Missões Populares*, São Paulo: Paulinas, 1996.

Moser, Antonio and Bernardino Leers, *Moral Theology: Dead Ends and Alternatives*, New York: Orbis 1990.

Moser, Antonio. 'Sexualidad' in Ignacio Ellacuria and Jon Sobrino (eds.), *Mysterium Liberationis*, II. San Salvador: UCA Editores, 1991.

Moura, Clovis, *Dialética radical do Brasil negro*, São Paulo: Anita, 1994.

MST, *O Movimento dos Trabalhadores Rurais Sem Terra: Uma Introdução*, São Paulo: MST, 1995.

MST, *Breve Histórico da Luta Pela Terra no Brasil*, Pôrto Alegre: MST, 1996.

Nagle, Robin, '"Pelo Direito de Ser Igreja": The Struggle of the Morro da Conceição' in John Burdick and W. E. Hewitt (eds.), *The Church at the Grassroots in Latin America: Perspectives on Thirty Years of Activism*, Westport, CA: Greenwood Press, 2000.

Nanne, Jaije and Monica Bergamo, 'Entrevista a Ivone Gebara: "El aborto no es pecado"', *Revista Conspirando*, 6, Deciembre 1993.

Neuhouser, Kevin, 'If I Had Abandoned My Children: Community Mobilization and Commitment to the Identity of Mother in Northeast Brazil', *Social Forces*, 77, 1, September 1998, 331–358.

Novaes, Regina, *De Corpo e Alma: Catolicismo, Classes Sociais e Conflitos no Campo*, Rio de Janeiro: Graphia, 1997.

Nuñes Hoffman and Leandro Sidinei, 'A Cruz e a bandeira: A construção do imaginário dos sem terra', master's thesis, Universidade Federal do Rio Grande do Sul, 1997.

Nuñes, Maria Jose F. Rosado, 'Autonomia das Mulheres vs. Contróle da Igreja: Uma Questão Insoluvel?', Trabalho apresentado na XXIII Conferencia da SISR, Québec, 1994.

Nuñes, Maria Jose F. Rosado, 'The Treatment of Abortion by the Catholic Church', *Estudos Feministas*, 5, 2, 1997, 413–417.

Nuñes, Maria Jose F. Rosado and Myriam Aldana Santin, *Aborto: Conversando a gente se Entende*, Sao Paulo: CDD, 1997.

Nuñes, Maria Jose F. Rosado, 'Women, Family and Catholicism in Brazil: The Issue of Power' in Sharm K. Houseknecht and Jerry G. Pankhurst (eds.), *Family, Religion and Social Change in Diverse Societies*, New York: Oxford Univeristy Press, 2000.

O'Brien, D. J., 'A Century of Catholic Social Teaching' in John A. Coleman (ed.), *100 Years of Catholic Social Thought*, Maryknoll: Orbis, 1991.

O'Connor, Frances B, *Like Bread, Their Voices Rise*, Notre Dame: Ave Maria Press, 1993.
O'Connor, Frances B. and Becky Drury, *The Female Face of Patriarchy: Oppression as Culture*, East Lansing: Michigan State University Press, 1999.
Orta, Andrew. 'From Theologies of Liberation to Theologies of Inculturation' in S. R. Pattnayak (ed.), *Organized Religion in the Political Transformation of Latin America*, Lanham Press, 1995, 97–124.
Ottman, Goetz, *Lost for Words? Brazilian Liberationism in the 1990s*, Pittsburgh: University of Pittsburgh Press, 2002.
Ottman, Goetz, 'Symbolic Contestation: Genesis, Death and Resurrection of the Liberationist Project in the Bairros of São Paulo', PhD dissertation, Australian National University, 1999.
Paiva, Vanilda, 'A Igreja Moderna no Brasil' in V. Paiva (ed.), *Igreja e Questão Agraria*, São Paulo: Edições Loyola, 1985, 52–67.
Pastoral da Juventude Rural do Brasil, *Credito para a Juventude Rural*, Pôrto Alegre: PJRB, 2001.
Pattanayak, S. R., *Organized Religion in the Political Transformation of Latin America*, Lanham, MD: University Press of America, 1995.
Perani, Claudio, 'Notas para um pastoral missionária', *Cadernos do CEAS*, 127, 1990, 74–83.
Perani, Claudio, 'O Inicio da Comissão Pastoral da Terra' in Ivo Poletto and Antonio Canuto (eds.), *Nas Pegadas do Povo da Terra*, São Paulo: Loyola, 2001, 47–53.
Peritore, N. Patrick, 'Socialism, Communism, and Liberation Theology in Brazil', Latin America Series, no. 15. Athens, Ohio: Center for International Studies, Ohio University, 1990.
Petersen, Anna, Manuel Vasquez and Philip Williams, 'Introduction: Christianity and Social Change in the Shadow of Globalization' in Anna Peterson et al. (eds.), *Christianity, Social Change, and Globalization in the Americas*, New Brunswick: Rutgers, 2001.
Petras, James and Henry Veltmeyer, 'Are Latin American Peasant Movements Still a Force for Change? Some New Paradigms Revisited', *The Journal of Peasant Studies*, 28, 2, January 2001, 83–118.
Pinassi, Maria et al., 'An Interview with João Pedro Stédile', *Latin American Perspectives*, 27, 5(114), September 2000, 46–62.
Poggi, Gianfranco, *Catholic Action in Italy*, Stanford: Stanford University Press, 1967.
Polletta, Francesca, 'Free Spaces and Collective Action', *Theory and Society*, 28, 1, February 1999, 1–38.
Poletto, Ivo, 'A CPT, A Igreja e os camponeses', in Comissão Pastoral da Terra, *Conquistar a terra, Reconstruir a Vida*, Petrópolis: Vozes, 1985, 29–85.
Poletto, Ivo, 'A Terra e a Vida em Tempos Neoliberais', in Secretariado Nacional da CPT, *A Luta pela Terra: A Comissão Pastoral da Terra 20 Anos Depois*, São Paulo: Paulus, 1996, 21–69.
Poletto, Ivo and Antonio Canuto (eds.), *Nas Pegadas do Povo da Terra*, São Paulo: Loyola, 2001.
Reichmann, Rebecca Lynn (ed.), *Race in Contemporary Brazil: From Indifference to Inequality*, University Park, PA: Pennsylvania State University Press, 1999.

Ribeiro, Lucia, 'Comunidades de Irmãs e Irmãos: A questão do gênero nas CEBs' in José Oscar Beozzo et al. (coord.), *CEBs: Povo de Deus, 2000 Anos de Caminhada, texto-base*, Paulo Afonso: Fonte Viva, 2000, 152–177.

Ribeiro, Lucia and Solange Luçan, 'Reprodução e Comunidades de Base: Duvidas e Certezas' in R. S. Oliveira and F. Caneiro (eds.), *Corpo: Meu bem, meu mal*, Rio de Janeiro: ISER, 1995.

Ribeiro, Lucia and Solange Luçan, *Entre (In)certezas e Contradições: Práticas Reprodutivas entre Mulheres das Comunidades Eclesiais de Base da Igreja Católica: O caso de Nova Iguaçu*, Rio de Janeiro: Editora Nau, 1997.

Ribeiro, Matilde, 'Black Brazilian Women: From Bertioga to Beijing', *Estudos Feministas*, 3, 2, 1995, 446–457.

Ribeiro de Oliveira, Pedro. *Religião e Dominação*, Petrópolis: Vozes, 1985.

Richard, Pablo, 'The Evangelization of Cultures' in Guillermo Cook (ed.), *Crosscurrents in Indigenous Spirituality*, Leiden: Brill, 1997, 225–232.

Richard, Pablo, 'A Theology of Life: Rebuilding Hope from the Perspective of the South' in K. C. Abraham and Bernadette Mbuy-Beya (eds.), *Spirituality of the Third World: A Cry for Life*, Maryknoll, New York: Orbis, 1994.

Richard, Pablo, *Fuerza espiriual de la Iglesia de los pobres*, San José: Editorial DEI, 1987.

Robles, Wilder, 'The Landless Rural Workers Movement (MST) in Brazil', *The Journal of Peasant Studies*, 28, 2, January 2001, 146–161.

Rocha-Coutinho, Maria Lucia, *Teçendo por Trás dos Panos: A mulher brasileira nas relações familiares*, Rio de Janeiro: Rocco, 1994.

Rochon, Thomas, *Culture Moves*, Chicago: Chicago University Press, 1999.

Rohner, Teodoro, *Atendimento Pastoral as Prostitutas*, São Paulo; Ediçóes Paulinas, 1987.

Rolim, Francisco Cartaxo, *Pentecostalismo no Brasil*, Petrópolis: Vozes, 1985.

Rosemberg, Fulvia, *Literatura infantil e ideologia*, São Paulo: Global, 1985.

Rosemberg, Fulvia, 'Relações raciais e rendimento escolar', *Cadernos de pesquisa*, 63, November 1987, 19–23.

Rufino, Alzira, '"I, Black Woman, Resist!"', *Gender and Development*, 3, 1, February 1995, 55–58.

Saffioti, Heleieth, 'Contribuições feministas para o estudo da violência de gênero', *Cadernos pagu*, 16, 2001, 115–136.

Sant'Anna, Rosangela, 'A fileira da catástrofe: o que a cor pode representar no sistema educacional?', Working Paper, Núcleo da Cor, Universidade Federal do Rio de Janeiro, 1996.

Santos, Andréa Paula dos, Suzana Ribeiro and José Carlos Sebe Bom Meihy, *Vozes da Marcha pela Terra*, São Paulo: Loyola, 1998.

Santos, Frei David dos, 'Uma contribuição ao debate em torno do rito católico afro-brasileiro', mimeo, São João de Meriti: Grupo dos Agentes do Pastoral do Negro, 1991.

Santos, Maria, 'The State, Feminism, and Gendered Citizenship: Constructing Rights in Women's Police Stations in São Paulo', PhD dissertation in political sociology, Berkeley: University of California, 1999.

Scarparo, Helena, *Cidadãs Brasileiras: o cotidiano de mulheres trabalhadoras*, Rio de Janeiro: Revara, 1996.

Schirmer, Jennifer, 'The Seeking of Truth and the Gendering of Consciousness: The Comadres of El Salvador and the Conavigua Widows of Guatemala', in Sarah A.

Radcliffe and Sallie Westwood (eds.), *Viva! Women and Popular Protest in Latin America*, New York: Routledge, 1993, 30–64.
Schneider, Ronald, *Brazil: Culture and Politics in a New Industrial Powerhouse*, Boulder, CO: Westview, 1996.
Schreiter, Robert, *Constructing Local Theologies*, Maryknoll: Orbis, 1985.
Schwade, Elisete, 'A Luta Nao Faz Parte da Vida: O Projeto Politico-Religioso de um Assentamento no Oeste Catarinense', Master's thesis, Mestrado, UFSC, 1993.
Secretariado Nacional da CPT, *A Luta pela Terra: A Comissão Pastoral da Terra 20 Anos Depois*, São Paulo: Paulus, 1996.
Serbin, Kenneth, 'Religious Tolerance, Church–State Relations, and the Challenge of Pluralism', in Paul Sigmund (ed.), *Religious Freedom and Evangelization in Latin America*, Maryknoll: Orbis, 1999.
Serbin, Kenneth, 'The Catholic Church, Religious Pluralism, and Democracy in Brazil' in Peter Kingstone and Timothy Power (eds.), *Democratic Brazil*. Pittsburgh: University of Pittsburgh Press, 2000.
Seuss, Paulo, *A Causa Indigena na Caminhada e a Proposta do CIMI: 1972–1989*, Petrópolis: Vozes, 1989.
Sheriff, Robin, *Dreaming Equality: Color, Race and Racism in Urban Brazil*, New Brunswick, NJ.: Rutgers University Press, 2001.
Sigmund, Paul, *Liberation Theology at the Crossroads*, New York: Oxford University Press, 1990.
Skidmore, Thomas, *Politics in Brazil, 1930–1964*, New York: Oxford University Press, 1967.
Skidmore, Thomas, *Brazil: Five Centuries of Change*, New York: Oxford, 1999.
Smith, Brian H., *Religious Politics in Latin America: Pentecostal vs. Catholic*, Notre Dame: University of Notre Dame Press, 1998.
Smith, Christian, *The Emergence of Liberation Theology: Radical Religion and Social Movement Theory*, Chicago: University of Chicago Press, 1991.
Smith, Christian, 'Correcting a Curious Neglect, or Bringing Religion Back In' in Christian Smith (ed.), *Disruptive Religion: the Force of Faith in Social Movement Activism*, New York: Routledge, 1996, 1–28.
Sobrino, Jon, 'Theology from amidst the Victims' in *The Future of Theology*, Grand Rapids: Eerdmans, 1996.
Stédile, João Pedro and Bernardo Mancano Fernandes, *Brava Gente: A Trajetório do MST e a Luta Pela Terra no Brasil*, São Paulo: Perseu Abramo, 1999.
Stephen, Lynn, *Women and Social Movements in Latin America*, Austin: University of Texas Press, 1997.
Strapazzon, João Paulo Lajus, *E o verbo se fez terra*, Chapecó: Grifos, 1998.
Tamez, Elsa, *Through Her Eyes: Women's Theology from Latin America*, Maryknoll: Orbis, 1989.
Tamez, Elsa, *The Amnesty of Grace*, Nashville: Abingdon Press, 1993.
Teixeira, Faustino Luiz Couto, *Os Encontros Intereclesiais de CEBs no Brasil*, São Paulo: Paulinas, 1996.
Turner, Victor, 'The Center Out There: The Pilgrim's Goal', *History of Religions*, 12, 1973, 191–230.
Turner, Victor, 'Pilgrimage and communitas', *Studia missionalia*, 23, 1974, 1–21.
Valente, Ana Lucia, *O negro e a igreja católica: o espaco concedido, um espaco reivindicado*, Campo Grande, MS: CECITEC, 1994.

Vasquez, Manuel, *The Brazilian Popular Church and the Crisis of Modernity*, Cambridge: Cambridge University Press, 1998.

Vasquez, Manuel and Ana Petersen, 'The New Evangelization in Latin American Perspective', *Cross Currents*, 48, Fall 1998, 311–329.

Veltmeyer, Henry and James Petras, 'The Social Dynamics of Brazil's Rural Landless Workers' Movement: Ten Hypotheses on Successful Leadership', *La Revue Canadienne de Sociologie et d'Anthropologie*, 39, 1, February 2002, 79–96.

Vieira Machado and Leda Maria, 'We Learned to Think Politically: The Influence of the Catholic Church and the Feminist Movement on the Emergence of the Health Movement of the Jardim Nordeste Area in São Paulo, Brazil' in Sarah A. Radcliffe and Sallie Westwood (eds.), *Viva! Women and Popular Protest in Latin America*, New York: Routledge, 1993, 88–111.

Vuola, Elina, *Limits of Liberation: Praxis as Method in Latin American Theology and Feminist Theology*, Helsinki: Suomalainen, 1997.

Warren, Jonathan, *Racial Revolutions*, Durham: Duke University Press, 2001.

Weller, Wivian, 'Identity Construction through the Hip-Hop Movement: A Comparative Analysis between Black Rappers in São Paulo and Turkish–German Rappers in Berlin', *Caderno CRH*, 32, January–June 2000, 213–232.

Willela, Wilza, 'Making Legal Abortion Available in Brazil', *Reproductive Health Matters*, 8, 16, 2000, 77–82.

Williams, Raymond, *Marxism and Literature*, New York: Oxford, 1977.

Yudice, George, 'Afro Reggae: Parlaying Culture into Social Justice', *Social Text*, 19, 4(69), Winter 2001, 53–65.

Index

Aboim, Maria, 79
abortion, 58, 75, 87–95, 139, 141; and rape, 87, 92, 93, 97 n.48; and Workers' Party, 87, 88, 92
activism, 107–11, 139, 140–141
affirmative action, 48
Africa, 20
African ancestry, 48–54
Afro-Brazilians, xi, 17–35. *See also* liturgy, afro
afro-descendentes, 45, 46
agente de pastoral negro. *See* APNs
agraciada, 25
Amorim, José, 48
AMZOL (Associção de Mulheres da Zona Este), 10, 86, 95
ancestry, 51, 52, 53
anti-authoritarianism, 6
anti-racism, 141. *See also* racism
APNs (*agente de pastoral negro*; Black Pastoral agents), 23–35, 48; and college entrance examinations, 38, 39; and racial identity, 53. *See also* pastoral agents
Apostolate of Prayer, 28
Arns, Paulo Evaristo, 5, 22, 79, 92
Assembly of God Church, 54
Associção de Mulheres da Zona Este (AMZOL), 10, 86, 95
Atabaque Cultura Negra e Teologia, 19
authority: household, 66–69, 139

batalhando (in the battle), 42
Benedito, 27
Bernadino, Dom, 125
Berryman, Philip, 7, 8
Betinho award, 46
Betto, Frei, 90–91

Bible, ix, 4. *See also* Exodus; Hebrews; Luke
Bingemer, Maria Clara, 60
birth control, 89, 91, 94. *See also* abortion
bishops, x, 1, 2, 3, 5, 6, 19, 22; black, 38. *See also* CNBB
black consciousness, 54
Black Pastoral, 9, 139, 141, 142; in the church, 17–35; in the secular world, 37–56
Black Pastoral agents. *See* APNs
blacks: in higher education, 39, 43
Boff, Leonardo, ix, 4, 5–6, 8, 13 n.29
brancas (whites), 19, 44
Brasil, Nunca Mais, 13 n.24
Brasilia, 125
Brotherhood Campaign, 24–25, 38, 79

Cabral, Bernardo, 130
Caldeira, Teresa, 70
Camara, Dom Helder, 2, 20
caminhada (path), 42, 86, 111, 113, 125, 141
candomblé, 27, 28, 32
Canuto, João, 116 n.15
capitalism, 4, 8, 88
capoeira, 28
Cardenal, Ernesto, ix, x, 14 n.57
Cardijn, Joseph, 2
carentes, 43. *See also* PVNC
Casaldáliga, Dom Pedro, 125–26
catechism, 122–24, 124, 125
Catholic Action groups, 2
Catholics for a Free Choice (CFC), 87
Católicas pelo Direito de Deridir (CDD), 10, 92, 94–95
CDD (*Católicas pelo Direito de Deridir*), 10, 92, 94–95

CEAP (Centro de Articulação de Populações Marginalizadas), 34 n.13, 56 n.19
CEBs (*comunidade eclesial de base*), x–xi, 2, 4, 5, 6–9, 10, 20; activism in, 110–11; Brotherhood Campaign and, 25; leadership and, 107–8; meetings, 35 n.26; *pastoral negro* and, 38; seminarians from, 19; on violence, 79–80; women in, 62–75, 80, 86, 89, 92–95, 141; youth and, 109

celebration (mass), 120–22

censorship, 5, 6

Centre of Indigenous Missions, 10
Centro de Articulação de Populações Marginalizadas (CEAP), 34 n.13, 56 n.19
Centro Feminista de Estudos e Assessoria (CFEMEA), 87
CFC (Catholics for a Free Choice), 87
CFEMEA (Centro Feminista de Estudos e Assessoria), 87
charismatic renewal, x, 6, 16 n.85, 58; women in, 94
Che, 133
Chiapas, x
Chiareli, Antonio, 121
childcare, 59
children: abuse of, 85
CIMI (Conselho indigenista Misionária; Missionary Consul for Indigenous Affairs), 4
citizenship rights, 41
civilian rule, 3
class, 17, 18, 19, 80
clergy, 1, 2, 5, 9, 21, 23, 84, 102, 104, 109, 121; on abortion, 139; black, 38; on domestic violence, 85; and land issues, 105, 106. *See also* priests
CNBB (Conferencia Nacional do Bispos do Brasil; National Brazilian Bishops' Conference), 4, 6, 19, 22, 24, 83, 84–85, 92, 103, 104
cognitive approach, 25, 26, 48

collectivism, 113, 140
college entrance examinations, 17, 37–48, 139. *See also* higher education; PVNC
colonization, 26
Comissão Pastoral da Terra. *See* CPT
communalism, 120
communion, 141
Community for Solidarity, 94
companheiros (comrades), 42
comunidade eclesial de base (CEBs). *See* CEBs
Conferencia Nacional do Bispos do Brasil (CNBB; National Brazilian Bishops' Conference), 4, 6, 19, 22, 24, 83, 84–85, 92, 103, 104
consciousness-raising: Black Pastoral and, 24–26, 48, 49, 53; and gender violence, 81; and land issues, 102, 121, 128, 129, 140; PVNC as, 41; of women, 52, 53, 141; in youth pastorals, 109
Conselho indigenista Misionária (CIMI; Missionary Consul for Indigenous Affairs), 4
Conspirando, 89–90
consumerism, 121, 122
Contins, Marcia, 44
CPT (Comissão Pastoral da Terra; Pastoral Land Commission), 4, 10, 140, 142; activism in, 110; agents, 119–26; catechism and, 122–24; MST relationship, 101–9, 112, 113, 114, 115 n.8, 125, 135; women's sector of, 91
crimes of passion, 79, 84
crosses, 129–32, 135, 142
culture, 26; African, 28; in liturgy, 31; values, 10
CUT, 111

da Silva, Benedita, 47–48
Daudelin, Jean, 6, 7
decolonization, 20
Della Porta, Donatella, 140
democracy, 5, 7; racial, 18, 21
De Theije, Marjo, 68
Dias, Ana, 7

discrimination, 19, 22, 45, 50; gender, 83, 139; of penal code against women, 84; racial, 21, 23, 139; sexual, 74
divorce, 80, 84
domestic violence, 79–87. *See also* rape
Drogus, Carol Ann, 62
drums, 27, 31–32, 49; in liturgy, 28

Earl, Jennifer, 10
Ecclesiogenesis: The Church that Is Born from the Poor, 5
Eckhart, Meister, 117 n.52
economic injustice, 81
economic issues, 18
Educafro, 10, 42, 46, 55 n.7, 141
education, 18; role of the Catholic church in, 39; of women, 59. *See also* higher education
educational quotas, 43, 45, 47–48
Efigenia, 27
Eldorado de Carajás, 112, 126, 133
elections, 5
Encontro das CEBs, 9
Encruzilhada Natalino, 103, 104, 131–32
Eucharist, 112–13
Exodus (book of the Bible), xi, 27, 104–5, 113–14, 116 n.29, 121–29, 135, 140, 142

family, 79, 80, 84–85
feminism, xi, 57, 72
Ferreira, Nelson, 125
food, 112; in liturgy, 27, 28
Francis, Saint, 133, 134
Free Trade Agreement of the Americas, 100
Freire, Paulo, 3
Frietzen, Father Arnildo, 102, 104

Garotinho, Anthony, 47
garra (courage), 42
Gaudium et spes, 3
Gebara, Ivone, 60, 62, 89–90, 91
gender relations, 57–78; in CEBs, 63–66; within the Church, 71–74; inequality of, 57–59, 61–66, 72–74, 81; politics of, 66–71; violence in, 19, 58, 80, 81, 84, 85, 95, 139. *See also* domestic violence
Genoino, José, 92
globalization, 15 n.78, 26
Goes, César, 106
Gonzaga, Father, 8
Gorgen, Frei Sergio, 107
greed, 4
Grupo Cultural Afro-Reggae, 34 n.13
Grupo de Reflexao sobre a Religião Negra e Indigena, 19
Gutierrez, Gustavo, 3, 13 n.29

Hebrews, 27, 121, 122–24, 128
Herzog, Vladimir, 3
Hewitt, W.E., 6, 7
higher education: Afro-Brazilians and, 37–48; blacks in, 39, 43; recruitment, 141; registration fees for, 46; Workers' Party and, 47–48. *See also* college entrance examinations; PVNC
Himmelkraut, Franz, 88
homosexuality, 85
housework, 59, 61, 66–69; politics of, 69–71
human rights, 3, 5

identity, 17, 20, 23, 37, 48, 51; Afro-Brazilian, 19; of APNs, 39; black, 20–21, 22, 50; Catholic, 44; MST and, 127–28, 130–31; *negro*, 48–49; PVNC's, 44; racial, 50, 53–54, 142
illiteracy, 17, 18
imperialism, 88
incest, 79
inclusivity, 45
INCRA (Instituto Nacional de Colonizaçãoe Reforma Agrária; National Institute of Colonization and Agrarian Reform), 99
inculturation, 26
indigenous rights, 142
individualism, 41, 71, 88, 113, 120, 121, 122, 124
Instituto do Negro Padre Batista, 19

Instituto Nacional de Colonizaçãoe Reforma Agrária (INCRA; National Institute of Colonization and Agrarian Reform), 99
Inter-American Development Bank, 47

Jacobs, Els, 70
Jesus, 29, 43, 124, 131
Jesus Christ, Liberator (Boff), 13 n.29
John Paul II, ix, 5–6, 26
Jósimo, Padre, 112, 133, 136 n.27
justice, 2, 3, 4, 6

Kubitchek, Juscelino, 1

Lacalle, Sáenz, 14 n.57
laity, 1, 2, 5, 6–7, 9, 109, 120; hierarchy of authority, 60; liturgies and, 27
land, 18, 102, 113, 121–22, 125, 131. *See also* MST
Landless Workers' Movement. *See* MST
leadership, 141, 142; black church, 38; and CEBs, 107–8; lay, 5; MST, 99–117; women and, 58, 61, 63, 66, 67, 71–73
legislation, 47–48
Leme, Cardinal, 1
lesbianism, 85
Libanio, João Batista, 6
libertaçao (liberation), 42
literacy campaigns, 2–3, 102
liturgy, 26, 112, 120, 121; afro, 17, 24–32, 112; European influences on, 28, 29, 31, 32
Lozano, Javier, 14 n.57
Luçan, Solange, 93, 94
Lucius, Saint, 133
Luiz, Bishop Dom, 125
Luke (book of the Bible), 70
luta (struggle), 42
Luzia, Saint, 133, 134–35

Machado, Maria das Dores, 89, 94
machismo, 58, 93
mães de santo, 29, 31
Maggie, Yvonne, 44
Malthus, 41–42

marches, 125, 128–29
Maria Miguel Battered Women's Counselling Centre, 86
Mariz, Cecilia, 89, 94
Marques, Father Luiz Carlos, 7
martyrs, 112, 124, 125, 126, 131, 133, 141
Marxism, x, 6, 8
Mary, Mother of God, Mother of the Poor (Gebara and Bingemer), 60
mass, 120–22, 124. *See also* afro liturgy
materialism, 6
McAdam, Doug, 140
MEB (Movimento de Educação de Base), 2–3
media, 18
Messias, Arthur, 47
Mesters, Carlos, 12 n.17
mestiço, 44, 48, 53
Meyer, David S., 10
military, 3, 4, 5, 18, 20, 102–3, 132
ministers of the Eucharist, 72, 73, 74
ministers of the Word, 72, 73, 74
missionaries, 86
Missionary Consul for Indigenous Affairs (CIMI; Conselho indigenista Misionária), 4
mística (spiritual commitment), 42, 111–12, 114, 130, 131
MMTR (Movimento de Mulheres Trabalhadoros Rurais; Women Rural Workers' Movement), 91
MNU (Movimento Negro Unifiçado), 21, 22
moreno, 19, 20, 21, 22, 48, 49–50, 51, 53; in PVNC, 44
mortality, 88, 89, 92
Moser, Antonio, 88
Moses, 104, 124, 127, 128, 130. *See also* Exodus (book of the Bible)
mothers' clubs, 89
Movimento de Educação de Base (MEB), 2–3
Movimento de Mulheres Trabalhadoros Rurais (MMTR; Women Rural Workers' Movement), 91

Movimento dos Trabalhadores Sem Terra. *See* MST
Movimento Negro Unifiçado (MNU), 21
MST (Movimento dos Trabalhadores Sem Terra; Landless Workers' Movement), x, 10, 11, 140, 141; CPT relationship, 101–9, 112, 113, 114, 115 n.8, 125, 135; leadership, 99–117; rank and file, 119–37
mulato, 48, 50
Mulher libertação, 83, 85, 87
music: in liturgy, 27

National Brazilian Bishops' Conference (CNBB; Conferencia Nacional do Bispos do Brasil), 4, 6, 19, 22, 24, 83, 84–85, 92, 103, 104
National Conference on Indigenous and Black Theology, 9–10
National Institute of Colonization and Agrarian Reform (INCRA: Instituto Nacional de Colonizaçãoe Reforma Agrária), 99
negros, 17, 20–22, 24, 37, 47, 50–53; within the church, 38–39; in higher education, 44–48; and PVNC, 43–45
new evangelization, 6
Nicaragua, ix
non-Christian religions, 16 n.85
núcleo, 40–45
Núcleo Resistencia, 40–42
Nuñes, Rosado, 88

Ogun, 27
Olodumaré, 27, 30
Olorum, 27, 29
oppositional consciousness, 127
oppression, 3, 4, 22, 139; black, 25; class, 58, 80; culture and, 26; economic, 82
orixás (spirits), 27–31
Oxalá, 29
Oxum, 27

pardo, 19, 20; in higher education, 38, 43, 47, 48; in PVNC, 44
Parlamento Latino-Americano Prize, 46
Partido dos Trabalhadores. *See* Workers' Party
Pastoral Afro-Brasileira, 19
pastoral agents, 2, 5, 8, 23, 26, 81–82, 91, 102, 111, 141; and land issues, 103, 106. *See also* APNs; CPT, agents
Pastoral de mulheres Marginalizades (PMM; pastoral of Marginalized Women), 10, 80–87, 95
Pastoral Land Commission. *See* CPT
Pastoral Negro, 17–35. *See also* Black Pastoral
pastoral of Marginalized Women (PMM; Pastoral de mulheres Marginalizades), 10, 80–87, 95
pastoral operaria (Workers Pastoral), 8
Peace and Justice Commission, 5, 13 n.24
Peasant Leagues, 2
Pentecostalism, x, 8, 16 n.85, 58, 75 n.8
People's Church, x, 20, 23, 71, 102, 112
Perseu Abramo Foundation, 79
pilgrimages, 43
pilgrimages for land (*romarias da terra*), 104, 124–26, 137 n.45
pleasure, 86
PMM (Pastoral de mulheres Marginalizades; pastoral of Marginalized Women), 10, 80–87, 95
political movements, 8, 22
politics: of authority in the household, 66–69; cultural, 17, 26; religious, 57; women in, 60
poor, 2–4, 6, 8, 18, 20, 22, 47, 81, 88, 101–2, 108–11, 125, 139, 141, 142; and abortion, 89–92; land issues and, 105. *See also* PVNC
poverty, 3, 17, 41, 80, 81, 82, 88, 93, 94
pretos, 20, 38, 44, 51

pre-vestibular courses, 10. *See also* PVNC
pre-vestibular para negros (PVN), 43–44
pre-vestibular para negros e carentes (PVNC), 37–48
priests, 120–21, 132. *See also* clergy
profético (prophetic), 42
prostitution, 19, 80–81, 82–83, 85
PT. *See* Workers' Party
PVN (*pre-vestibular para negros*), 43–44
PVNC (*pre-vestibular para negros e carentes*), 37–48, 54

Quadragesimo Anno, 12 n.12
Quadrangular Church, 75 n.8

race, 17, 20–21, 23, 24, 37, 139; and identity, 50, 53–54, 142
racism, 18, 19, 22, 23, 25, 41, 48, 52; anti-black, 11, 17–35, 139; within the church, 22; internalized, 52
Rainha, José, 107
rape, 61, 79, 80, 82, 84, 85; abortion and, 87, 92, 93, 97 n.48. *See also* domestic violence
rationalism, x
Rede Mulher (Women's Network), 80
Rede Vida, 46
reproduction rate, 59
reproductive rights, 57, 61
Rerum Novarum, 12 n.12
Ribeiro, Lucia, 93, 94
ritual, 26, 31, 130, 131
Rocha-Coutinho, Maria Lucia, 59
Rodriguez, Nicholas Lopez, 14 n.57
Romaria das Aguas, 137 n.27
romarias da terra (pilgrimages for land), 104, 124–26, 137 n.45

saints, 9, 27, 30, 133–35, 142
Sampaio, Tania Mara V., 91
Sandinistas, ix, 8
Santas Missoes Populares, 9
Santos, Frei David Raimundo Dos, 25, 26, 38, 39, 43, 45
Santos, Ivanir dos, 56
Sarney, José, 104

see-judge-act method, 2, 3, 92
seminaries, 19–23, 139
sex, 80, 88
sexism, 82
sexual abuse, 82
sexuality, 85, 86, 88, 89
sexual violence, 57, 61, 75, 79, 80, 82, 83, 84. *See also* domestic violence
slavery, 17, 18, 24, 50, 86
Sobrino, Jon, 8
social change, 26, 54
socialism, ix, 2, 4, 8
social justice, ix, 6, 9, 39, 81, 88, 108, 140, 141
social movement outcomes, 10, 11–12, 54, 140
social movements, x, 3, 4, 86, 107, 135, 139, 140, 142. *See also* MST
spirituality, 6, 8, 86, 112
spousal abuse, 79. *See also* domestic violence
state repression, 3
Stédile, João Pedro, 102, 107
strikes, 4

tambor, 31
tambor de Mina, 29, 30
terreiros, 29, 31–32
theological writing, 3
A Theology of Liberation (Guttierrez), 13 n.29
Tiçao, Padre, 8
torture, 5

umbanda, 27
Union of Rural Workers, 116 n.15
unions, 2, 4, 6, 8, 12 n.12, 101, 119
United Nations, 91
United Nations Third Conference on Racism, 47–48
United States: black identity from, 20–21
Universal Church of the Kingdom of God, 75 n.8
universalism, 45
urbanization, 1

Vargas, Getúlio, 1

Vatican, ix, 5–6
Vatican II, 19, 102
violence, 3, 79–80; domestic, 79–87; gender, 19, 58, 80, 81, 84, 85, 95, 139; police, 127, 131; sexual, 57, 61, 75, 79, 81, 82, 83, 84. *See also* rape

Whittier, Nancy, 10
women, 11, 139, 141, 142; and abortion, 87–95; afro religiosity and, 28; Black, 18–19; in charismatic renewal, 94; and domestic violence, 79–87; education of, 59; and leadership, 58, 61, 63, 66, 67, 71–73; in liturgy, 27; ordination of, 75 n.8, 96 n.27; Pentecostal, 75 n.8; racial identity and, 50–53; roles of, 57–78; in secular activities, 65–66; spirituality and, 86; status of, 58–60; stereotypes of, 59; treatment within the church, 71–74
women-only groups, 80, 85
Women Rural Workers' Movement (MMTR: Movimento de Mulheres Trabalhadoros Rurais), 91
Women's Network (*Rede Mulher*), 80
Workers' Party (PT; Partido dos Trabalhadores), 4, 8, 15 n.75, 111, 119, 142; abortion and, 87, 88, 92; higher education and, 47–48
Workers Pastoral (*pastoral operaria*), 8

Yemenja, 30
youth: and catechism, 122; in CEBs, 109
youth groups, 107
Youth Land Pastoral, 140, 141
youth pastorals, 107, 108–9, 114; activism in, 110

Zapatistas, x
Zumbi, 24, 27, 28, 38, 50, 112, 133, 136 n.26

For Product Safety Concerns and Information please contact our EU
representative GPSR@taylorandfrancis.com
Taylor & Francis Verlag GmbH, Kaufingerstraße 24, 80331 München, Germany

www.ingramcontent.com/pod-product-compliance
Lightning Source LLC
Chambersburg PA
CBHW071400290426
44108CB00014B/1629